Selfscapes, Selfhoods, and Subjectivities

This book explores cross-cultural similarities and differences of human sub-jectivity and selfhood through the concept of *selfscapes*.

Utilizing an ethnographic and person-centered approach to the study of human subjectivity, *Selfscapes, Selfhoods, and Subjectivities* demonstrates that autopoietic processes are informed by the constraints of a social and material ecology acting on a particular person and by how that person is remembering and habitually responding to that history of engagement with the world. While the co-constitution of social and historical circumstance and individual reac-tivity and memory is universal, the way an autopoietic process unfolds within any given social ecology will vary, sometimes greatly, from person to person.

Drawing on a broad theoretical base, this book is essential reading for an-thropologists, psychoanalysts, social psychologists, and anyone seeking to un-derstand the varieties and particularities of human subjectivity and selfhood.

Douglas W. Hollan is Distinguished Professor and Luckman Distinguished Teacher in the Department of Anthropology at UCLA and a research psycho-analyst affiliated with the New Center for Psychoanalysis in Los Angeles.

'For more than three decades, Douglas Hollan has made vital contributions to our understanding of the self in cultural context. His work is characterized by ethnographic engagement with the social world, psychodynamic attunement to the self, and a humanistic commitment to respect the complexity of experience. Hollan is a master of person-centered ethnography and in this collection of seminal essays, he shows how attention to both the social world and to psychological dynamics can reveal the person as an active agent fashioning a durable and generative self. Building on his ethnographic and clinical experience, he uses the concept of *selfscape* to articulate and explore the looping effects between self-constitution and cultural affordances. This work will be enlivening, enriching, and sustaining for scholars in the social sciences and humanities and for mental health practitioners who seek to better understand the interplay of psyche and culture.'

Laurence J. Kirmayer, *Distinguished James McGill*
Professor & Director, Division of Social &
Transcultural Psychiatry, McGill University

'Douglas Hollan, a leading contemporary voice in psychoanalytic anthropology and person-centered ethnography, has written a book that is urgently needed in anthropology, psychology, and all fields that study persons-in-culture. He offers an approach that successfully navigates the Scylla of psychological reductionism on one side, and the Charybdis of cultural and structural reductionism, on the other. Psychologists and psychoanalysts typically focus on the individual's intrapsychic, interpersonal, and neurobiological characteristics while downplaying the social-structural, cultural, political-economic, and material contexts that are just as influential in shaping the self. Many social theorists and researchers have tried to rectify this lack of attention to context by emphasizing the social and cultural formation of the person. But in doing so, they go too far in the opposite direction: They neglect the complexity and singularity of human mental life as well as the active, dynamic nature of human subjectivity. Prof. Hollan has long recognized that the study of persons must move beyond these bifurcations. Here, he presents a more integrative approach, one that illuminates individual human experience in its complexity and particularity, as well as its formation within sociopolitical and cultural contexts. Many social and psychological researchers are seeking ways to theorize and study the whole person, and they will find this book to be both useful and inspiring.'

Suzanne R. Kirschner, *Professor Emerita of Psychology*
College of the Holy Cross

'Douglas Hollan's unique immersion as both Anthropologist and Psycho-analyst resulted in a career-long engagement with human subjectivity. In this volume of his essays, he shares his profound and useful insights about person-centered ethnography and the multiple sources, in addition to early childhood experiences, of self construction: selfscapes. Hollan offers us a rich and nuanced new methodology of the mind—one important both to anthropological researchers and to mental health practitioners. A critical contribution for both.'

Jeffrey Prager, Ph.D., *Research Professor of Sociology,*
UCLA, Training and Supervising Analyst,
New Center for Psychoanalysis, ICP

'At least since the early 20th century, anthropologists have drawn upon Freud, and Freud turned to anthropology, in one of the most fruitful cross-disciplinary dialogues either field has engaged. In his insightful, elegantly written and deeply absorbing Selfscapes, Selfhoods, and Subjectivities, anthropologist and psychoanalyst Douglas Hollan exemplifies and fur-ther entwines these disciplines. He gives us a beautifully fine-tuned account of the ways that individual selves experience and act within and thereby create environments, describing how this ever-creative in-teractive process works in human life and giving us vivid, on-the-ground examples of individuals. Scholars and clinicians from these two fields and from the social sciencies and clinical practices more broadly, as well as anyone who is interested in their own subjectivity in its relation to their own social being, will delight in and gain enormous understanding from reading this book.'

Nancy J. Chodorow, *Professor Emerita, Department of Sociology,*
University of California, Berkeley, Author,
The Psychoanalytic Ear and the Sociological Eye

Selfscapes, Selfhoods, and Subjectivities

Perspectives from Anthropology
and Psychoanalysis

Douglas W. Hollan

Routledge
Taylor & Francis Group

LONDON AND NEW YORK

Designed cover image: Getty Images

First published 2026
by Routledge
4 Park Square, Milton Park, Abingdon, Oxon OX14 4RN

and by Routledge
605 Third Avenue, New York, NY 10158

*Routledge is an imprint of the Taylor & Francis Group,
an informa business*

British Library Cataloguing-in-Publication Data
A catalogue record for this book is available from the British Library

Library of Congress Cataloging-in-Publication Data
Names: Hollan, Douglas Wood author
Title: Human subjectivity, selfhood and selfscapes : perspectives from
   psychoanalysis and anthropology / Douglas Hollan.
Description: Abingdon, Oxon ; New York, NY : Routledge, 2025. |
Includes bibliographical references and index.
Identifiers: LCCN 2025012770 (print) | LCCN 2025012771 (ebook) |
ISBN 9781032866635 hardback | ISBN 9781032867748 paperback |
ISBN 9781003529118 ebook
Subjects: LCSH: Self | Subjectivity--Psychological aspects |
   Ethnopsychology | Personality and culture
Classification: LCC BF697 .H527 2025 (print) | LCC BF697 (ebook)
LC record available at https://lccn.loc.gov/2025012770
LC ebook record available at https://lccn.loc.gov/2025012771

ISBN: 978-1-032-86663-5 (hbk)
ISBN: 978-1-032-86774-8 (pbk)
ISBN: 978-1-003-52911-8 (ebk)

DOI: 10.4324/9781003529118

Typeset in Optima
by KnowledgeWorks Global Ltd.

for Inma and Jack,
mi familia

Contents

Acknowledgments

The articles and book chapters that make up the bulk of this book were written over a 30-year period, and there are many people to thank. First and foremost, I want to thank all the people in my anthropological and psychoanalytic work who have been willing to sit and talk to me about their lives and experiences. Without their collaboration, there would be no book. I am forever indebted to you all.

I also want to thank the many teachers and colleagues who have helped to inspire and nurture this work over the years. My former teachers and mentors at the University of California, San Diego, Mel Spiro, Bob Levy, Ted Schwartz, Gananath Obeyesekere, and Roy D'Andrade all raised important questions for me about human subjectivity that I continue think about all these years later. As both anthropologists and psychoanalysts, Mel Spiro and Bob Levy in particular, showed me how anthropology and psychoanalysis could be integrated in important and interesting ways, and Bob Levy, with his groundbreaking book, *Tahitians: Mind and Experience in the Society Islands*, gave me my love for and devotion to person-centered ethnography. Jane Wellenkamp and I went to graduate school together, conducted Indonesian fieldwork together, and wrote two books together on Toraja life and experience together. My personal and intellectual debt to her is incalculable and goes without saying.

All chapters in this book were written while I was a faculty member in the Department of Anthropology at the University of California, Los Angeles. I am grateful to the Department and to the University of California for supporting my own subfield of medical and psychological anthropology at UCLA and for surrounding me with many inspiring colleagues. I am particularly grateful to the Mind, Medicine, and Culture group in the Department of Anthropology at UCLA, a collection of faculty and graduate students who have met weekly over the past 25 years to discuss and debate important issues in psychological and medical anthropology and to support each other's research. Without doubt, my participation in MMAC has been the most enjoyable and enriching part of my academic life. I wish I could name and thank personally all the brilliant graduate students who have passed through MMAC over the last 25 years and who have helped shape my thinking about human subjectivity and many other things, but alas, there are just too many. It needs to be said, however, that any of us who have played the academic game for as long as I have know that a big part of our longevity is due to the graduate students who challenge our thinking and keep us informed about the latest developments in our fields. Many thanks to all of you.

I owe a particular intellectual debt to my fellow MMAC faculty, including visiting faculty, from whose thinking and perspectives I have learned so much over the years. Many thanks to Allen Johnson, Tom Weisner, Carole Browner, Elinor Ochs, Linda Garro, Jason Throop, Can Aciksoz, Rob Lemelson, Cheryl Mattingly, and Steve Lopez.

It is rare for an anthropologist to receive full training in psychoanalysis. For that privilege, I want to thank the Southern California Psychoanalytic Institute, now the New Center for Psychoanalysis, for its generous support, both financial and intellectual. The institutes deferred the costs of my personal analysis, training, and supervision, and without that support, I would not have become a licensed research psychoanalyst. A special thanks to Peter Loewenberg, a professor emeritus of history at UCLA and a co-founder and tireless supporter of the research psychoanalytic training program at SCPI and NCP, for encouraging me to begin psychoanalytic training even as an untenured assistant professor, and who reassured me that one day, it would all work out. I am also forever indebted to Richard Rosenstein, my training analyst, whose kindness and empathy were always front and center, and to Jona Perlmutter, Doryann Lebe, and Saul Brown, who supervised my training cases. For several years, Jeff Prager, research professor in the Department of Sociology at UCLA and a fellow research psychoanalyst who also trained at SCPI and NCP, and I shared an analytic office together. Thanks to Jeff for many enjoyable conversations about the academic and analytic work we were each doing.

When I talked to Nancy Chodorow, Professor Emerita of Sociology at the University of California, Berkeley, and a psychoanalyst, about the possibility of pulling some of my articles and chapters together for a book, she recommended I talk with the editor, Kates Hawes, at Routledge. Thanks to Nancy for that recommendation, and to Kate, Alice Maher, and all the production people at Routledge for getting this book over the finish line.

I first met Dr. Robert Ross, psychiatrist and psychoanalyst, when we started psychoanalytic training together in 1990. Despite big differences in our backgrounds and upbringing, we hit it off immediately and have since hung out together almost weekly for the last 35 years. It is difficult for me to express how much I have benefited and learned from Robert's wisdom and insights, about psychiatry and psychoanalysis, but also about many other things, including many of the ideas in this book. I feel very fortunate to have had his friendship and encouragement over all these years. I owe you, Robert.

I also owe a lot to my lifelong friend, Mike Miller. Mike and I grew up together in San Antonio, Texas. We went to middle school and high school together and eventually went to undergraduate school at the University of Texas together. Fortunately for me, he ended up in Los Angeles about the same time I started teaching at UCLA. I have had more fun laughing and joking with

Mike than anyone else in my life, and his humor and abiding friendship has helped me get through some of the darkest moments of my personal and professional life. Everyone should have a lifelong friend like Mike.

I dedicate this book to Inma and Jack. Without them, I would probably be under a table somewhere...

I am grateful to the following for permission to publish: *The Journal of Anthropological Research* for Chapter 2, "Cross-Cultural Differences in the Self" (1992); *American Anthropologist* for Chapter 3, "Constructivist Models of Mind, Contemporary Psychoanalysis, and the Development of Culture Theory" (2000); *Ethos* for Chapter 4, "On the Varieties and Particularities of Cultural Experience" (2012); Bloomsbury Press, for Chapter 5, "Emotional Entrainment in Crowds and Other Social Formations" (2019); State University of New York Press for Chapter 6, "Selfscape Dreams" (2003); Berghahn Books for Chapter 7, "Selfscapes of Well-Being in a Rural Indonesia Village" (2008); *Ethos* for Chapter 8, "From Ghosts to Ancestors (and Back Again): On the Cultural and Psychodynamic Mediation of Selfscapes" (2014); and Routledge for Chapter 9, "Relational but Also Singular: On the Varieties and Particularities of Selfscapes" (2023).

1 Selfscapes, Selfhoods, and Subjectivities

It Takes the Whole of Us

How and why do people think, feel, sense, imagine, desire, hope, create, moralize, fantasize, dream about, act upon, and experience the world in the ways they do? What are the varieties and particularities of these kinds of experiencing and emotional engagements, and what are their existential dimensions? How do particular kinds of historical, social, cultural, economic, political, and material circumstances affect the ways in which people experience and engage with the world, and in turn, to what extent do people's experiences of and engagements with the world mirror, expand upon, subvert, transform, or transcend that world? What are the relationships between waking and less wakeful or altered forms of consciousness, including dreaming and drug- or alcohol-induced states, and how are these relationships affected by social and material conditions? How do people's past engagements with the world affect their experiencing of present and future engagements, and in turn, how do their present engagements with the world affect or transform their memories of and emotional reactions to their past engagements? What are the kinds of historical, social, and material circumstances that contribute to human experiences of illness and suffering—physical, mental, or emotional—and what are the circumstances that mitigate or alleviate such experiences, or which promote human experiences of happiness and well-being? In short, what is like to be "psychically alive" as a human being (Chodorow 2020: 252)?

Humans have long pondered the nature and variability of their own self-consciousness and the extent to which that awareness of self is or is not *the* defining characteristic of the species, or rather one that we share in various degrees with other life forms. While curiosity about self-awareness and self-consciousness is ancient, the systematic and multidisciplinary study of selfhood has accelerated over the past hundred years. Many of these more recent studies reflect both the strengths and weaknesses of the psy- and socially oriented disciplines from which they emerge: the psy-oriented studies capturing important aspects of the intrapsychic, intrapersonal, corporeal, and neurobiological variables affecting human experiencing and subjectivity, but often ignoring or underplaying the extent to which these same variables are affected by such things as race, class, gender, language, history, and other environmental circumstances and contextual factors. And the more socially

DOI: 10.4324/9781003529118-1

oriented studies doing the reverse: capturing well how human subjectivities are always affected by the social, political, and material worlds from which they emerge and in which they remain entangled throughout life, but ignoring or downplaying aspects of human experiencing and self-consciousness that may be more universal or individually variable—either possibility belying the notion that human subjectivity could ever be as directly and unambiguously reflective of social attitudes and perspectives as some socially oriented theorists would suggest.

This chasm in perspectives becomes even more acute for someone like myself who has been trained in both anthropology and psychoanalysis—this despite the fact that my own small, subfield of anthropology, "psychological anthropology," has, since the early seminal work of Ruth Benedict (1934), Edward Sapir (1949), and Irving Hallowell (1955), among others, attempted to bridge and integrate insights from both the psy- and socially oriented disciplines.[1] Wearing my anthropological hat, I have often been in the position of reminding my psychoanalytic colleagues that we should not be too quick to presume that a person's troubles are rooted in their childhood experience when there may be many other more contemporary reasons why a person struggles, or which amplify and aggravate the troubles related to childhood. One example of this that remains particularly salient for me occurred during a clinical discussion of an untenured professor's troubles at a time when I was still an untenured, assistant professor myself. As my psychoanalytic colleagues discussed and analyzed what aspects of early family experience and their internalization might have contributed to this man's struggles, it became evident to me that these same colleagues, most of whom were clinical psychologists or psychiatrists, did not have a clue about how the tenure system at universities worked and how demanding, stressful, and anxiety-provoking it could be for someone who did you yet have tenure. Whatever troubles related to childhood and family experience this man might have had, they could not be separated from the current and ongoing precarity of his employment and career situation.

But conversely, with my psychoanalytic hat on, I have become acutely aware of how much social theory is premised on the assumption of a curiously unitary, fully conscious, yet relatively passive subjectivity, one easily buffeted and shaped by the social and material forces from which it emerges and one that is relatively homogenous with other subjectivities from the same time and place—as if people do not have to live with the consequences of their idiosyncratic life histories and its effects on their future life experience. As if their waking consciousness and motivations are not occasionally, or frequently, ruptured by dream and religious or spiritual experiences, illness episodes, and states of modified consciousness or intoxication brought on by medicinal substances or by drugs and foods of various types. Such roilings and fluctuations of subjectivity find a limited role in most social theories, and yet without taking them into account, we cannot comprehend how a Toraja man in the highlands of Sulawesi so earnestly advocates for the wisdom of the gods and ancestors despite his own conversion to Christianity and criticism of important elements of traditional Toraja culture (Chapter 9). Nor can we understand why a white, middle-class American laid off in the midst of the recession of 2007–2008 experiences and dreams about his loss of employment as a literal mugging and assault (Chapter 5).

Only a much more systemic, ecologically oriented model of subjectivity can help close this conceptual gap between the social and psy-oriented disciplines as currently practiced. One that encourages us to recognize the phenomenological truth that the sense of self and subjectivity arise only *in relation to* their entanglements with a non-self world, but also reminds us that once in existence, subjectivity is not an empty shell waiting to be filled by its entanglements in a transparent, linear way, but rather an evolving sense of experiencing engaged in an active process of autopoiesis. This process of self-fashioning is a spiraling one in which inborn proclivities and memories of and reactions to past experiences affect the experiencing of contemporary entanglements and imaginings of and aspirations for, or a fear and avoidance of, the future. But also the reverse, one in which contemporary experiences and imaginings of and aspirations for the future feed back into how past experiences are remembered and reconfigured experientially. Such a spiraling, looping form of subjectivity, one in which past, present, and future are comingled and linked through emotional and imaginative associations, defies easy modeling by either the psy- or socially oriented disciplines when taken alone.

Gregory Bateson's (1972) notion of an ecology of mind and experience was an early effort to provide just such a model of the systemic, ecologically embedded nature of human subjectivity and selfhood, emphasizing that self-awareness emerges from a vast network of feedforward and feedback loops interlinking body/brain processes to an equally dynamic environmental landscape of family, culture, politics, and the material world, including other species—most of the vast network remaining outside conscious self-awareness most of the time. The self-system in this model is a fractionated one that is organized dynamically, temporarily, hierarchically, and developmentally. Lower-level subsystems of subjectivity and consciousness may or may not come together to form a superordinate self that is aware, or not, of its constituent parts. Lower-level subsystems may or may not remain separate from other parts of self-organization and function relatively independently and autonomously. In any or all of these cases, the organization of the self-system, and the border between what is conscious in subjectivity and what is unconscious or less than fully conscious, is responsive to and contingent upon both the intrapersonal and extrapersonal processes from which it emerges. Such a conceptualization of human subjectivity and selfhood brings attention to how profoundly the material, symbolic, and interpersonal world affects the organization and experiencing of selfhood, but also underscores that self-consciousness is never a mere reflection of or container for the non-self world, but rather that experiences are actively constructed out of numerous and varied self-states and memory-laden perceptions. Constructions that are not only influenced by cultural, linguistic, political, and material variables of various kinds, but also by the genetic, neural, creative, and imaginative intrapersonal and intrapsychic capacities, and limitations, of individual people.

While Bateson's ecological model captures well how body/brain and environmental interactions co-constitute human subjectivity and consciousness, it is a model that remains relatively abstract and conceptual, and Bateson himself did not closely investigate the experiential dynamics of everyday human life—especially with regard to how individual differences in biology, genetics, neural organization, and psychodynamics might affect the degree to which and the manner in which people are affected by their culturally constituted worlds. And the reverse, how variations in culturally constituted worlds might affect aspects of individual embodiment. To help facilitate the kind of empirical, grounded investigation of these dynamics by myself and others that Bateson himself never pursued, all of the chapters in the second part of this book develop and utilize the concept of "selfscapes."

Drawing on Bateson's notion of an ecology of mind and on Damasio's work on embodied mind and emotion (1994, 1999, 2010), a selfscape is the self-system's implicit moment by moment mapping of its own representations of its own past embodied experiences onto the space and time of the contemporary culturally constituted world. The "self" part of the term underscores that though the dynamic, looping, recursive, autopoietic interplay of the phenomenal field remains open to and dependent upon its transactions with the broader world, the distinction between one's own bodily organism and body/mind and all other objects in the world maintains itself throughout life, producing and regulating an intraself topography and organization of memory and emotional reactivity (Thompson 2007). The "scape" part of the terms refers to both the intraself and extraself terrains that the self-system simultaneously maps and represents throughout the day and night and from which a contingent and dynamic sense of self emerges moment to moment. "Selfscape" is, then, a bridging and integrating concept that is meant to capture both the integrity of self-systems and their experiential accretions over time, but also their contingency and looping dynamism in relation to their transactions with the world. It is thus a concept that invites investigations of human subjectivity from either the psy- or socially oriented disciplines, yet reminds investigators of either stripe that whether one begins with a primary interest in the extrapersonal -scapes of a selfcape or its intrapersonal -scapes, one must always be concerned with how either set of -scapes is linked to and affected by the others.

Illuminating Human Selfscapes: Person-Centered Ethnography

While selfscapes can be investigated from a variety of disciplinary perspectives and using a variety of methodologies, my own training in anthropology and psychoanalysis has led me to use person-centered ethnography (Hollan 2001, 2005, 2025; Levy and Hollan 2015) in my own work—an approach and style of research that I think can be particularly fruitful for anyone interested in how human subjectivities unfold in ongoing, naturally occurring behavior. Person-centered ethnography refers to ethnographic attempts to describe, represent, and analyze human behavior and subjective experience from the point of view of the acting, intending, and attentive subject. Yet unlike most other forms of ethnography focusing on group characteristics and dynamics, person-centered ethnography attempts to actively explore, rather than to assume, the emotional force (Spiro 1984) and cognitive saliency (D'Andrade 1984) of the social, cultural, political, economic, and material forces that entangles a person. The focus in such work is not only on the culturally constituted behavioral environment in which a person "thinks, is motivated to act, and satisfies his [sic] needs" (Hallowell 1955: 88), but also on how people are reacting to, embodying, internalizing, and transforming that environment. This involves the kind of participant observation or deep hanging out that social and cultural anthropologists are known for, in which the participant observer follows people through their normal routines in life, observing what they do and do not do, who or what they associate with and who or what they avoid, and the extent to which they conform or not to conventional expectations of how people of their social, cultural, and racial type should be acting, feeling, and thinking.

But beyond observing overt behavior, person-centered ethnography also involves attempting to explore how people are experiencing, assessing, and reacting to their entanglements with other people and the larger behavioral environment. For many person-centered ethnographers, including myself, this involves engaging people in extended, repeated, open-ended conversations in which they reflect on their life engagements, including how their current entanglements may be evoking memories of the past and fantasies or imaginings of the future. And the reverse: how people's memories, fantasies, and dream experiences may be affecting the way they engage with other people and the larger, non-self world. Such conversations resemble psychoanalytic sessions in some ways, in which an analyst encourages a person to express and reflect on whatever crosses their mind and pays close attention to, among other things, how a person's wish or desire may reinforce or contradict moral conscience; the extent to which someone is consciously aware or not of conflicting desires or goals; the way in which someone may avoid certain topics of discussion, but actively promote others; who or what someone identifies with and who or what they may be repelled by; the extent to which someone consciously assumes responsibility for different aspects of their behavior or attributes such responsibility to beings or forces outside their conscious control. Indeed, from an anthropological point of view, it is the value and significance placed on the long-term, non-judgmental engagement with and observation of another person's flow of consciousness and awareness and unawareness that is the most important legacy of psychoanalysis to the study of humans.

In other respects, though, person-centered conversations differ from psychoanalytic sessions in important ways. Perhaps most significantly, person-centered interviewees are not self-identified "patients." They do not come to the ethnographer for comprehension of or relief from their pain and suffering, and so they are not motivated to bare their thoughts and feelings in the same way a patient might—though they may, and often do, find it gratifying to be listened to with patience and respect (Levy and Hollan 2015). And unlike an analyst or other healer, an ethnographer is not usually attempting to intervene in or help change an interviewee's subjectivity, but rather, to observe its naturally occurring ebbs and flows in relation to the non-self world.

It is through this dual process of observing a person's overt behavior in relation to their emotional reactions to, reflections on, and fantasies and imaginings about that behavior, and vice versa, that we can begin to get a handle on the looping process of autopoiesis, in which past, present, and future intermingle in non-linear, spiraling ways. By taking advantage of people's human capacity to reflect on themselves and their experiences (Rapport 2015), we learn things about them that we can learn in no other way. We learn what they think about, feel, imagine, or obsess on and how these preoccupations affect their overt behavior, if at all. We learn how overdetermined and motivationally complex conventional behaviors can be, and how they can be used to divert attention from, or secretly gratify, other, less socially acceptable preoccupations or concerns. We learn that what people are willing and able to tell us about themselves and their experiences changes as our relationships with them deepen and evolve over time. We learn what parts of people's behavior they have conscious awareness of and what parts they do not, and how those parts are dynamically related. We learn what people most value, enjoy, fear, or dread in their lives and why. By illuminating the complexities, paradoxes, and contradictions of human subjectivities, person-centered ethnography gives us a window onto the varieties and particularities of human selfscapes as they shape and are shaped by the non-self world.

Spatial and Temporal Aspects of Selfscapes

While the concept of selfscapes gets us away from misleading notions overemphasizing either the universal or social aspects of human subjectivity, it does not itself attempt to predict the relative value or importance of either intrapersonal or extrapersonal factors affecting consciousness and subjectivity. Rather, it suggests that the relative value or importance of both factors must be actively investigated, leaving open the possibility that one or the other may play an inordinate role in shaping or influencing any given selfscape. For example, when Joao Biehl (2005) first met Catarina in his person-centered study of the dire living conditions he found at a residential institution in Brazil, he assumed that much of Catarina's impaired gait and disjointed language could be explained by the malnourishment, neglect, and overmedication that she shared with many of the other impoverished residents. Although Biehl was told by caretakers and staff that Catarina was a "mad" woman who spoke only nonsense, he began to realize that her words, gestures, and writings were more meaningful than he had been led to believe, and so he followed up on her intimations that she had once had a family that had "forgotten" her, and that her impairments of gait and balance were shared with other members of this absent family. Biehl eventually found and visited members of Catarina's extended family and learned that several of them did indeed also suffer a form of degenerative ataxia, later identified as Machado-Joseph disease. That finding helped explain why Catarina was experiencing the kind of language and balance problems that she was.

Similarly, the selfscape concept does not suggest any particular value or importance placed on the past, the present, or the future in shaping or influencing a selfscape, but rather, leaves open the possibility that any of these temporalities may strongly influence a given person's subjectivity, depending on both cultural and experiential factors. While some people may be haunted by their past experiences and seemingly stuck or frozen within them, as trauma victims sometimes are, others may be so focused on and aspirational for a future life that it is as if they have no past at all. Other people may be more prone to seize the day and live without much regard to either past or future, while yet others might get stuck in the past for some part of their lives and then unstuck and then stuck again. The experiential possibilities here are endless and cannot be known in advance for any given person. The selfscape concept does not obscure these kinds of experiential complexities and dynamics but rather draws attention to them so that they may be investigated more actively and explicitly. For example, in Chapter 5, I discuss how George's economic precarity in the aftermath of the 2007–2008 recession triggered dreams and memories of himself as a victim of bullying and assault, unable to defend himself. These dreams and memories then looped into the way he experienced his lay-off and rehiring as a temporary contract worker as itself a type of aggressive assault—a type of experiencing that was unique to his own background and upbringing.

Ecologies of Selfscapes and the Interpersonal World

If human subjectivities are as particular and varied as the selfcape concept suggests, then we must abandon the idea that we will ever be able to generalize much about them from either a psy- or socially oriented perspective alone. Rather, we need to be thinking about how selfscapes are situated within dense, interconnected, mutually influenced and shaped material, behavioral, and symbolic ecologies in which even small changes in one part of the ecology must necessarily affect other parts. Such effects may be large or small or negligible, depending on the degree of integration or insularity of various parts of the self-system. For example, a person who is discriminated against within a static race-based social hierarchy may not be able to escape the double consciousness (DuBois 1903; Fanon 1952) that such hierarchies often create—an identification with both the oppressed and the oppressor—even with the counterbalancing benefits of wealth, education, therapy, etc. But on the other hand, the subjective consequences of a contingent and unexpected historical event, such as Nene'na Tandi's conversion to becoming a firm believer in the retributory justice of the Toraja gods and ancestors in the aftermath of his near starvation in New Guinea (Chapter 9), may ramify throughout a community. In Nene'na Tandi's case, he became an astute diagnostician of the signs and indexes of retribution directed toward himself and others. His self-consciousness about these issues led him to inhabit and enact Toraja conceptions of ancestral figures, morality, and justice in a particularly animated way that went far beyond that of most of his fellow villagers. He thereby created a particular kind of world for himself and his fellows, one that was, in some ways, unlike any other Toraja world either before or since.

This last example suggests just how important the immediate interpersonal world is in mediating any person's engagements with other elements of the non-self world—though one that is largely ignored or downplayed in contemporary discussions of human subjectivity outside of psychoanalysis or clinical psychology. As I discuss further in Chapter 9, people live, act, and experience in behavioral environments not just of competing norms, values, classes, institutions, and ways of labeling and conceptualizing things like gender and race, but environments in which the people around them have animated these various elements in different ways and with varying degrees of conviction and emotional intensity. In one's proximate social environment, it matters very much *who* one's co-actors and interlocutors are and how they *inhabit* that environment, not just what formal rules, norms, ideologies, or statuses they may be enacting overtly in the current moment. The people around one may amplify or mute all or some of the other elements of one's immediate behavioral environment, or alternately and inconsistently amplify or mute them, with varying consequences for how people engage with and experience their non-self worlds. There is a dynamism, complexity, and unexpectedness to human action and reaction at this level of analysis that the selfscape concept attempts to highlight rather than to obscure. A single generous or empathic person in someone's circle of intimate companions can help compensate for structural, material, and psychological deprivations of numerous kinds. A single excessively angry or manipulative person in one's proximate behavioral environment may dilute or completely neutralize and eliminate the advantages of an otherwise privileged social and material position. Do the people around one encourage one's imagination and emotional reactivity, or do they constrain or inhibit them? The way we learn to interpret, react to, and sometimes internalize many aspects of the non-self world is often strongly influenced by the way the people us around interpret, react to, and internalize that world—whether we end up consciously or unconsciously reproducing some or all of these influences or by consciously or unconsciously defining ourselves in opposition to some or all of them. The interpersonal world, then, must be considered a central, mediating element of the experiential topography that the selfscape maps and reacts to, not a marginal one.

The Subjectivity and Experiential Potentials of Groups

Human consciousness emerges at a particular time and place within a complex and dynamic material, social, and symbolic ecology. Although every person's selfscape remains relationally entangled in this dense ecological matrix until the moment of its death, the person´s experiencing of the matrix and of their received circumstances will be singular and unique because their positionality and spiraling autopoiesis within the matrix is singular and unique. This is true no matter how rigid or structured a person's proximate ecological matrix might be, because while families, cultures, religions, nation states, and other groups may attempt to encourage or enforce overt conformity to local values, customs, or rules, the *experiencing* and *inhabiting* of such conventional behaviors is much more difficult to socialize or control. Overt enactments of behavior can be given relatively direct feedback and critique. One can be told, "do it this way," or "don't do it that way." But the emotions and imaginings interpolated within such enactments are not so easily controlled or contained. As I mention in Chapter 4, one can be taught that some form of behavior communicates respect, but experience it as humiliating to others or to oneself. One can be taught that some form of behavior should be joyful, but experience it as unimaginably tragic or poignant. And all of this can change over time. The expansiveness, particularity, and variegated nature of personal experience will always overflow the social or cultural forms into which it is poured or within which it is instantiated.

In Chapter 3, I refer to these experiential overflows as the *subjectivity* or *experiential potentials* of a group. Groups large and small often work hard to contain such subjectivity potentials, fearing that they may lead to social or political disorder, pathology, or worse. Yet ironically, it is this large and variable pool of emotions, cognitions, mental models, and imaginings within groups that, in part, allows them to adapt to changing social, material, and technological conditions, as Gananath Obeyesekere (1981, 1990) and others have argued. Subjectivities that are considered marginal, suboptimal, or idiosyncratic in a group today may prove to be highly valued under new or changing conditions. I give several illustrations of this among the Toraja of Indonesia in Chapter 3, but other examples are not hard to find. In *Radical Hope: Ethics in the Face of Cultural Devastation* (2006), Jonathan Lear discusses how Crow elders in the late 1870s and beyond drew on the dream images and experiences of the youthful Plenty Coup to help them evaluate and respond to devastating losses of culture and livelihood at the hands of the United States government and settler colonialists. The Crow, like many people around the world, believed that dream experiences could be valuable sources of information about how an individual or group was relating to other humans and non-humans, and to the world at large. Even as a child, Plenty Coup was recognized as someone who was gifted at dreaming, and Crow elders considered several of his dreams to be prophetic. One dream seemed to foretell the coming loss of a traditional way of life and the radical changes that the Crow would have to adopt in order to survive. As Lear observes, Plenty Coup's dream "did not predict any particular event, but the change of the world order. It was prophetic in the sense that the tribe used it to face up to a radically different future" (Lear 2006: 68).

What is notable here is that rather than dismiss or ridicule the dreams of a small boy, Crow elders recognized that Plenty Coup had something valuable to impart to them. They realized that Plenty Coup's dreaming mind was attuned to the changing circumstances of the world in a way that they and other Crow were not, and that they could learn from his unique awareness. What was once a fleeting state of mind and subjectivity was becoming a central tenet of Crow survival and change.

Of course, many, if not most, elements of a group's subjectivity potential—passing thoughts and feelings, night and daydreams, fantasies and imaginings—remain just that, a behavioral potential, states of subjectivity and awareness that are fleeting and never become widely shared or observable through overt behavior. Yet such states of mind and subjectivity are also a key source of any group's dynamics of either statis or change. This is a way of thinking about the importance of "diversity" in a group of people that goes far beyond the usual politics of advantaged and disadvantaged groups. It is the recognition that the emerging state of the world is co-constituted by existing circumstances, however structured and constrained by cultural, political, and material factors, and by the ways those circumstances are differentially perceived, understood, and interpreted by people variously and uniquely placed within them. Within such a dynamic social ecology, no person's contributions of subjectivity and awareness are without significance or value because in some way, for good or ill, they all afford or constrain other elements of the dynamic ecology. They thus play a part, however broad or limited, in what eventually emerges from the overall social ecology. While any socio-ecological system, any human community, is always more than the sum of its parts, it would be a different system or community if any of its parts, if any of its selfscapes, were replaced or lost.

Peopling of the Selfscapes

The concept of selfscapes is meant to help us understand how human subjectivity and consciousness emerges and changes over time. But it would be ironic, indeed, if the concept came to overshadow the actual people who inspired its conception and development—a complaint I myself have made about several other theories of human subjectivity. My thoughts about selfscapes have emerged from my years-long, person-centered engagement with a variety of people in both anthropological and psychoanalytic contexts. Through this style of work and research, I have developed an appreciation of how human subjectivity is always informed by *both* the constraints of the social ecology acting on and affecting a particular person *and* by how that person is remembering and habitually responding, or not, to that history of engagement with the world. While this mutual influence and co-constitution between historical circumstance and individual reactivity and memory is universal, the way this autopoietic process unfolds will vary, sometimes greatly, from person to person. Which is why throughout this book I do not refer to a generalized groups of people or to an abstract process of human subjectivity formation and experience, but rather to the subjectivity formation and experience of individual people with individual names and identities—though for the sake of privacy, all the names in this book are pseudonyms and the social identities of some people have been changed in some respects or disguised.

Readers will meet three people recurrently throughout the book, two from the Toraja highlands of Sulawesi in Indonesia and one from the Los Angeles area of the United States. I got to know both Nene'na Tandi (Chapters 2, 3, 7, 9) and Nene'na Limbong (Chapters 2, 3, 5, 6, 8) while conducting fieldwork in Toraja in the 1980s and 1990s. Although Nene'na Tandi and Nene'na Limbong were roughly the same age, grew up in the same small village, spoke the same languages, were exposed to the same social and cultural influences, and were both rice farmers, Nene'na Limbong had more economic security and status than Nene'na Tandi and had many more of his own biological children—children being an important additional source of economic and social security in Toraja. Such differences led to important differences in life and subjective experience between the two men, despite having grown up near to one another in the same small, relatively insular community—differences that I explore and discuss throughout the book.

Another person who appears throughout the book is a man I met through my research psychoanalytic practice. He is a white, middle class, U.S. citizen who appears in Chapters 3, 5, 6, and 9. In Chapters 3 and 6, he appears under the pseudonym of Steve, and in Chapters 5 and 9, I refer to him as George. Though Steve, or George, struggled for many years trying to come to terms with a traumatic childhood and upbringing, it was his deep commitment to our work together that allowed the two of us to grasp aspects of his emerging autopoietic subjectivity that we would have missed or misunderstood otherwise. Like all the other individual people I mention in this book, his lived experience informs the concept of selfscapes and yet far exceeds it. It is because of this that I argue that all experiences of selfhood and subjectivity are singular as well as being relationally constituted. If it is true, as John Donne has written, that "no man is an island entire of itself," it is equally true, as William James has observed, that the elementary psychic fact is not *"thought* or *this thought* or *that thought,* but *my thought,* every thought being owned. Neither contemporaneity, no proximity in space, nor similarity of quality and content are able to fuse thoughts together sundered by this barrier of belonging to different personal minds. The breaches between such thoughts are the most absolute breaches in nature" (James 2021: 97). It is this singularity and insularity of subjective experience that makes the use of personal names and identities so necessary when discussing human selfhood, subjectivity, and selfscapes.

The person-centered focus on the life experience of individual people in different times and places allows us to see not only how a selfscape may vary by its entanglements with a historically specific social and material ecology, but also how the experience and memory of those relational entanglements, how they are actually lived and inhabited, may take on a life of their own, affecting other people and the surrounding world in both predictable and unpredictable ways. To be sure, the worries and concerns of Steve (George) in southern California were very different than those of the rice farmers Nene'na Tandi and Nene'na Limbong in Toraja. Yet Nene'na Tandi and Nene'na Limbong inhabited their common world in different ways, just as Steve (George) experienced his layoff during the 2007-08 recession in his own particular way (Chapter 5). A person-centered perspective on selfscapes illuminates such experiential complexities rather than obscures them.

It Takes the Whole of Us

While William James, whom I reference above and in Chapters 4 and 9, did not use formal ecological concepts in his psychological and philosophical writings, his radically empiricist approach to human subjectivity and consciousness—recognizing that people's ideas and practices are more closely tied to or follow from their proclivities, desires, and unique positioning in the world than commonly thought—resonates with such concepts and with how I have conceptualized selfscapes. From the point of view of "radical empiricism," "Prima facie the world is a pluralism (James 2019: vii)," including all of the people who co-constitute and inhabit it. For James, individual people are sites of emergent streams of consciousness and subjectivity in which impingements and influences from the world meet the experientially shaped imaginative capacities of the person, a meeting in which both person and world may or may not be transformed—the world overwhelming people at times, but people also at times imposing them*selves* on the world and other people. This is a perspective that highlights, rather than underplays or ignores, the contingency and uniqueness of human experience and subjectivity, noting that the "unsharable feeling which each of us has of the pinch of his [sic] individual destiny as he privately feels it rolling out on fortune's wheel may be disparaged for its egotism, may be sneered at as unscientific, but it is the one thing that fills up the measure of our concrete reality, and any would-be existent that should lack such a feeling, or its analogue, would be a piece of reality only half made up" (James 1982: 499–500).

While James underscores the contingency and uniqueness of human subjectivity in passages such as this one, he is not claiming that experience or subjectivity is locked away in the inner recesses of an isolated mind. Rather, he is merely acknowledging the cross-cultural, existential fact that things happen to one person, even within the same local world, that do not happen to another and that this difference in happenings and developmental history continues to leave its mark on the way people go on to interact with one another and experience the world. The selfscape concept resonates strongly with this emphasis on the contingency and uniqueness of human subjectivity, yet goes beyond James to spell out more explicitly how and why this contingency and uniqueness is related to the dynamics of particular and variable social ecologies.

James's view of the human condition more generally also resonates with the notion of selfscapes and with some of the ecological concepts that underly it. For James, the human condition is not a static condition or state, but one that is dynamic and emergent, and one in which every person, everywhere has something to contribute: "No two of us have identical difficulties, nor should we be expected to work out identical solutions. Each, from his [sic] peculiar angle of observation, takes in a certain sphere of fact and trouble, which each must deal with in a unique manner. Each attitude being a syllable in human nature's total message, it takes the whole of us to spell the meaning out completely" (James 1982: 487).

As both an anthropologist and a psychoanalyst, I take this perspective seriously. The lives of all people are an experiment in becoming human, and all such experiments have value and are worthy of acknowledgment and consideration. The concept of selfscapes is meant to underscore not only the varieties and particularities of these experiments in becoming, but also the fact that no single life, no single selfscape alone can tell us what it means to be human or reveal all its potentialities. It does, indeed, take the whole of us to spell out the meanings, and possibilities, of human experiencing.

Organization of the Book

The book is divided into two main parts. In Part I, *Orienting Concepts*, I include some of my earlier work sketching out thoughts and ideas that I later develop into the concept of selfscapes. Several of these chapters express my dissatisfaction with theorists who exaggerate either the social (Chapters 2 and 4) or universal (Chapter 5) aspects of human subjectivity and selfhood. All chapters in Part I also make the case for the use of person-centered ethnography and the listening and observational approach of psychoanalysis as important tools in the study of human subjectivity and experiences of selfhood.

In Part II, I introduce the concept of selfscapes and illustrate their dynamics with ethnographic and clinical material. Chapter 6 illustrates how dreams both reflect and inform the dynamics of selfscapes, and how they mediate interior scapes of memory and emotion with the cultural and social-scapes of the world. Chapter 7 uses a typical day in the life of Nene'na Tandi to illustrate how the dynamics of a selfscape may change throughout the course of a day and night, and with it, the sense of wellness and unwellness. Chapter 8 uses one of Nene'na Limbong's dreams to illustrate how an emergent selfscape is informed by both the intrapersonal scapes of memory and emotion and the social and cultural-scapes of interpersonal and worldly engagements. Chapter 9 makes the case that while selfscapes are always relationally constituted and entangled with other people and with the world, their looping processes of autopoiesis lead to experiences of the world and other people that are always unique and singular.

Note

1 For some other recent efforts to bridge the psy- and socially oriented disciplines (see Kirmayer et al. 2015, 2020; Worthman et al. 2024a, 2024b).

References

Bateson, G. 1972. *Steps to an Ecology of Mind*. Chicago: University of Chicago Press.
Benedict, R. 1934. *Patterns of Culture*. Boston: Houghton Mifflin.
Biehl, J. 2005. *Vita: Life in a Zone of Social Abandonment*. Berkeley: University of California Press.
Chodorow, N.J. 2020. *The Psychoanalytic Ear and the Sociological Eye: Toward an American Independent Tradition*. New York: Routledge.
Damasio, A. 1994. *Descartes' Error: Emotion, Reason, and the Human Brain*. New York: Avon.
Damasio, A. 1999. *The Feeling of What Happens: Body and Emotion in the Making of Consciousness*. New York: Harcourt Brace.
Damasio, A. 2010. *Self Comes to Mind: Constructing the Conscious Brain*. New York: Pantheon.
D'Andrade, R.G. 1984. Cultural Meaning Systems. In *Culture Theory: Essays on Mind, Self, and Emotion*, edited by R.A. Shweder and R.A. LeVine, pp. 88–119. Cambridge: Cambridge University Press.
DuBois, W.E.B. 1903. *The Souls of Black Folks: Essays and Sketches*. Chicago: A.C. McClurg and Company.
Fanon, F. 1952. *Black Skin, White Masks*. New York: Grove Press.
Hallowell, A.I. 1955. *Culture and Experience*. Philadelphia: University of Pennsylvania Press.
Hollan, D. 2001. Developments in Person-Centered Ethnography. In *The Psychology of Cultural Experience*, edited by C.C. Moore and H.F. Mathews, pp. 48–67. Cambridge: Cambridge University Press.
Hollan, D. 2005. Setting a New Standard: The Person-Centered Interviewing and Observation of Robert I. Levy. *Ethos* 33(4):475–489.
Hollan, D. 2025. Person-Centered Ethnography: Exploring Complex Personhood. In *Cambridge Handbook of Psychological Anthropology*, edited by T. Low. Cambridge: Cambridge University Press.
James, W. 1982[1902]. *The Varieties of Religious Experience: A Study in Human Nature*. New York: Penguin Books.
James, W. 2019. *Essays in Radical Empiricism*. Whithorn, UK: Anodos Books.
James, W. 2021[1890]. *The Principles of Psychology*. New York: Henry Holt.
Kirmayer, L.J., R. Lemelson, and C.A. Cummings, eds. 2015. *Re-Visioning Psychiatry: Cultural Phenomenology, Critical Neuroscience, and Global Mental Health*. Cambridge: Cambridge University Press.
Kirmayer, L.J., C.M. Worthman, S. Kitayama, R. Lemelson, and C.A. Cummings, eds. 2020. *Culture, Mind, and Brain: Emerging Concepts, Models, and Applications*. Cambridge: Cambridge University Press.
Lear, J. 2006. *Radical Hope: Ethics in the Face of Cultural Devastation*. Boston: Harvard University Press.

Levy, R.I., and D.W. Hollan. 2015. Person-Centered Interviewing and Observation. In *Handbook of Methods in Cultural Anthropology*, edited by R. Bernard and C.C. Gravlee, pp. 313–342. New York: Rowman & Littlefield.

Obeyesekere, G. 1981. *Medusa's Hair: An Essay on Personal and Religious Experience*. Chicago: University of Chicago Press.

Obeyesekere, G. 1990. *The Work of Culture: Symbolic Transformation in Psychoanalysis and Anthropology*. Chicago: University of Chicago Press.

Rapport, N. 2015. Extraordinary Encounter? The Interview as an Ironic Moment. In *Extraordinary Encounters: Authenticity and the Interview*, edited by K. Smith, J. Staple, and N. Rapport, pp. 175–187. New York: Berghahn.

Sapir, E. 1949. *Culture, Language, and Personality*. Berkeley: University of California Press.

Spiro, M.E. 1984. Some Reflections on Cultural Determinism and Relativism With Special Reference to Emotion and Reason. In *Culture Theory: Essays on Mind, Self, and Emotion*, edited by R.A. Shweder and R.A. LeVine, pp. 323–346. Cambridge: Cambridge University Press.

Thompson, E. 2007. *Mind in Life: Biology, Phenomenology, and the Sciences of Mind*. Cambridge: Harvard University Press.

Worthman, C.M., C.A. Cummings, and D. Lende. 2024a. The Landscapes of Lives I: An Action Landscape Approach to Practices and the Interface of Individual and Society. *Ethos* 52(2):149–165.

Worthman, C.M., C.A. Cummings, and D. Lende. 2024b. The Landscapes of Lives II: How Social Actors Navigate Dynamic Action Landscapes. *Ethos* 52(2):166–185.

Part I
Orienting Concepts

2 Cross-Cultural Differences in the Self

Marsella, Devos, and Hsu (1985: ix) note a renewed interest in the study of the self. While such interest is evident in psychology and philosophy, it seems to be especially strong in anthropology, where recent work on the self includes ethnographies (e.g., Keeler 1987; Myers 1979; Rosaldo 1980), collections of articles (e.g., Carrithers et al. 1985; Dieterlen 1973; ed. 1979; Heelas and Lock 1981; Levy and Rosaldo 1983; Marsella et al. 1985; Shweder and LeVine 1984; Stigler, Shweder, and Herdt 1990; White and Kirkpatrick 1985), chapters in texts or books (e.g., Bock 1988; Crapanzano 1990; LeVine 1982), and at least one extensive review of the literature (Fogelson 1979).[1]

As Howard points out for the collection edited by White and Kirkpatrick (1985), much of the recent anthropological work on person, self, and other aspects of ethnopsychology has been in the revisionist vein of Mead (1928) and Malinowski (1951): it purports to demonstrate the culture-boundedness of Western conceptions and theories of person, self, and emotion by presenting data from around the world which appear to contradict them. "The aim is to release 'scientific' psychology, which should be universal, from the shackles imposed on it by Western 'folk'·psychology, which is culturally constricted" (Howard 1985: 403).

Anthropologists have argued, for example, that Western conceptions of the person as a discrete, autonomous, and individuated locus of personal will and responsibility—an "egocentric reductionist" view of the individual-in-society (Shweder and Bourne 1984)—misrepresent notions of the person in many nonWestern societies. Geertz (1984: 126), for instance, has noted:

> The Western conception of the person as a bounded, unique, more or less integrated motivational and cognitive universe, a dynamic center of awareness, emotion, judgment, and action organized into a distinctive whole and set contrastively both against other such wholes and against a social and natural background is, however incorrigible it may seem to us, a rather peculiar idea within the context of the world's cultures.

In many non-Western societies, it has been argued, views of the person are much more "sociocentric organic" in nature (Shweder and

DOI: 10.4324/9781003529118-3

Bourne 1984: 193). The person is seen as so inextricably woven into a fabric of culturally prescribed social roles, patterns of interpersonal behavior, and corporate identities that it is more appropriate to speak of the person as the "person-in-relationships," rather than as a discrete, well-bounded unit (cf. Howard 1985: 414).

Geertz and Shweder and Bourne use the term "person" in the work cited above to refer, at least in part, to a locus of subjective experience. Used in this way, the concept closely resembles what Hallowell refers to as "self." According to Hallowell (1959: 52), the self is that part of consciousness that comes into play when human beings begin to take themselves as an object. As such, it is an *experiential* datum that, unlike the Freudian "ego," can be directly described and talked about by actors, not merely deduced or postulated from psychological or cultural theory. In this chapter, I limit my focus to anthropological studies of "self" in Hallowell's sense of the word.[2]

The notion that concepts of the self vary by culture is now accepted by many, if not most, social and cultural anthropologists. Yet the theoretical and methodological implications of such a finding remain obscure. For example, when we say that concepts of the self vary by culture, do we mean only that different cultures have different ways of conceptualizing and talking about the self, or do we mean something more: that aspects of subjective experience also vary considerably?[3]

Anthropologists are often not explicit on this issue. They frequently fail to clearly and unequivocally address such questions as: To what extent are selves culturally constituted? If selves are only partially constituted by culture, what other factors play a part in their makeup? Are those other factors—social, biopsychological, etc.—universal in nature? Even if all selves are at least partly culturally constituted, are some selves more culturally constituted than others? Some researchers have argued that the experiential self must vary as much as the cultural models within which it is embedded, because the latter largely constitute the former. According to this position, since "the metaphors by which people live and the world views to which they subscribe mediate the relationship between what one thinks about and how one thinks" (Shweder and Bourne 1984: 189) and since "cultural models ... provide a basis for the organization of activities, responses, perceptions, and experiences by the conscious self" (Rosaldo 1984: 140), it is reasonable to assume that (usually) there is little or no distance between cultural models or theories of selfhood and the experiential self. Indeed, Lutz (1987: 308) has argued that such questions as "Does any particular ethnotheoretical model have an effect on the way people feel and behave?" and "How does the structure of ethnotheory acquire direction and force?"—which presuppose some gap between cultural conceptions and the self, emotions, and other psychological processes—are both unanswerable and culture-bound. They are, according to Lutz, suggested by our own Western theories of the mind, based on Cartesian dualisms, which emphasize, among other things, a split between self and social persona.

While the above position aptly points out how Western conceptions may distort cross-cultural research, other anthropologists have cautioned that the relationship between cultural conceptions of the self and "actual" subjective experience may be highly problematic. Howard (1985) notes, for example, that despite our American model of the self as separate, independent, and autonomous, experientially we seem to extend ourselves beyond the boundaries of the skin through such processes as empathy, identification, and personal space extension. Furthermore, he asks, despite evidence that many non-Westerners

> do not normally distinguish themselves as individualized entities in ordinary discourse, does this mean that they do not have a clear conception of themselves as unique individuals? If so, how do they deal with the corporal reality of the body—the fact that it urinates and defecates and experiences hunger, thirst, and sexual urges?
>
> (Howard 1985: 414)

Howard is arguing here that the sharp contrasts which are often drawn between Western and non-Western experiential selves have probably been exaggerated. I would agree and suggest that this occurs, in part, because some researchers (e.g., Dumont 1970; Geertz 1973) may too readily assume a close correspondence, or even identity, between cultural models or theories and subjective experience. There are at least three problems with this assumption.

The first concerns "cultural models," the presupposed, taken-for-granted, commonsensical, and widely shared assumptions which a group of people hold about the world and its objects (see Holland and Quinn 1987 for an excellent general discussion). Cultural models (of selves or anything else) present a simplified and often idealized conception of objects and processes in which much of the blooming, buzzing complexity of phenomena is either suppressed or ignored. Such models are often implicit, rather than explicit, and may be partial, situational, ad hoc, or inconsistent in nature (Keesing 1987). If cultural models of the self, like most other types of cultural models, are simplified and/or idealized, then we should not mistakenly assume that they encompass all aspects of the experiential self or that they alone should serve as the basis for a comparison of the self.

Second, by too readily assuming the cognitive and emotional "saliency" (Spiro 1984) of cultural discourse and conceptions, one may fail to recognize that cultural models are merely "ideas, *premises* by which people guide their lives, *and only to the extent a people lives by them do they have force*" (Shweder and Bourne 1984: 193; second emphasis added). One way people actually "live by" a cultural model of the self is by maintaining childrearing practices which result in deep intuitions about the model's inherent truth and correctness. Consider, for example, socialization for autonomy in the United States. By extending the rights of privacy to even very young children,

American parents repeatedly assert, through concrete interactions, the value of autonomy and independence.

> And, where are these "assertions" redundantly (even if tacitly) reiterated? Well, the assertion is there in the respect shown by a parent for a child's "security blanket." It's there as well when an adult asks a three-year-old "What do you want to eat for dinner?" and again in the knock on the door before entering the child's personal space, his private bedroom, another replica of the assertion.
>
> (Shweder and Bourne 1984: 194)

The extent to which a people actually "lives by" or practices a given model of the self is a question that should be investigated empirically, since the possibility exists that the model or some part of it will *not* be integrated into everyday experience.

Third, by emphasizing a one-to-one correspondence between cultural models and the experiential self, one underplays the extent to which aspects of subjective experience are also a product of psychobiological propensities (Hallowell 1955, 1959) and social encounters (Blumer 1969; Cooley 1922; Mead 1934) which may actually run counter to, or contradict, ideal cultural representations. For example, a child raised in an ostensibly "egocentric" society may yet be treated in such a way as to deny or discourage the emergence of a sense of initiative and autonomy. This, in turn, may lead to the development of individually constituted self-concepts which are at odds with the ideal sense of self promoted by the culture at large. Thus, cultural discourse and ideal conceptions "may not coincide neatly with personal experience and may ignore, obscure, and even misrepresent aspects of experience" (Wellenkamp 1988a: 488; see also Levy 1984: 218–228).

The position I am developing here is based on the view that while cultural and linguistic categories provide one important means by which the self is conceptualized and talked about and must surely influence the way the self is constructed (see, e.g., Hallowell 1955; Lakoff and Johnson 1980; Lutz 1982, 1985; Rosaldo 1980, 1984), cultural models and conceptions of the self should not be conflated with the experiential self.[4] Self-concepts may also be derived from one's own personal and social experience. Such individually constituted self-concepts may or may not be widely shared and they may or may not coincide with or reinforce self-concepts which are culturally constituted. Just as one cannot assume that cultural models of the self are merely projections of individual phenomenology, one cannot assume that an individual's experiential self can be reduced to the concepts and terms which are used to talk about it (cf. Bock 1988: 199). While the two are no doubt intimately and dynamically related, the extent to which they influence and shape one another should remain an empirical question (cf. Wellenkamp 1988a). This teasing apart of culture and subjective experience is fraught with difficulty (e.g., How is the report of an experience related to the experience reported upon?). Yet I agree with Keesing (1982: 31) that "with strategic interviews, projective tests, dreams, and other psychological methods, we *can* separate out the strands of individual experience from the cultural designs into which they are woven."

This distinction between cultural concepts or theories of the self and aspects of subjective experience which may escape such models is often lost or confused in recent discussions, yet it is not without precedent. Mauss, for example, in his article "A Category of the Human Mind: The Notion of Person; The Notion of Self" (1985), made clear that he was concerned with examining cultural variations in the *concept* of the self, not the experiential self, which he believed to be much less culturally variable:

> I shall leave aside everything which relates to the "self" (moi), the conscious personality as such. Let me merely say that it is plain, at least to us, that there has never existed a human being who has not been aware, not only of his body, but also at the same time of his individuality, both spiritual and physical... .

> My subject is entirely different, and independent of this. It is one related to social history. Over the centuries, in numerous societies, how has it slowly evolved—not the sense of "self" (moi)—but the notion or concept that men in different ages have formed of it?
> (Mauss 1985: 3; cf. Theodore Schwartz's comments
> quoted in Shweder 1984: 13–14)

In the next two sections, I illustrate some of these methodological and theoretical points by examining some discrepancies between ideal cultural models and aspects of subjective experience in both Toraja (South Sulawesi, Indonesia) and the United States. My intent here is to illustrate, in programmatic fashion, the complexity of the relationship between cultural models and the self as a locus of subjective experience, not to develop a comprehensive or conclusive analysis of either the Torajan or American experiential self.

Much of the data I present comes from the use of open-ended interviews conducted with a select group of American and Torajan respondents.[5] In a review of three recent works based on in-depth interviewing,[6] Marcus and Fischer (1986: 54) note that the mark of such contemporary approaches is the "display of discourse—self-reflective commentaries on experience, emotion, and self; on dreams, remembrances, associations, metaphors, distortions, and displacements; on transferences and compulsive behavior repetitions— *all of which reveal a behaviorally and conceptually significant level of reality reflecting, contrasting with, or obscured by public cultural forms*" (emphasis added). The following passage from Levy and Wellenkamp (1989) provides further elaboration of this point. What they have to say about the advantages of the open interview in the anthropological investigation of emotional experience also applies to the study of subjective experience in general.

> Such interviews provide two kinds of information about emotion. Individuals being interviewed are used in part as *informants,* providing their own interpretations of phenomena related to emotion. At the same time they may serve as *respondents,* objects of systematic study in themselves, in which their discourse—and in particular the *forms* of that discourse and their behavior as they talk—indicates something about the organization of emotion in that particular individual.. . . Many aspects of form can be put to analytic use here—facial expression and body language (capable of being recorded by video tape) as well as paralinguistic features, and a rich field of thematic clumpings, distortions, evasions, hesitations, slips of the tongue, and confusions, all amply illustrated and easily discernible in a close listening to tape recordings of interviews.
>
> (Levy and Wellenkamp 1989: 223–24)

While Abu-Lughod (1986) has recently demonstrated that different aspects of the self may be culturally elaborated in different contexts, my point in this chapter is somewhat different: that aspects of the experiential self are sometimes left undeveloped and unelaborated because they are only poorly understood or because they directly contradict other, more highly valued experiences. The open interview data I present should make clear that while there are significant differences between Toraja and American experiential selves, the differences are not of the magnitude that one might suppose from an examination of ideal cultural models alone.

Throughout my discussion, I focus on the individuated/relational dimension of the experiential self: that is, the extent to which the self is clearly individuated and distinguished from others in the behavioral environment or identified and merged with them. There are two reasons for this. First, the "self" is a global term that refers to several aspects or dimensions of subjective experience (Gergen 1971). For example, one could focus on the self's orientation in space and time, the evaluation of self, the sense of being "in control" as opposed to being "under control" (Heelas 1981; Lock 1981), the differences in what is considered "inside" the self or "outside" the self, etc. The failure to clearly specify which aspect of the self one is concerned with is yet another source of confusion in the contemporary literature. Thus, "self" is a term that gains analytical utility only to the extent that its referents are carefully specified and delimited. Second, the individuated/relational dimension of the self is most frequently described and commented upon in the anthropological literature and is the aspect of self for which comparable data are most readily available. Both the American and Toraja data sets illustrate the complexities of the self/other relationship, though both were originally collected for other purposes.[7]

The Relational Self in the United States

In research Jane Wellenkamp and I conducted some years ago (Wellenkamp and Hollan, 1981), we attempted to elicit salient aspects of middle-class American beliefs regarding death and bereavement by interviewing undergraduate students who had recently experienced a death in their families. Among other things, we were struck by the extent to which students relied upon notions of self-sufficiency, autonomy, and independence to cope with the experience of grief and loss. For example, each of our respondents believed that it was important to show "strength" in the wake of a death. To be "strong," one had to control the public display of one's emotions as well as actively master or resolve one's private sense of grief so that a normal lifestyle could be resumed as quickly as possible. According to one woman, even the death of a very close relative cannot be allowed to threaten one's sense of self-sufficiency and autonomy:

> Well, it's like our family is a boat. We've made a flotilla. And we've tied up to each other. And then these ties are all cut off [by a death in the family]... . But you just have to say that I don't need any of these ties at all. I can stand on my own.

Later in the same interview, she goes on to assert that in order to "stand on one's own," one has to develop "spine," so that one can avoid positions of dependency vis-à-vis other people.

Similar sentiments were voiced by another woman who argued that one has a duty to oneself to carry on after the death of a relative. Others may die and fade away, but oneself must and should persevere:

> Go on and keep your life rolling. Don't let it stand still because of that [a death in the family]. *Your* life is still there. And you should always watch out for yourself. When something like that happens [the death], it also makes you appreciate yourself more. At least you have yourself. That's what you'll always have. And you should never forfeit it.

Such statements about the need for strength and self-control in the face of a relative's death were complemented by negative evaluations of those who did not show such "spine." One respondent concluded a moving description of her mother's emotionally volatile reaction to the death of the respondent's sister by saying, "She really wasn't that strong."

Thus, according to the cultural model articulated by our undergraduate students, the self should be "strong" and independent and should not be compromised by the deaths of other people. And indeed, our respondents had actively sought to comply with such expectations when faced with a death in their own families. Yet other interview data clearly suggest that such losses did in fact present a strong challenge to the integrity and independence of our respondents' selves. They also indicate that Americans experience themselves to be more intertwined with one another, and so less impermeable, than the cultural model would suggest. For example, students occasionally displayed a fleeting recognition, cultural models to the contrary notwithstanding, that the death of a significant other also involved a partial "death" of one's own self:

> You think about your time with them [the dead person] and what you'll miss about them. Like I think about going to the beach and playing tennis with her [a recently dead sister]. And gossiping with her. And that's the part I miss because it makes me sad. Because I think everyone has a tendency to think about what they'll miss from that person [the one who has died]. You realize that they're gone and that a part of you had gone with them. And that can hurt.

Similarly:

> You're stripped of a certain role [when someone dies]. One of the people you relate with is gone. And so that side of you is gone. And you're kind of empty and reaching out for something.

Musings such as these seek to describe and articulate subjective experiences which are only poorly understood and conceptualized. The nature of these experiences is given more exact formulation by the sociologist Vernon (1970: 133):

> We are speaking here not of biological death, but rather of the death or cessation of behavior patterns–of a social death. Without doubt, part of one's way of behaving dies, or is no longer possible, when another individual with whom the behavior has been integrated is no longer there to react. Part of one's self, or his self-definition, dies when the other with whom one has been interacting dies. A particular reflected or mirror image is no longer there to receive.

It appears, then, that feelings of loss and emptiness during periods of bereavement betray aspects of the American experiential self which are only poorly accounted for, if not actually denied, by the ideal cultural model: namely, that the self is at least partly constituted by the "others" with whom it interacts and that the boundaries between self and other may remain somewhat fluid and indistinct. This is, of course, a point that G.H. Mead (1934) and the symbolic interactionists (e.g., Blumer 1969) have made repeatedly.

Autonomous Aspects of the Toraja Self

The Sa'dan Toraja (henceforth called the "Toraja") number approximately 350,000 and live in the interior mountainous regions of South Sulawesi, Indonesia. They are primarily wet-rice farmers who also cultivate small gardens of sweet potatoes, cassava, and assorted vegetables. Traditionally, Toraja society was stratified into three primary groups: nobles, commoners, and slaves or dependents. Although one's position within this hierarchy was theoretically ascribed at birth, status and prestige could also be achieved by slaughtering livestock at community feasts. Since the development of a cash economy, however, even former dependents are now heavily involved in the competitive slaughter of livestock. The traditional religion of the Toraja, *Alukta*, is based on the veneration and propitiation of spirits and deceased ancestors. Yet at least 50 percent of older adults and almost all Toraja under the age of 20 have now converted to Christianity.[8]

The Toraja are a strongly "sociocentric" people. Like many other Austronesian-speaking groups, they place a high value on affiliation and alliance within the community and strongly criticize self-serving, boasting, "pushy" behavior. The statuses and identities of individual villagers are not only tied to generations of ancestors who have preceded them, but also, through a system of teknonymy, to the generations of children and grandchildren that follow. The belief that the sins and "mistakes" of individuals may be visited upon the family or community as a whole, or on the generations to follow (Hollan 1988a), also serves to link the fate and prosperity of one to the moral behavior of all.

Toraja notions of the ideal person also reflect a concern with community and relatedness. People with *penaa melo*, "good breath," are said to be sensitive to the needs and concerns of others. They give generously and willingly—within the bounds of reciprocity—when asked for help, and they are at pains to avoid giving offense. Should disagreements arise, they strive for consensus and shun confrontational behavior. They are thought scrupulously honest in economic affairs, but they quite properly dissemble when brute facts and "sharp" words would serve only to embarrass or anger. Above all else, people with penaa melo are said to recognize that the peace and well-being of the community must come before individual interests; identity and self-esteem are affirmed within the community, not apart from it.

Open interview data[9] confirm that the interrelatedness of Toraja selves is often experientially "real" as well as culturally valued. For example, many of my respondents found it difficult to make evaluations of their own behavior without at the same time analyzing its effects on neighbors and kin. When Ambe'na ("Father of") Patu is asked what part of his character or behavior he would change if he could, he replies:

> [beginning to laugh] It depends on other people. If other people want us to change, we can change.... We may feel that our behavior/attitudes are good, but if other people don't like them they may say, "Don't act like that...." How are we ourselves to know how to change? Only other people can know that, you know? So if other people don't like us, we can try to change. We can try to change whatever behavior/attitudes are not liked.

This concern with, and openness to, others' opinions of oneself is also suggested by Indo'na ("Mother of") Rante:

> With regard to one's behavior/attitudes, it changes everyday. (Is that easy or difficult?) Easy! We think to ourselves, "Don't act like this or that [in ways people disapprove of], act like this [in ways people approve of]." It is the same when we instruct our children: "Don't act like that [inappropriately], act like your mother and father." That way, people don't criticize. That's how we maintain good behavior/attitudes.

Such statements suggest the extent to which the individual's sense of conscience and moral awareness are directly linked to the evaluations and opinions of others (cf. Levy 1973; Shore 1982).

Yet while Toraja culture and society clearly encourage the interrelatedness and identification of self with others, such embeddedness is not always sought or achieved. In the following pages, I discuss a number of contexts in which respondents express, directly or indirectly, a sense of their own autonomy or protest vigorously when that autonomy is challenged. While such expressions are partially supported by a general understanding that it is wrong to coerce people to do things against their will (Hollan 1990: 372–376), they are usually limited to relatively private settings, and they are less clearly articulated, and more morally ambiguous, than expressions of the sociocentric self.

1 One such expression involves occasional resistance to requests for aid or assistance. On the one hand, the Toraja are fond of saying that maturity and proper "understanding" necessarily eventuate in cooperative, unselfish, compliant behavior. Children are not always cooperative and compliant, and are often selfish, because they do not yet "know" the rules of proper behavior. The notion is, if one understands that relationships within the village are reciprocal and interdependent, then one *will be* responsive to the needs of others. Yet respondents also state that others cannot, and should not, take their cooperation and compliance for granted. They often asserted in the open interviews that they cannot be forced to do that which they do not wish to do. Such feelings of self-assertive defiance are especially evident when respondents imagined themselves replying to a request for assistance with a resounding "I don't want to!"[10]

The point here is not that the Toraja merely *claim* to identify with the needs of others. In fact, the Toraja *are* extremely cooperative and compliant. And when they do, rarely, refuse the requests of others, they do so in a culturally appropriate, nonconfrontational manner: they assiduously avoid the person asking for aid or assistance until the request is dropped or forgotten. The point, rather, is that when the Toraja *do* respond to the wishes and requests of others, as they usually do, they do so, in their own minds, because they *choose* to cooperate—not because they are incapable of resistance, self-assertion, or autonomy (cf. Levy 1973: 460).

2 Respondents also express a sense of autonomy when they state that they have extensive knowledge of the nature of the relationships, both human and supernatural, in which they are embedded. By claiming, as they frequently did in private contexts, that they "know everything" about politics, religion, customs, etc., they sought to *use* these relationships to satisfy their own personal needs and desires, rather than to be submerged and dominated by them. Several men, for example, claimed that their knowledge of omens, dream interpretation, astrology, and special magical amulets called *balo'* enabled them to manipulate the life-enhancing powers of the gods and ancestors to insure the fertility of their crops and livestock. They were thus capable of feeling *in* control, not just *under* control (cf. Heelas 1981; Lock 1981).

3 Open interview data indicate that the botanical metaphors which the Toraja often use to suggest that a group of people have mutual interests and a common identity may also be employed to *deny* how separate and autonomous the interests and identities of that group may actually be. In the passage below, Nene'na ("Grandfather of") Tandi uses a conventional metaphor in an effort to convince his parents that they cannot disinherit him simply because he chooses to exercise his independence and become a member of the Christian church:

> There is not a person in the world who can be separated from his parents. Just like trees. There is not a leaf that can be separated from the tree [it grew from]. All of them, even if they fall, fall beneath the tree. They do not fall away from the tree. I [the leaf] am the same to you [his parents, the tree].

4 Aspects of an autonomous self are also evident during certain dream experiences in which respondents envision themselves looming above and dominating those around them.[11] While some such dreams are culturally prescribed ways of validating claims to positions of power and influence, they also may be interpreted as expressions of an individual, autonomous self which stands apart from the crowd.

Nene'na Limbong reported two such dreams. In one, he found himself high atop a mountain. As he raised his arms perpendicular to his body, he discovered that he loomed above the landscape and that his hands reached to the farthest corners of Tana Toraja, dominating all those around him. In the second dream, an important government official asks several men to prove their worthiness to lead the village by climbing to the top of a tall pole. Nene'na Limbong watches other men try and fail in this task before he himself successfully reaches the top and is given the leadership of the village. Here, quite graphically, Nene'na Limbong asserts a dominant, commanding self.

As in the United States case, aspects of the Toraja experiential self— in this case autonomous aspects—are not readily inferred from an analysis of ideal cultural models alone. Such discrepancies suggest that the relationship between ideal cultural conceptions and subjective experience is complex and problematic and requires active investigation.

Discussion and Conclusion

I have argued that by too readily assuming a close correspondence between ideal cultural conceptions of the self—which are often simplified and idealized—and subjective experience, some researchers have tended to exaggerate the differences between a closed, individuated, autonomous, egocentric, "Western" self and an open, relational, interdependent, sociocentric, "non-Western" self (cf. Carucci 1987; Ewing 1990, 1991; Kleinman 1986; McHugh 1989; Mines 1988; Rosenberger 1989; Stephenson 1989). Using nondirective interview techniques which allow one to explore both valued and disvalued aspects of the experiential self, I have shown that one can find evidence, *in some contexts,* of an independent, autonomous self among the "sociocentric" Toraja of Indonesia and of an interdependent, relational self among "egocentric" Americans in the United States.

Rather than continue to focus on broad contrasts between "Western" and "non-Western" selves, I suggest, first, that we begin to examine in greater detail *degrees* of egocentrism or sociocentrism, openness or closedness, individuation or relation, etc., *within specific contexts* in both Western and non-Western societies. We might also begin to analyze more closely the different ways in which societies develop or fail to develop different aspects of the experiential self, for example, through such processes as "hypocognition" or "hypercognition" (Levy 1973, 1984). Only by making more subtle and detailed analyses of regional and intraregional variation will we begin to discern the ways in which different types of human reflexivity are related to different types of sociocultural systems.[12]

Second, partly as a result of the tendency to confuse ideal-typical models and theories of the self with the experiential self, current research often focuses on culturally valued dimensions of the self to the exclusion of those dimensions that are disvalued or those that are valued, or tolerated, only in narrowly defined contexts. This constricted focus not only oversimplifies the complexity of the human self, which is often characterized by multiple and contradictory facets (Gergen 1971), but it also leaves unexamined a fascinating area of research: the differential manner in which disvalued or disapproved dimensions of the self, some of which may be unconscious,[13] are culturally organized, expressed or suppressed, and managed. Closer examination of culturally disvalued dimensions of the self would also demand that we begin to analyze the ways in which different dimensions of the self, both valued and disvalued, are mutually defined and interrelated.[14]

Anthropologists have clearly demonstrated that cultural models of the self may vary significantly from culture to culture. The task now is to investigate both the manner and the extent to which these various models are actually "lived by" and thereby to ascertain the range of the experiential self as well.

Notes

1 Funding for parts of this research was provided by the National Science Foundation; the National Institute for Mental Health; The Wenner-Gren Foundation for Anthropological Research; Sigma Xi, The Scientific Research Society; and the Office of Graduate Studies and Research, University of California, San Diego. Sponsorship in Indonesia was provided by Lembaga Ilmu Pengetahuan Indonesia in Jakarta and by Universitas Hasanuddin in Ujung Pandang. Jane Wellenkamp's comments and suggestions have been invaluable. I have also benefited from the comments of Robert Levy, anonymous JAR reviewers, and the editor.

2 The inconsistent and imprecise use of terminology has been one of the banes of ethnopsychological research (see Harris 1989).

3 The relationship between cultural variation and individual psychology has been critical to the cross-cultural study of cognition and emotion as well. As Cole and Scribner (1974:172) note, for example:

> So long as we are concerned with demonstrating that human cultural groups differ enormously in their beliefs and theories about the world and in their actual products and technical accomplishments there can be no question: there are marked and multitudinous differences. But are these differences the result of differences in basic cognitive processes or are they merely the expressions of the many products that a universal human mind can manufacture, given variations and conditions of life and culturally valued acts?

And Wellenkamp (1988a:487) has observed:

> Even preliminary work in the ethnopsychology of emotion reveals the wide diversity in ways of talking about emotions. When the Javanese say that a group of villagers beat to death a reckless driver because they were "startled" by his behavior or when an Ilongot says, "[Since] I couldn't kill my wife, I just decided to forget my anger," are we to conclude that their emotional lives are very different from our own?

4 See Spiro (1984:324–25) for a more detailed discussion of the problems which result from conflating culture and phenomena which are partially constituted by culture and partially constituted by noncultural processes.

5 All of the interviews in both the United States and Indonesia were tape-recorded and transcribed. The quotations that follow are direct quotes taken from these Interviews.

6 These are Levy (1973), Kracke (1978), and Obeyesekere (1981). Levy interviewed rural and urban Tahitians, Kracke interviewed Kagwahiv political leaders and their followers, and Obeyesekere interviewed religious specialists in Sri Lanka.

7 The American data were collected during a study of loss and bereavement in the United States. The Toraja data were collected for the purpose of writing a "person-centered" ethnography.

8 For a more comprehensive description of Toraja life, see Bigalke (1981), Hollan (1984, 1988a, 1988b), Nooy-Palm (1979, 1986), Volkman (1985), and Wellenkamp (1984, 1988a, 1988b).

9 All of the quotations in this section are taken from a series of in-depth, open-ended life history interviews that Jane Wellenkamp (1984, 1988a, 1988b, 1991, 1992) and I (Hollan 1984, 1988a, 1988b, 1989, 1990, 1992) conducted with 11 Toraja of varying social and economic backgrounds. Wellenkamp interviewed the women and I interviewed the men. For a profile of individual respondents and a description of the interviewing techniques and procedures, see Hollan and Wellenkamp (1994).

10 I want to emphasize that this is a response that informants *imagine* themselves making. In fact, I never saw anyone blatantly and rudely reject a request for assistance in this way. Yet even if such feelings of defiance are not openly expressed, they obviously belie the assertion that members of "organic cultures" must necessarily "feel at ease in regulating and being regulated" (Shweder and Bourne 1984:194). It is probably more accurate to say that they feel at ease being regulated in certain contexts and at certain times.

11 For a brief ethnography of Toraja dreams, see Hollan (1989).

12 Gaines (1984) has shown, for example, that within "the West," there are significant differences between the "referential" self-concepts of the Northern European culture areas and the "indexical" self-concepts of the Latin Mediterranean culture areas. It remains to be seen whether such cultural differences also reflect significant differences in individual phenomenology.

13 It is, of course, awkward to speak of unconscious aspects of the self, since reflexive awareness implies consciousness. Yet we know that representations of the self and other which are out of awareness *do* shape human behavior in important ways. The challenge, then, is to develop a model of mind and consciousness which integrates various aspects of the self, those that are conscious and at least partly culturally constituted and those that may be individually constituted (though perhaps widely shared) and out of awareness. Unfortunately, neither anthropologists nor psychoanalysts have responded to this challenge. The former deal almost exclusively with culturally constituted aspects of the self, while the latter spend most of their time investigating aspects of self which are unconscious or out of awareness.

14 Melford Spiro has addressed such issues in several places (e.g., 1965, 1978, 1984). See also Thomas Hay (1977:78), who has argued that among the Ojibwa, a "conscious self-concept of helplessness is derived from the unconscious self-concept [of anger and hostility] through repression and projection"; Abu-Lughod (1986), who shows how the Bedouin come to value both the vulnerability and; invulnerability of the self in different contexts; and Rosenberger (1989), who analyzes the bipolar nature of the Japanese self.

REFERENCES

Abu-Lughod, L. 1986. *Veiled Sentiments: Honor and Poetry in a Bedouin Society*. Berkeley: University of California Press.

Bigalke, T. 1981. A Social History of "Tana Toraja," 1870–1965. Ph.D diss., University of Wisconsin, Madison.

Bock, P. 1988. *Rethinking Psychological Anthropology: Continuity and Change in Human Action*. New York: W.H. Freeman and Company.

Blumer, H. 1969. *Symbolic Interactionism*. Englewood Cliffs, N.J: Prentice-Hall, Inc.

Carrithers, M., S. Collins, and S. Lukes, eds., 1985. *The Category of the Person*. Cambridge, Eng: Cambridge University Press.

Carucci, L.M. 1987. The Person as an Individual in the Pacific. Paper presented in the symposium "Cultural Meaning and Self Representation" at the 86th Annual Meeting of the American Anthropological Association, November 18–22, Chicago, Ill.

Cole, M., and S. Scribner. 1974. *Culture and Thought: A Psychological Introduction*. New York: Wiley.

Cooley, C.H. 1922. *Human Nature and the Social Order*. New York: Scribner's.

Crapanzano, V. 1990. On Self Characterization. In *Cultural Psychology: Essays on Comparative Human Development*, edited by J.W. Stigler, R.A. Shweder, and G. Herdt, pp. 401–423. Cambridge, Eng.: Cambridge University Press.

Dieterlen, G., ed., 1973. *La notion de la personne en Afrique noire*. Paris: CNRS.

Dumont, L. 1970. *Homo Hierarchicus*. Chicago: University of Chicago Press.

Cross-Cultural Differences in the Self 33

Ewing, K.P. 1990. The Illusion of Wholeness: Culture, Self, and the Experience of In-consistency. *Ethos* 18:251–278.

Ewing, K.P. 1991. Can Psychoanalytic Theories Explain the Pakistani Woman? Intra-psychic Autonomy and Interpersonal Engagement in the Extended Family. *Ethos* 19:131–160.

Fogelson, R.D. 1979. Person, Self, and Identity: Some Anthropological Retrospects, Circumspects, and Prospects. In *Psychological Theories of the Self*, edited by B. Lee, pp. 67–109. New York: Plenum Press.

Gaines, A.D. 1984. Cultural Definitions, Behavior, and the Person in American Soci-ety. In *Cultural Conceptions of Mental Health and Therapy*, edited by A.J. Marsella and G.M. White, pp. 167–92. Dordrecht, Neth.: D. Reidel Publishing Co.

Geertz, C. 1973. Person, Time, and Conduct in Bali. In *The Interpretation of Cultures*, edited by C. Geertz, pp. 360–411. New York: Basic Books.

Geertz, C. 1984. From the Native's Point of View: On the Nature of Anthropological Understanding. In *Culture Theory: Essays on Mind, Self, and Emotion*, edited by R.A. Shweder and R.A. LeVine, pp. 123–136. Cambridge, Eng.: Cambridge Uni-versity Press.

Gergen, K.J. 1971. *The Concept of Self*. New York: Holt, Rinehart and Winston, Inc.

Hallowell, A.I. 1955, The Self and Its Behavioral Environment. In *Culture and Experi-ence*, edited by A.I. Hallowell, pp. 75–110. Philadelphia: University of Pennsylva-nia Press.

Hallowell, A.I. 1959. Behavioral Evolution and the Emergence of the Self. In *Evolu-tion and Anthropology: A Centennial Appraisal*, edited by B.J. Meggars, pp. 36–60. Washington, D.C.: Anthropological Society of Washington.

Harris, G.G. 1989. Concepts of Individual, Self, and Person in Description and Analy-sis. *American Anthropologist* 91:599–612.

Hay, T. 1977. The Development of Some Aspects of the Ojibwa Self and Its Behavioral Environment. *Ethos* 5:71–89.

Heelas, P.L.F. 1981. The Model Applied: Anthropology and Indigenous Psychologies. In *Indigenous Psychologies*, edited by P.L.F. Heelas and A.J. Lock, pp. 39–63. New York: Academic Press.

Heelas, P.L.F., and A.J. Lock, eds., 1981. *Indigenous Psychologies: The Anthropology of Self*. New York: Academic Press.

Hollan, D. 1984, "Disruptive" Behavior in a Toraja Community. Ph.D. diss., University of California, San Diego.

Hollan, D. 1988a. Pockets Full of Mistakes: The Personal Consequences of Religious Change in a Toraja Village. *Oceania* 58:275–289.

Hollan, D. 1988b. Staying "Cool" in Toraja: Informal Strategies for the Management of Anger and Hostility in a Nonviolent Society. *Ethos* 16:52–71.

Hollan, D. 1989. The Personal Use of Dream Beliefs in the Toraja Highlands. *Ethos* 17:166–86.

Hollan, D. 1990. Indignant Suicide in the Pacific: An Example from the Toraja High-lands of Indonesia. *Culture, Medicine, and Psychiatry* 14:365–379.

Hollan, D. 1992. Emotion Work and the Value of Emotional Equanimity Among the Toraja. *Ethnology* 31:45–56.

Holland, D., and N. Quinn, eds., 1987. *Cultural Models in Language and Thought*. Cambridge, Eng: Cambridge University Press.

Hollan, D., and J.C Wellenkamp, 1994, Contentment and Suffering: Culture and Expe-rience in Toraja. New York: Columbia University Press.

Howard, A. 1985. Ethnopsychology and the Prospects for a Cultural Psychology. In *Person, Self, and Experience*, edited by G.M. White and J. Kirkpatrick, pp. 401–420. Berkeley: University of California Press.

Keeler, W. 1987. *Javanese Shadow Plays, Javanese Selves*. Princeton, N.J: Princeton University Press.

Keesing, R. 1982. Prologue: Toward a Multidimensional Understanding of Male Initiation. In *Rituals of Manhood*, edited by G.H. Herdt, pp. 2–43. Berkeley: University of California Press.

Keesing, R. 1987. Models, "Folk" and "Cultural": Paradigms Regained? In *Cultural Models in Language and Thought*, edited by D. Holland and N. Quinn, pp. 369–393. Cambridge, Eng.: Cambridge University Press.

Kleinman, A. 1986. *Social Origins of Distress and Disease: Depression, Neurasthenia, and Pain in Modern China*. New Haven, Conn: Yale University Press.

Kracke, W. 1978. *Force and Persuasion: Leadership in an Amazonian Society*. Chicago: University of Chicago Press.

Lakoff, G., and M. Johnson. 1980. *Metaphors We Live By*. Chicago: University of Chicago Press.

Lee, B. ed., 1979. *Psychosocial Theories of the Self*. New York: Plenum Press.

LeVine, R. 1982. Culture, Behavior, and Personality. 2nd ed. Chicago: Aldine.

Levy, R.I. 1973. *Tahitians: Mind and Experience in the Society Islands*. Chicago: University of Chicago Press.

Levy, R.I. 1984. Emotion, Knowing, and Culture. In *Culture Theory*, edited by R.A. Shweder and R.A. LeVine, pp. 214–237. Cambridge, Eng.: Cambridge University Press.

Levy, R.I., and M.Z. Rosaldo, eds., 1983. Special Issue Devoted to Self and Emotion. *Ethos* 11(3):127–209.

Levy, R.I., and J.C. Wellenkamp. 1989. Methodology in the Anthropological Study of Emotion. In *Emotion: Theory, Research, and Experience*, vol. 4: The Measurement of Emotions, edited by R. Plutchik and H. Kellerman, pp. 205–232. New York: Academic Press.

Lock, A.J. 1981. Universals in Human Conception. In *Indigenous Psychologies*, edited by P.L.F. Heelas and A.J. Lock, pp. 19–36. New York: Academic Press.

Lutz, C. 1982. The Domain of Emotion Words on Ifaluk. *American Ethnologist* 9(1):113–28.

Lutz, C. 1985. Ethnopsychology Compared to What? Explaining Behavior and Consciousness Among the Ifaluk. In *Person, Self, and Experience: Exploring Pacific Ethnopsychologies*, edited by G.M. White and J. Kirkpatrick, pp. 35–79. Berkeley: University of California Press.

Lutz, C. 1987. Goals, Events, and Understanding in Ifaluk Emotion Theory. In *Cultural Models in Language and Thought*, edited by D. Holland and N. Quinn, pp. 290–312. Cambridge, Eng.: Cambridge University Press.

McHugh, E.L. 1989. Concepts of the Person Among the Gurungs of Nepal. *American Ethnologist* 16:75–86.

Malinowski, B. 1951. *Sex and Repression in Savage Society*. New York: Humanities Press.

Marcus, G.E., and M.M.J. Fischer. 1986. *Anthropology as Cultural Critique: An Experimental Moment in the Human Sciences*. Chicago: University of Chicago Press.

Marsella, A.J., G. DeVos, and F.L.K. Hsu, eds., 1985. *Culture and Self: Asian and Western Perspectives*. New York: Tavistock Publications.

Mauss, M., 1985. A Category of the Human Mind: The Notion of Person; The Notion of Self. In *The Category of the Person*, edited by M. Carrithers, S. Collins, and S. Lukes, pp. 1–25. Cambridge, Eng.: Cambridge University Press.

Mead, G.H. 1934. *Mind, Self, and Society*. Chicago: University of Chicago Press.

Mead, M. 1928. *Coming of Age in Samoa*. New York: Morrow.

Mines, M. 1988. Conceptualizing the Person: Hierarchical Society and Individual Autonomy in India. *American Anthropologist* 90:568–579.

Myers, F. 1979. *Pintupi Country, Pintupi Self: Sentiment, Place, and Politics Among Western Desert Aborigines*. Washington, D.C.: Smithsonian Institution Press.

Nooy-Palm, H. 1979. The Sa'dan Toraja: A Study of Their Social Life and Religion, vol. 1: *Organization, Symbols, and Beliefs*. The Hague: Martinus Nijhoff.

Nooy-Palm, H. 1986. The Sa'dan Toraja: A Study of Their Social Life and Religion, vol. 2: *Rituals of the East and West*. Dordrecht, Neth.: Foris Publications.

Obeyesekere, G. 1981. *Medusa's Hair: An Essay on Personal Symbols and Religious Experience*. Chicago: University of Chicago Press.

Rosaldo, M. 1980. *Knowledge and Passion: Ilongot Notions of Self and Social Life*. Cambridge, Eng: Cambridge University Press.

Rosaldo, M. 1984. Toward an Anthropology of Self and Feeling. In *Culture Theory*, edited by R.A. Shweder and R.A. LeVine, pp. 137–157. Cambridge, Eng.: Cambridge University Press.

Rosenberger, N.R. 1989. Dialectic Balance in the Polar Model of Self: The Japanese Case. *Ethos* 17:88–113.

Shore, B. 1982. *Sala'ilua: A Samoan Mystery*. New York: Columbia University Press.

Shweder, R.A. 1984. Preview: A Colloquy of Cultural Theorists. In *Culture Theory*, edited by R.A. Shweder and R.A. LeVine, pp. 1–24. Cambridge, Eng.: Cambridge University Press.

Shweder, R.A., and E.J. Bourne. 1984. Does the Concept of the Person Vary Cross-Culturally? In *Culture Theory*, edited by R.A. Shweder and R.A. LeVine, pp. 158–199. Cambridge, Eng.: Cambridge University Press.

Shweder, R.A., and R.A. LeVine, eds., 1984. *Culture Theory: Essays on Mind, Self, and Emotion*. Cambridge, Eng: Cambridge University Press.

Spiro, M. E., 1965. Religious Systems in Culturally Constituted Defense Mechanisms. In *Context and Meaning in Anthropology*, edited by M.E. Spiro, pp. 100–113. New York: The Free Press.

Spiro, M.E. 1978. *Burmese Supernaturalism*. Expanded ed. Philadelphia: Institute for the Study of Human Issues.

Spiro, M.E. 1984, Some Reflections on Cultural Determinism and Relativism With Special Reference to Emotion and Reason. In *Culture Theory*, edited by R.A. Shweder and R.A. LeVine, pp. 323–346. Cambridge, Eng.: Cambridge University Press.

Stephenson, P.H. 1989. Going to McDonald's in Leiden: Reflections on the Concept of Self and Society in the Netherlands. *Ethos* 17:226–247.

Stigler, J.W., R.A. Shweder, and G. Herdt, eds., 1990. *Cultural Psychology: Essays on Comparative Human Development*. Cambridge, Eng: Cambridge University Press.

Vernon, G. 1970. *Sociology of Death*. New York: Ronald Press.

Volkman, T. 1985. *Feasts of Honor: Ritual and Change in the Toraja Highlands*. Chicago: University of Illinois Press.

Wellenkamp, J.C. 1984. A Psychocultural Study of Loss and Death among the Toraja. Ph.D. diss., University of California, San Diego.

Wellenkamp, J.C. 1988a. Notions of Grief and Catharsis Among the Toraja. *American Ethnologist* 15:486–500.

Wellenkamp, J.C. 1988b. Order and Disorder in Toraja Thought and Ritual. *Ethology* 27:311–326.

Wellenkamp, J.C. 1991. Fallen Leaves: Death and Grieving in Toraja. In *Coping With the Final Tragedy*, edited by D. Counts and D. Counts, pp. 113–134. Amityville, NY.: Baywood Publishing Co.

Wellenkamp, J.C. 1992. Variations in the Social and Cultural Organization of Emotions: The Meaning of Crying and the Importance of Compassion in Toraja, Indonesia. In *Social Perspectives on Emotion*, edited by D.D. Franks and V. Gecas, pp. 189–216. Greenwich, Conn.: JAI Press.

Wellenkamp, J.C., and D. Hollan. 1981. The Influence of American Concepts of the Self on the Experience of Bereavement. Paper presented at the Kroeber Anthropological Society, Spring 1981, Berkeley, California.

White, G.M., and J. Kirkpatrick, eds., 1985. *Person, Self, and Experience: Exploring Pacific Ethnopsychologies*. Berkeley: University of California Press.

3   Constructivist Models of Mind, Contemporary Psychoanalysis, and the Development of Culture Theory

In developing theories of culture and cultural transmission, anthropologists have always made assumptions about how people learn, think, feel, and are motivated to act—even if those assumptions have remained implicit and un-examined (Bock 1988). These underlying assumptions about human psychology and the development of mind, whether implicit or explicit, shape our conceptualizations of culture and how we imagine the ways in which, and the extent to which, culture influences human behavior. If we assume that the mind is an empty vessel into which understandings about the world are poured or upon which they are inscribed by habit and practice, our conceptualizations of culture will differ from those that develop if we assume that the mind resists being inscribed by social experience or responds to social experience in selective ways only.

Currently, researchers in a number of fields are contributing to the development of a dynamic model of mind that acknowledges the contributions of biology and social experience to the construction of human consciousness and subjectivity. In this paper, I examine this emerging model and I discuss its implications for the development of culture theory. Although the model I discuss draws upon work in anthropology, psychology, psychiatry, and the neurosciences. I focus primarily on how the model is emerging within the field of contemporary psychoanalysis, which is one of my own areas of expertise.

I begin by discussing how recent research on trauma,[1] dissociation,[2] and the modular organization of cognitive and emotional processes[3] has been integrated into psychoanalytic conceptualizations of human consciousness and subjectivity. I discuss, as well, why these newer conceptualizations are helpful in accounting for a wide range of clinical and ethnographic phenomena.

In the second part of the paper, I discuss the implications of a constructivist model of mind for the development of culture theory. I argue that theories of culture must reflect the fluidity and complexity of the psychological states that underlie the cultural process, and I suggest that even highly conventional models of action, thought, and feeling are rarely, if ever, internalized, appropriated, or reproduced without some degree of

DOI: 10.4324/9781003529118-4

modification, refashioning, and personalization. This constant and dynamic refashioning of received ideas and practices eventuates in an experiential or subjectivity potential that enhances a population's ability to adapt to social, economic, and environmental change. I conclude by discussing some of the factors that limit cultural and psychological fluidity, and I propose person-centered ethnography as one of the methods by which we can explore the complex relations among culture, mind, and behavior.

Contemporary Psychoanalytic Models of Mind

Recently, Donnel Stern (1996) has identified two models of mind that crop up, in various guises, throughout the psychoanalytic literature. The first and earlier is what Stern refers to as the "beach ball" model of consciousness: our consciousness, of ourselves and other things, floats on top of an ocean of unconsciousness like a beach ball on water. And like a ball on water, our experience will remain conscious until we exert force (repression) to push it into the ocean of unconsciousness. As Stern points out (1996: 256), a major assumption here is that our experience is or should be conscious until we do something to make it unconscious. A second, related assumption is that our consciousness is or should be whole and undivided, because that is the nature of consciousness and self-awareness until it is broken up, pushed down, and repressed.

As Johnson and Price-Williams note (1996: 79), this beach ball model of human consciousness[4] and self-awareness captures well the sense we sometimes have that there are hidden forces within us that "push" for expression. What it does not explain well, however, is who or what is doing the pushing down and repressing and why: "The problem is that there is a basic paradox in our current views of the cohesive self with respect to repression: How can a self hide important information from itself about itself? Who is the deceiver and who the deceived?" (Johnson and Price-Williams 1996: 80).

It is important to note here that Stern has simplified the traditional psychoanalytic model of mind,[5] drawing together threads from a number of different authors and works to make a point. Indeed, some might argue that he has presented a caricature of the traditional model, ignoring its subtlety and complexity. But Stern's beach ball metaphor does capture several important underlying assumptions of an earlier psychoanalytic model of the mind. And as Johnson and Price-Williams (1996) and Johnson (1998) note, it is a metaphor of mind that is both enlightening and misleading at the same time.

The second, more recent model Stern identifies draws on the notion of dissociation as a key explanatory concept (see also Bromberg 1994, 1996a, 1996b, 1998). The basic, underlying assumptions of this second model are quite different than the first. Rather than assume that experience will be conscious unless or until pushed out of awareness, the "constructivist" model assumes the opposite:

> What if the natural state of experience is to remain outside awareness? What if action and effort arc required not to keep experience out of consciousness, but to bring it in? What if being aware *is* less like letting the beach ball do its thing than having to grab a rock from the bottom and drag it to the surface?
>
> (Stern 1996: 256)

According to this model, consciousness of ourselves and other things must be actively constructed out of our myriad engagements with the world. Many of our engagements will remain unconceptualized, unverbalized, and out-side conscious awareness unless or until they gain representation through complex symbolic processes.[6] Here, self-awareness, once developed, is not a seamless, unfractionated whole, but rather the end product of a complicated series of feedforward and feedback loops within a broad and open system of information exchange. This self-system encompasses the synaptic structure of the brain, intrapersonal processes of memory and symbol formation, and interpersonal, self-other configurations as organized and shaped through fa-milial, social, and historical processes.[7]

According to this second model, "the self" is organized hierarchically, dy-namically, and temporally. Lower level subsystems may or may not come together to form a superordinate self (or selves) that is (or are) aware of its (or their) constituent parts. Lower-level subsystems may or may not remain separate from other parts of self-organization and function relatively inde-pendently and autonomously. In any or all of these cases, the organization of the self-system, and the border between what is conscious and unconscious, is highly responsive to both the intrapersonal and extrapersonal processes within which it is embedded.

What are the advantages, if any, of the second model over the first in help-ing us to conceptualize the relationships among culture, mind, and behav-ior? In my view, there are several. First, the constructivist model allows us to see more clearly that while splits and divisions in human consciousness certainly may be indicative of pathology, they also appear to be inherent to the organization of the self and mind. Thus, they may serve, under certain circumstances, to enhance survival, adaptation, and communication (Slavin 1990; Slavin and Kriegman 1992). Slavin argues, for example, that divisions in consciousness seem adaptive, perhaps even necessary, for an environ-ment in which individuals who are heavily dependent (both behaviorally and psychologically) upon their relationships to other people must yet find ways of maintaining and protecting their own vital interests and views. From this point of view, splits or divisions of consciousness could divert, and then pre-serve for future motivation or developmental growth, vital interests and needs of the individual that are inexpressible and unrealizable because (at least temporarily) they are in conflict with the social and emotional needs of others (Slavin 1990: 318–319).

Recent anthropological work on spirit possession would support the idea that splits in human consciousness may serve positive and adaptive social and psychological purposes (see especially Lambek 1981, 1989, 1996). A number of the chapters in a recent volume on contemporary spirit beliefs in the Pacific (Mageo and Howard 1996) demonstrate that spirit possession idioms often give expression to marginalized voices and points of view. They open a cultural arena for the public discussion of morality and power relationships, and they offer the possibility for the renegotiation of status, wealth, and hierarchy. As a system of communication, possession idioms and behavior may provide a means by which otherwise unknowable, suppressed, or repressed knowledge about a community, often conflictual in nature, is directly or indirectly expressed (see Hollan 1996).

Furthermore, while splits in consciousness typical of possession behavior *may* express illness or pathological states of mind (see Spiro 1997: 118–135), this is probably the exception rather than the rule. As Levy, Mageo, and Howard note:

> Full possession behavior is highly skillful. It requires a mastery of role playing and of subtle, specialized kinds of communally significant communication. It is wrong to interpret it as "pathology," incompetence or breakdown in the same sense as schizophrenic psychosis or senility. Possessed individuals operate as competent persons in the moral realm in established webs of communication. They are essentially thought of and act as though they contain and exhibit a possessing person who is radically different and discontinuous from the possessed person. Both persons are mind-bearing actors, with communicative competence, intentions, and all the characteristics of selfhood.... It [possession] is a culturally crafted coping behavior that is useful because it is understood and responded to helpfully.
>
> (1996: 17–18)

Second, the constructivist model of mind, although it readily accounts for "repression" as we normally use that term—that is, the (in some sense) willful pushing away of unpleasant or disruptive thoughts or feelings by a higher order, superordinate self (Johnson 1998)—also readily allows us to conceptualize a number of other ways that we may "not know" about our own motivations and psychological processes. For some time, we have known that many neurophysiological and autonomic nervous processes involved in homeostatic regulation normally function outside of conscious self-awareness. We now know that many cognitive and emotional processes are equally conscious-free, though the information these processes convey may affect self-awareness in complex and myriad ways. For example, people with certain kinds of brain damage due to accident, stroke, or lesions do much better on recognition tasks of names, objects, people, and locales than they consciously believe they are capable of (Damasio 1994, 1999; LeDoux 1996; Ramachandran 1998). In other words, as Damasio notes (1994: 41), "the brain knows more than the conscious mind reveals."

Further, within the last several years a number of trauma researchers[8] have shown how certain types of experiences can be so overwhelming for us, so shattering of our normal, everyday expectations, that they never become cognitively and linguistically processed and represented at all. Or if they do become processed and represented, they are stripped of their emotional force and meaning. Such experiences cannot be pushed away or "repressed" by a higher-order, superordinate self because they were never integrated into the higher levels of self-organization to begin with.

This is a very different way of "not knowing" about one's experience than the process of repression. But it would be incorrect to think that it occurs only in the aftermath of "trauma" per se, Sullivan (1953) has used the term "not-me" to refer to aspects of personal experience, found in all people and in all cultures, that have been lost to awareness as a result of encountering strong negative evaluations during the course of socialization. The anxiety that comes to be associated with these aspects of experience can be so overwhelming that it can be likened to "a blow to the head," effectively interrupting the normal process by which experience comes to be cognized, remembered, and integrated into self-organization:

> The not-me is literally the organization of experience with significant people that has been subjected to such intense anxiety, and anxiety so suddenly precipitated, that it was impossible for the then relatively rudimentary person to make any sense, to develop any true grasp on, the particular circumstances which dictated the experience of this intense anxiety. As I have said, very intense anxiety precipitated by a sudden, intense, negative emotional reaction on the part of the significant environment has more than a little in common with a blow to the head. It tends to erase any possibility elaborating the exact circumstances of its occurrence, and about the most the person can remember in retrospect is a somewhat fenestrated account of the event in the immediate neighborhood.
>
> (Sullivan 1953: 314)

The vast majority of not-me experiences very likely consist of thoughts, feelings, and behaviors that are culturally disvalued, and so more likely to be negatively sanctioned by caretakers. Thus in a place like Toraja, Indonesia (located in the highlands of South Sulawesi), where social hierarchy is still acknowledged and valued, not-me experiences are more likely to be associated with inappropriate assertions and expressions of anger (see Hollan 1988, 1992a), status, rank, and entitlement than with displays of shame, deference, or fear of others.

However, not-me experiences also may cut against the cultural grain and be linked to more idiosyncratic upbringings. For many years, one of my analysands, Steve, experienced intense, unverbalizable anxiety whenever he began to act or feel in ways that removed him from the emotional orbit of his parents. He had "learned" that such centrifugal movements brought on the ire and anxiety of his parents, despite the fact that both he and his parents were members of a culture that places a high value on independence, self-sufficiency, and autonomy. He could not feel himself to be separate from his parents without also experiencing intense anxiety and dread. The fact that Steve's culture denigrates prolonged attachment between parents and children has not enabled him to free himself from his parents; it has merely made his continued connection to them that much more humiliating and debilitating.

But the constructivist model also encompasses the nontrauma- and non-anxiety-related "forgetting" of experience so brilliantly elucidated by Ernest Schachtel (1949) in his essay, "On Memory and Childhood Amnesia." Schachtel suggests that much experience is lost and forgotten not because it is actively repressed (as a result of intrapsychic conflict) or dissociated (as a result of trauma or socialization experiences), but because it never finds its way into culturally and familially mediated schemas and "cliches" that give form, structure, and persistence to self-related memory. That is, while our families and cultures encourage us to remember certain types of experiences by providing us with the cognitive and linguistic resources necessary to capture and encode them, many other of our experiences do not receive such memory-enhancing resources. As a result, they are "forgotten." Like traumatic experiences, linguistically and cognitively "starved" experiences are never integrated into higher order, conscious levels of self organization.

Schachtel's insights about the cultural shaping of personal experience and its effects on human consciousness have been further developed by Levy (1984).[9] Levy points out that cultures shape personal experiences not only through starving them of cognitive and linguistic representations, which he refers to as "hypocognition," but also by categorizing and labeling them in great detail, which he refers to as "hypercognition." These processes represent two different ways of shaping and controlling emotion and personal experience. In the latter, awareness of certain types of experience is heightened and focused by drawing close attention to them. In the former, experience is flattened or made difficult to access through lack of representation.

Levy notes that examples of hyper- and hypocognition can be found in all cultures; what varies are the types of experiences and emotions that are accentuated or not. In Tahiti, for example, anger is hypercognized while grief, dependency feelings, and guilt receive relatively little linguistic and cognitive representation. As a consequence, Tahitians articulate feelings of anger and frustration more easily than feelings of interpersonal loss and grief. Grief tends to be expressed only indirectly, through symptoms of physical illness and other somatic complaints (Levy 1973).

While Schachtel argues that cognitive and linguistic starvation alone may rob consciousness of certain types of awareness and memory, Levy suggests that the "state of hypocognition and processes of dynamic repression have a systematic and amplifying relationship to each other" (Levy 1984: 228). That is, the effects of hypocognition may enhance those of dynamic, intrapsychic repression and vice versa.

Constructivist models of the mind remind us of the variety of ways people may "not know" about their own motives and behavior, including lack of awareness due to brain damage or to nonconscious processing of cognitive and emotional processes, repression, dissociation as a result of trauma and not-me experiences, and culturally influenced hyper- and hypocognition. While it is likely that individuals come to construct consciousness of themselves in different ways, depending upon their culture and their individual life circumstances and experiences, it is also likely that several modes of "not knowing" will be entailed within any given individual's construction. The challenge, then, is to acknowledge and represent as faithfully as possible the complexity and overdetermination of fluctuating states of self-consciousness.[10]

A third advantage of the constructivist model is that it more readily accounts for the observation that the unconscious mind often seems highly organized, self-like, and intentionally motivated, and that its boundary with the conscious part of the mind often seems fluid and permeable, rather than rigid and unbreachable (Weiss and Sampson 1986). For example, when my analysand, Steve, repeatedly refers to himself as a marionette, he senses—sometimes very clearly, sometimes not very clearly at all—that there is a puppeteer part of himself that acts as if it had a mind of its own, complete with will and intentions. He can identify and observe the behavioral consequences of this hidden willfulness, but he has difficulty identifying its source. When he looks, it is gone.

Such complex yet unconscious motivations and intentions can be found in spirit possession phenomena as well, in which the possessed person's everyday persona is temporarily replaced by the equally complex and developed persona of another. As Levy, Mageo, and Howard note (1996: 18), possession behavior, much like theatre or any other form of dramatic performance, requires the presence of an audience and involves the display of skillful communicative acts. The alternative voices that emerge through these acts are meaningful and interpretable, not senseless.

Examples such as these suggest that the human unconscious is, at least in parts, as highly organized and complex as the conscious part of the mind. Desires, wishes, and impulses do not spring into psychological existence in raw or pure form, but rather always appear embedded in an interpersonal matrix (see Mitchell 1988). The desire or impulse, that is, is only experienced as part of a self-system, or in relation to the self-system, if experienced outside of it. *I* desire. *I* wish. *I* feel driven and overwhelmed. But this sense of self, its quality and affective valence, only emerges in interaction with other people, whose evaluations and responsiveness (or lack thereof) deeply affect its constitution and its own evaluation of itself and its wishes and impulses.[11]

The embeddedness of wishes and desires in relational matrices, both past and present, helps us account, in tum, for the fact that our conscious awareness of our motives and behavior may vary from context to context and from person to person. Self-related desires, wishes, and behavior that come into conflict with certain people in certain circumstances may not come into conflict with them under different circumstances or with different people even in the same circumstances.[12] Possessed people often express knowledge about people and events in a family or community that they appear to be unaware of when not possessed. When speaking with me, my analysand Steve expresses feelings of love and sexual longing for women—evinced by his talk, his dreams, and his reports of physical stirrings—that he claims not to feel or experience when he is around his parents.[13]

Thus, whether or not self-related wishes. desires, and behaviors become repressed, dissociated, or "not known" about in the other ways described above depends upon the self-other configurations, both past and present, in which they arise and with which they become engaged. Davies (1996b) puts it this way:

> If indeed, the internal psychic structure of the mind evolves out of an ever present yet constantly changing system of affective, cognitive. and physiologically based self-experiences in ongoing interactive and dia- logic discourse with a host of significant internally and externally de- rived objects, then what is conscious and what is unconscious at any particular point in time will emerge fluidly out of the particular con- stellation of self- and object-related experience that crystallizes in the foreground of interpersonal experience at any given moment. We deal not with one unconscious, but with multiple levels of consciousness and unconsciousness—a multiply organized, associationally linked net- work of meaning attribution and understanding. Within such an interac- tive, dynamic system, past experience infuses the present, and present experience evokes state-dependent memories of formative interactive representations.
>
> (p. 562)

The idea that the human unconscious may be organized around complex self-other configurations in potential or actual conflict with one another is not new in psychoanalysis, as many of its contemporary proponents[14] read- ily acknowledge. Johnson and Price-Williams (1996: 79–89) have identified related ideas in Kohut (1977), with his ideas of vertical splits in the self, the "non-self," and "disavowed" aspects of the self; in Jung (1964), with his notion of the "shadow" self; and in Winnicott (1965), with the distinction he draws between the "true" and "false" self. But related ideas can also be found in Janet (1890), with his notion of the "subconscious" self that coexists with the conscious self, and following from Janet, the early Breuer and Freud ([1893–95] 1955), with their description of a "second consciousness." They can also be found in the distinction that Sullivan (1953, 1956) draws among the "good me," the "bad me," and the "not me"; Fairbairn's (1952) and Guntrip's (1968) articulation of splits between and among the "libidinal," "antilibidinal," and "central" egos: and more recently, in Weiss and Sampson's (1986) notion that the human unconscious, in a highly organized and volitional way, actively seeks to disconfirm its own pathological beliefs.

My point here is not to present an exhaustive survey of psychoanalytic ideas on "vertical" splits in the self—others, no doubt, could be referenced—but to suggest that contemporary views of the "relational unconscious" further develop and make explicit what has remained undeveloped and implicit in several other bodies of psychoanalytic work.

Constructivist models of the mind broaden our view of the sources of intrapsychic conflict in human life. Moving beyond the notion that conflict arises from the clash among id, ego, and superego, such models suggest how self-other configurations, some of which may be culturally or individually specific, become internalized and alienated from one another. According to these models, deep divisions within the self can arise not only from the repression of id-like desires, but also from "the clash between contrasting and often incompatible self-organizations and self-other relationships" (Mitchell 1993: 104). Steve, for example, is torn between a part of himself that wishes to remain loyal to his parents and another part that wishes to be free and autonomous.

Related to this, constructivism reopens the question of the relative importance of intrapersonal versus extrapersonal factors in human psychological experience and illustrates how complex the relationship between these factors can become (see also Strauss and Quinn 1997). While reasserting the significance of external factors like trauma, emotional deprivation, and emotional impingement on the development of intrapsychic conflict, constructivist models also reunderscore how the mind is never a mere reflection of outside events. Rather, they posit that impressions of the world are constructed out of numerous and varied perceptions and self-states. Such constructions are influenced not only by cultural and linguistic variables, but also by the creative and imaginative capacities (or limitations) of the individual.

Constructivist theory does not, therefore, lend itself to simplistic explanations of psychological experience that overgeneralize the importance of either intrapersonal or extrapersonal variables. Rather, it challenges us to examine closely, case by case, their relative influence, to study the conditions under which, and the developmental stages in which, the mind is both an organizer and a product of experience.

Implications for the Development of Culture Theory

Models of the mind that incorporate notions of constructivism draw upon and in turn support the view that the sense of a unitary self, when it exists, is woven out of a variety of self-states (see, for example, Damasio 1999: Ewing 1990), which are themselves embedded within specific self-other configurations. Theoretically, such models readily accommodate the idea that the overall tapestry of selfconsciousness will be greatly affected by the warp of cultural values, attitudes, and narrative and linguistic resources. Self-states that are culturally valued and encouraged, or linguistically and narratively marked, are more likely to be woven into self-consciousness than those that are not (see, for example, Bruner 1990; Kirmayer 1996; Spence l982), as Schachtel (1949) suggested long ago.

However, such models also suggest that cultural values, schemas, and narratives are never internalized wholesale. Attitudes and values, towards oneself as well as to other people and objects in the world, are learned within specific, affectively charged (or affectively impoverished) self-other configurations. This emotionally charged learning affects the extent to which cultural forms become motivationally salient as well as the extent to which they come into conflict with self-states and personal mental models that are not socially encouraged or approved. As Spiro (1997) notes, people are "psychologically preadapted" to find some types of cultural beliefs and practices to be far more emotionally salient and compelling than others. Thus the finer weave of both consciousness and unconsciousness, and the boundary between them, is probably much more varied from individual to individual than many cultural theorists would suppose.

Let me expand upon this point. Bradd Shore notes in his recent book, *Culture in Mind: Cognition, Culture, and the Problem of Meaning* (1996), that one of the primary challenges of psychocultural anthropology is to explain how widely shared, culturally constituted, public models of the world and human experience find their way into the minds of individual actors and become "born again" as *mental* models with motivational force and salience. Conversely, it must explain how it is that mental models within the minds of individual actors eventually become externalized and "instituted" as public, cultural forms. Shore points out that many cultural anthropologists have assumed that these outside-in and inside-out psychocultural processes are fairly straightforward and unproblematic: instituted cultural models somehow come to imprint themselves upon the minds of individuals in uniform fashion and, in turn, individuals with highly similar mental models enact routinized, public behavior. Strauss (1992) refers to this simplified view of cultural reproduction as the "fax model" of cultural internalization.

But as Shore, and before him Spiro (1951), Schwartz (1978), Strauss (1992), and Linger (1994) suggest, things are not so simple. Internalized cultural models sometimes conflict with one another, generating a sense of confusion and ambivalence on the part of individual actors. And generally speaking, there is not a simple one-to-one correspondence between an instituted cultural model and its cognitive analogue within the mind of a given individual. But perhaps even more significantly, individual actors develop *personal*, sometimes highly idiosyncratic mental models of the world (based on their own, highly personal experience) that may affect the way they learn and internalize, or reject or change or modify, more culturally constituted forms of thinking and behaving.

Shore does a superb job, in a general and theoretical way, of pointing out the complexities of psychocultural processes. He notes, for example, how personal mental models may undermine or contradict "conventional" mental models. And he suggests how the richness and variegated nature of personal experience will always overflow the mental models into which it is poured or within which it is instantiated. However, most of his ethnographic examples demonstrate how cultural forms come to be reproduced with relatively little change or modification. They fail to illustrate how the integration of, or conflict between, conventional and personal mental models will affect which instituted cultural models gain motivational force and which do not. Nor do they illustrate how integration of, or conflict between, conventional and personal mental models will lead to the modification of existing cultural forms.

This is where contemporary psychoanalytic models of the mind become particularly helpful to cultural theorists because they focus our attention on the affectively charged microcontexts of learning. They remind us that how individuals learn and what they become conscious of is dependent not only upon the instituted cultural models they are exposed to but also upon how and when and where that exposure takes place, an exposure that is never the same for any two individuals, even those growing up within the same household (see Sulloway 1996) or small community.

The implications here for a theory of psychocultural process are significant. Because no two individuals internalize instituted cultural models in the same way, and because their subjectivity, consciousness, and self-states therefore vary, the reproduction of culture necessarily must be a highly dynamic process subject to constant, even if subtle, modification and change. Further, the varieties of subjectivity, consciousness, and self-states that necessarily must underlie psychocultural process (even if often masked by overt forms of conventional behavior) do not compromise social and cultural adaptation, but rather very likely enhance it, by providing a ready pool of emotions, cognitions, and mental models, which, under changing circumstances, could prove useful in motivating new forms of behavior.

Unlike the genetic potential of a population, which can only be brought into the play of adaptation in the aftermath of a generational time lag, the *experiential* or *subjectivity potential* of a population may be tapped much more quickly. Subjectivities and self-states that are marginal or subdominant today may prove to be adaptive in the wake of technological or social change in the future. Obeyesekere (1981, 1990) is one of the few anthropologists who has attempted to document, with the necessary individual case studies, how the subjectivity potential of a population comes into play in the process of cultural change (see also Wallace 1956, 1972). He has shown how individuals refashion preexisting cultural idioms along the lines of more idiosyncratic, personal mental models of the world and then use these new, refashioned idioms to rationalize and motivate innovative forms of behavior—a process he refers to as "subjectification" (Obeyesekere 1981:137). Let me use some Toraja examples to illustrate these ideas further.

Up until 25 or 30 years ago, most Toraja men practiced two forms of bodily scarification to mark their transition from youthhood to manhood: *ma'baruk*, the scarification of the forearm with burning embers, and *ma'tille*, supercision, or the longitudinal cutting of the foreskin of the penis (see Hollan and Wellenkamp 1996). Both practices usually were performed during the time that boys herded buffalo together, when they were between the ages of about 10 and the mid-teens. And both were cultural idioms through which boys could communicate that they had become bold enough and mature enough to begin courting young women.

Although both ma'baruk and ma'tille appear to symbolize masculinity in a fairly straightforward and uniform way, my extensive, long-term interviews with seven men indicate that, in fact, these practices are internalized and embodied by Toraja men in quite distinct ways. Let us first consider ma'baruk.

Formerly, one of the ways young Toraja men demonstrated courage and masculinity was by scarring the top of their forearms with burning embers. Although all of the men I interviewed over the age of 30 or so had ma'baruk scars, the number and visibility of these scars varied from individual to individual. Some of the men had several large, prominent scars on both arms, while others had only one small, faint scar on one or both arms. This variation is significant because it indexes, graphically and directly on the body, differences in these men's tolerance of physical pain; their attitudes and beliefs about masculinity; and their commitment to, and emotional involvement with, a received cultural practice.

For example, although both Nene'na[15] Tandi and Nene'na Limbong had several, large scars on both arms, the significance of these scars for each man's sense of masculinity was different. Nene'na Limbong, a high-status, wealthy man who is very much concerned with preserving his traditional entitlements, believes the scars demonstrate his courage, his toughness, and the power and force of his personal choice:

Ma'baruk causes great pain. But we tolerate it.... We tolerate it.... [The pain] of ma'baruk is worse [than the pain of supercision] because we sit for an hour [with burning embers on the arm]. It is truly painful, but we just sit. Sometimes the arm must be held [so that the embers remain in place long enough to cause a burn]. *Did you cry?* No! Because we chose to do it ourselves.

In contrast, Nene'na Tandi, a lower-status man who has long envied and criticized the privileges of people like Nene'na Limbong, emphasizes how his prominent ma'baruk scars demonstrate not his toughness but, rather, his cleverness in discovering a way of burning himself *without* experiencing pain:

> Here are three, and here are three [pointing to the scars on both arms]. I did them all at one time. *All at one time?* Yes. I was probably ten years old. But I didn't just sit [as he burned himself]. I ran, so that the wind would blow [and cool the wound]. When we ran, the fright would disappear. But if we just sat, we had to be frightened. If we ran, we didn't feel anything. *You didn't cry?* No. I didn' t feel pain. I didn't feel anything.

Both Ambe'na[16] Patu and To Minaa[17] Sattu, on the other hand, have only one or two barely visible scars. Ambe'na Patu is clear that his motivation for burning himself was limited to wanting to be like his friends, and he jokes about his low tolerance for pain:

> I saw my friends do it, and so I wanted to do it, too. Here's one, and here's one [pointing out one on each arm].... I thought there were more, but I guess they're gone now. I guess they've disappeared [still inspecting his arms]. There were some who were frightened and brushed them [the embers] off [laughing loudly].... I didn' t want to be burned anymore.... The embers were placed [on the arm], and before they had a chance to burn, they were brushed off [continues laughing]. Even before we had a chance to run [to distract themselves from the pain], they [the embers] were brushed off [continues laughing].

To Minaa Sattu is equally forthright in explaining his lack of prominent scars and his fear of being burned:

> We were supposed to leave them [the embers] until they burned. But this one [his single, faint scar] is small. Before the ember had a chance to burn, I brushed it off [laughing loudly]. If a boy is brave, yes [he leaves the ember to burn].

It is clear that these men literally embody their ma'baruk scars in different ways, and that the personal meanings of the scars also vary from man to man. Only Nene'na Limbong seems deeply proud of the scars as a symbol of his physical courage, boldness, and masculinity. The other men openly admit their fear of burning themselves, and only Nene'na Tandi was able to overcome his fright enough to scar himself in a clearly visible and unambiguous way. We see here the lack of emotional valence that ma'baruk has for several of the men, and the marginal role it plays in the construction of their sense of masculinity. It should not surprise us, then, that Toraja men abandoned the practice of burning themselves rather quickly once it came under criticism from non-Toraja Indonesians as a primitive, backwards custom.

Supercision, unlike ma'baruk, cannot be practiced in degrees. One is either supercised or one is not. And almost all Toraja men are, in fact, supercised. However, even here, where the overt behavior of men seems so standardized and uniform, I discovered that individuals react to and appropriate the supercision experience in distinct ways, depending upon their prior experiences and personality dispositions. Some men are very neutral and matter-of-fact in their description of the procedure. They note that there was a chance that their penises might have been injured during the procedure but go on to say that the chances were actually quite remote and inconsequential. They are proud of the fact that they have been supercised, but do not see it as any great achievement. Others *do* comment on the dangers of the operation, however, and underscore how brave and bold boys must be to endure it. They also emphasize how long and painful the recovery period is, and how important it is that the wound be properly cleansed and bandaged. Still others laugh and joke about the possible mutilation of the penis during ma'tille, as if to both admit their fear of the operation and deny it at the same time. Thus, even a standardized and uniform cultural practice like supercision can be "subjectified" in distinct and nontrivial ways, and so have a variable, and perhaps unpredictable, impact on the future behavior and experience of a community.

Let us consider one final example of how a cultural practice is personalized in the course of its appropriation. Most adult Toraja men appear to be deeply involved in the competitive slaughter of water buffalo at elaborate funeral ceremonies, this being one important means by which they maintain or enhance their status and prestige within the community (see Hollan and Wellenkamp 1994; Volkman 1985). Based on my observations of his public behavior, Nene'na Tandi appeared to be as committed to this pursuit as anyone else. He was always in attendance at local funerals. He always carefully monitored the distribution of meat at funerals to make certain that he would not be humiliated by receiving less than his own fair share or by allowing others to receive more than their status warranted. And he always attempted to associate himself with the high-status individuals in attendance, thereby publicly demonstrating to others that he was worthy of acknowledgment and respect.

Yet during the course of my interviews with him, it became apparent that he was more ambivalent about his involvement in slaughtering activities than his outward behavior had indicated. As a man of commoner birth and the owner of limited rice land, and as the stepfather of only one daughter, he had neither the wealth nor the extended family support to pursue slaughtering activities as successfully as other men in the community. As a result, he had become envious and resentful of these other men and contemptuous of the whole meat-dividing process:

> Why should we get angry [about the politics of meat]? This meat—indeed, people call it meat, but I think of it as shit. Shit. Once we eat it, it becomes shit, right? It doesn't increase our wealth. After eating it, we sleep, and the next morning we go to the edge of the village and defecate. If it's like that, why get upset about it? *But some people say it's the most important....* . Those are people who try to be big. Rich people. For one day [the day of the slaughtering], they can be rich. But they don't stay rich. Those who stay rich, ah, they sell pigs, they have nice houses. Ah, those are the happy ones. [Those are the ones] who are truly rich. But those who are rich only for an hour or two. . . I look at them [and think], they're all stupid.

Although Nene'na Tandi participates in a highly visible cultural practice, we see that his participation is shot through with ambivalence. His anger and resentment towards those who benefit more from slaughtering than he does suggest that he is ready to subvert or abandon the practice if alternative ways of asserting status and prestige begin to emerge. And indeed, Nene'na Tandi was a very early convert to the Protestant Church when it entered this part of Toraja, and he has been a longtime and vocal advocate for a more modernist, egalitarian point of view within the village.

These examples suggest that conventional models of action and feeling—even those that require highly standardized forms of behavior such as the practice of ma'tille—are rarely, if ever, internalized or appropriated without some degree of modification, refashioning, and personalization. While it is useful from a theoretical point of view to contrast appropriations that involve relatively extensive modifications from those that do not,[18] we must keep in mind that the subjectification of cultural idioms is very likely the rule, rather than the exception. Although I emphasize this personalization of the cultural process even more than Obeyesekere (1981, 1990) does, it is a notion that is implicit, if not highlighted, in the work of several other contemporary psychocultural theorists (see, for example, Briggs 1998; Chodorow 1999; Shore 1996; Spiro l997; Strauss and Quinn 1997).

Discussion

I have argued that cultural processes must be highly dynamic and ever changing because the minds and self-states of the people who embody and enact them are. I have argued, as well, that the efflorescence of personal meanings that intermingle with received cultural ideas and practices eventuate in an experiential or subjectivity potential for a population that very likely enhances, rather than compromises, its adaptation and survival. As Wallace (1970) and

Schwartz (1978) pointed out long ago, social and cultural processes *organize* experiential and subjective diversity; they do not eliminate it.

The subjectivity potential of a population allows it to adapt relatively quickly to changing social and historical circumstances, within the lifetimes of a single generation. People who appear to be marginal to a social and cultural system today may be "psychologically preadapted" (Spiro 1997) to thrive under newer, changing conditions. Nene'na Tandi, who was marginal to the feasting system of allocating status, prestige, and leadership in Toraja (and was angry and resentful as a result), easily and readily embraced Christianity and other forms of "modernity" that have swept through the Toraja highlands in recent decades. The ease with which he has adopted these newer cultural patterns, and the compelling way in which he is able to articulate their advantages, have helped the whole village learn to cope with the rapidly changing social and economic conditions of contemporary Indonesia.

While I have emphasized the dynamism of psychocultural processes, I would certainly not wish to deny that overt cultural patterns, symbols, and institutions may be highly "durable" (Strauss and Quinn 1997) and persist over long periods of time. The existence and influence of political, military, economic, and bureaucratic interest groups and the social necessity of a modicum of coherence in everyday life ensure that cultural patterns are perpetuated. Furthermore, particular appropriations of cultural idioms, once internalized, may themselves become highly resistant to change, as individual actors begin to perceive the world in ways that reinforce their initial subjectifications.[19] But periods of apparent cultural stability and persistence are themselves the products of social and psychological processes in dynamic, not inert, equilibrium. Under changing conditions, even apparently widespread and entrenched customs, like the Toraja practice of ma'baruk, can give way quickly.

Further, the persistence of cultural symbols and behaviors does not mean that their meanings and motivational salience remain static. Different Toraja men experience the practice of supercision in different ways and carry away from it different senses of what it means to be male and masculine in Toraja society. The American flag remains an important symbol of national unity and identity in the United States, yet it means something different to pre- and post-Vietnam War generations.

The models of mind I have reviewed here suggest that human consciousness is constructed out of our many and varied engagements in the world. They suggest, further, that these engagements become organized around self-other configurations that slip into and out of awareness depending upon the interpersonal matrices from which they emerge and with which they become engaged. However, I do not wish to imply that the human self-system is infinitely divisible and or that it cannot be integrated at very high levels. Indeed, elsewhere (Hollan 1992b) I have argued that anthropologists have exaggerated the extent to which self-experience varies cross-culturally (see also Spiro 1993).

Hallowell (1959) pointed out long ago that human societies could not have emerged without the evolution of a self-system that allows people to evaluate their behavior relative to the norms of society and to the behavior of other people. Such evaluation, in any society, requires a high degree of continuity in self-experience and identity (see also Slavin and Kriegman 1992): if the people we are today cannot be held accountable for the acts we committed yesterday or if the people we are tomorrow cannot he held accountable for the acts we commit today, organized social life would not be possible. Cultures provide variable orientations to the self as it grows and develops (see Hallowell 1955), and this leads to some variation in self-experience (see, for example, Hollan and Wellenkamp 1994, 1996). But no culture can tolerate extensive, dramatic shifts in day-to-day identity, even those that encourage altered states of consciousness in circumscribed ritual or religious contexts.

My point here is that anywhere in the world, self-fragmentation and dissociation cannot go beyond a certain point without being labeled pathological. From an evolutionary point of view, it appears that the self can be neither too unitary and brittle nor too loose and fragmented:

> Although the coexistence of "multiple versions of the self" that we observe introspectively and clinically may thus represent crystallizations of different interactional schemes, this multiplicity may also signal the existence of an inner, functional limit on the process of self-integration.... The cost of our human strategy for structuring the self in a provisional fashion–around a sometimes precarious confederation of alternate self/other schemas—lies in the everpresent risk of states of relative disintegration, fragmentation, or identity diffusion. The maintenance of self-cohesion ... should thus be one of the most central ongoing activities of the psyche.... [but] the strivings of such an evolved "superordinate self" would emanate ... not primarily from a fragmentation induced by trauma or environmental failure to fully provide its mirroring (selfobject) functions. Rather, its intrinsic strivings would emanate from the very design of the self-system.
>
> (Slavin and Kriegman 1992: 204–205, quoted in Bromberg 1996b: 513–514)

It is also well to remember that organized senses of self and other apparently begin to emerge in infant life much earlier than we had once imagined (Stern 1985) and that our current interest in extreme and exaggerated states of self-fragmentation may itself be culturally and historically bound (see, for example, Hacking 1995; Young 1995).

Finally, constructivist models of the mind raise very important methodological issues for anthropologists and all others attempting to develop theories of how the mind works in context. If states of consciousness and unconsciousness truly are as shifting and fluid as some recent psychoanalytic work would suggest, how do we go about studying them? Although this is a complex question that could be the subject of an entire paper or book, it would seem that only fine-grained observational and interactional methods that follow individuals through both space and time and across different cultural domains could come close to capturing the fluctuating states of the mind posited by some recent psychoanalytic theories. Many investigative strategies could prove useful here, but perhaps especially those of person-centered ethnography.

As I have noted elsewhere (Hollan 1997, 2001; Levy and Hollan 1998), person-centered ethnographers attempt to develop experience-near ways of describing and analyzing human behavior, subjective experience, and psychological processes. A primary focus is on the individual and on how the individual's psychological and subjective experience both shapes, and is shaped by, social and cultural processes. In contrast to standard ethnography that "produces a cultural description analogous to a map or aerial photograph of a community," person-centered ethnography "tells us what it is like to live there—what features are salient to its inhabitants" (LeVine 1982: 293). An effort is made to represent human behavior and subjective experience from the point of view of the acting, intending, and attentive subject; to actively explore the emotional saliency and motivational force of cultural symbols and beliefs (rather than to assume such saliency and force); and to avoid unnecessary reliance on overly abstract, experience-distant constructs.

Person-centered ethnographers explore the phenomenological world and culturally constituted behavioral environment of actors through the use of extensive, open-ended interviews (Hollan and Wellenkamp 1994, 1996; Levy 1973, 1990; Parish 1994, 1996; Strauss and Quinn 1997), they make close observations of people's behavior at different times and in different settings in order to determine what is at stake for them in the course of their daily lives (Kleinman and Kleinman 1991; Wikan 1990), and they examine how subjective experience is embodied, and conversely, how the senses and perceptions of the body are culturally elaborated into the experience of self and other (Csordas 1994; Desjarlais 1992). It is through these and related methodologies that we come to appreciate just how complex and dynamic the human subject is.

Theories of culture must account for this complexity and dynamism, not explain it away. They must come to terms with an actor whose consciousness and self-states are fluid and dynamic, whose motives are overdetermined and sometimes contradictory, and whose ways of "not knowing" about their own actions and intentions are labyrinthine. A complex model of the actor must be at the center of social and culture theory. If culture theory does not follow and account for the actor, the actor, assuredly, will elude the assumptions and expectations of theory.

Acknowledgments

An abbreviated version of this paper was presented at the Fifth Biennial Meeting of the Society for Psychological Anthropology in San Diego, California, October 1997. I wish to thank the discussants of that earlier paper, Vincent

Crapanzano, Stanley Kurtz, and Melford Spiro, for their helpful comments and criticisms. Alan Fiske and Allen Johnson also read an earlier version of this paper. I thank them for their interest and suggestions. I also have benefited from the incisive comments of six anonymous reviewers.

Notes

1 See, for example, Davies (1996a, 1996b); Davies and Frawley (1992, 1994); Hegeman (1995a, 1995b); Herman (1992); van der Kolk (1987, 1989); and van der Kolk and van der Hart (1989).

2 See, for example, Bromberg (1994, 1996a, 1996b, 1998); Castillo (1994a, 1994b); Kirmayer (1994, 1996); Spiegel (1994); and Stern (1996, 1997).

3 See, for example, Damasio (1994, 1999); Dennett (1991); Edelman (1992); Hinton (1999); LeDoux (1996); Pinker (1997); and Ramachandran (1998).

4 Johnson and Price-Williams do not use the "beach ball" term, but they seem to be referring to a similar set of assumptions. In a later publication, Johnson (1998) uses the metaphor of an angler's float, rather than a beach ball, to refer to many of the same assumptions.

5 For a more extensive discussion of the traditional psychoanalytic model of the mind, see Johnson (1998).

6 Stern uses Fingarette's work on self-deception (1969) as his point of departure for this discussion. He then answers the question "But which engagements do we spell out and which ones do we avoid?" by saying, "We spell out those engagements that are either consistent with the stories we are telling about ourselves–our personal narratives–or that further these storylines in directions we want them to go. Other engagements are not spelled out" (Stern 1996:257).

7 Such a conceptualization of the self-system is reminiscent of Bateson's attempt (1972) to develop an ecology of mind.

8 See note 1.

9 See also Connerton (1989).

10 Although contemporary models of the mind have the potential to illuminate the variety and complexity of ways that people do·"not know" things about themselves, many students of culture and psychology continue to write as if people's minds come to be dominated by a single mode of disavowal or lack of self-knowledge. Does this emphasis on singularity reflect descriptive phenomenology? Or does it reflect the theorist's need to impose certainty and understanding on the flux and complexity of shifting states of consciousness'?

11 This type of argument draws heavily upon the earlier work of G. H. Mead (1934).

12 Hence the possibility for the resolution of conflict and therapeutic change.

13 For many years now, Sieve and his parents implicitly have abided by a "don't ask, don't tell" rule. Steve's parents do not ask him about his life apart from them, and he does not tell them anything about it.

14 The current version of these ideas are most clearly articulated by the interpersonal school of American psychoanalysis. See, for example, Mitchell (1988, 1993) and the journal, *Psychoanalytic Dialogues*.

15 *Nene'na* is a teknonym meaning "Grandfather of."

16 *Ambe'na* is a teknonym meaning·"Father of."

17 *To Minaa* is the title of one type of Toraja ritual specialist.

18 Obeyesckere (1981:51, 77–78) use the term *objectification* to refer to appropriations of cultural idioms that do not involve modification and refashioning. In objectification, the cultural or conventional models of the world that an individual appropriates match up very closely with his or her own preexisting, personal

mental models of the world. See also Spiro's notion (1997) of "psychological preadaptation."
19 Strauss and Quinn (1997) provide an excellent discussion of factors that contribute to both the persistence and change of actors' perceptions of the world.

References

Bateson, G. 1972. *Steps to an Ecology of Mind*. New York: Ballantine Books.

Bock, P.K. 1988. *Rethinking Psychological Anthropology: Continuity and Change in the Study of Human Action*. New York: Freeman.

Breuer, J., and S. Freud [1893–95] 1955. Studies in Hysteria. In *Standard Edition of the Complete Psychological Works of Sigmund Freud*, vol. 2, edited by J. Strachey, pp. 1–335, London: Hogarth Press.

Briggs, J. 1998. *Inuit Morality Play: The Emotional Education of a Three-Year Old*. New Haven, CT: Yale University Press.

Bromberg, P.M. 1994. "Speak! That I May See You": Some Reflections on Dissociation, Reality, and Psychoanalytic Listening. *Psychoanalytic Dialogues* 4:517–547.

Bromberg, P.M. 1996a. Hysteria, Dissociation and Cure: Emmy von No. Revisited. *Psychoanalytic Dialogues* 6:55–71.

Bromberg, P.M. 1996b. Standing in the Spaces: The Multiplicity of Self and the Psychoanalytic Relationship. *Contemporary Psychoanalysis* 32:509–535.

Bromberg, P.M. 1998. *Standing in the Spaces: Essays on Clinical Process, Trauma and Dissociation*. Hillsdale, NJ: Analytic Press.

Bruner, J. 1990. *Acts of Meaning*. Cambridge, MA: Harvard University Press.

Castillo, R.J. 1994a. Spirit Possession in South Asia, Dissociation or Hysteria? Part I: Theoretical Background. *Culture, Medicine, and Psychiatry* 18:1–21.

Castillo, R.J. 1994b. Spirit Possession in South Asia, Dissociation or Hysteria? Part II: Case Histories. *Culture, Medicine, and Psychiatry* 18:141–162.

Chodorow, N.J. 1999. *The Power of Feelings: Personal Meaning in Psycho-Analysis, Gender, and Culture*. New Haven, CT: Yale University Press.

Connerton, P. 1989. *How Societies Remember*. Cambridge: Cambridge University Press.

Csordas, T.J. 1994. *The Sacred Self: A Cultural Phenomenology of Charismatic Healing*. Berkeley: University of California Press.

Damasio, A.R. 1994. *Descartes' Error: Emotion, Reason, and the Human Brain*. New York: Avon Books, Inc.

Damasio, A.R. 1999. *The Feeling of What Happens: Body and Emotion in the Making of Consciousness*. New York: Harcourt Brace.

Davies, J.M. 1996a. Dissociation, Repression, and Reality Testing in the Countertransfcrence: The Controversy Over Memory and False Memory in the Psychoanalytic Treatment of Adult Survivors of Childhood Sexual Abuse. *Psychoanalytic Dialogues* 6:189–218.

Davies, J.M. 1996b. Linking the "Pre-Analytic" With the Postclassical: Integration, Dissociation, and the Multiplicity of Unconscious Process. *Contemporary Psychoanalysis* 32:553–576.

Davies, J.M., and M.G. Frawley. 1992. Dissociative Processes and Transference-Countertransference Paradigms in the Psychoanalytically Oriented Treatment of Adult Survivors of Childhood Sexual Abuse. *Psychoanalytic Dialogues* 2:5–36.

Davies, J.M., and M.G. Frawley. 1994. *Treating the Adult Survivor of Childhood Sexual Abuse: A Psychoanalytic Perspective*. New York: Basic Books.

Dennett, D.C. 1991. *Consciousness Explained*. New York: Little, Brown and Company.

Desjarlais, R.R. 1992. *Body and Emotion: The Aesthetics of Illness and Healing in the Nepal Himalayas*. Philadelphia: University of Pennsylvania Press.

Edelman, G.M. 1992. *Bright Air, Brilliant Fire: On the Matter of the Mind*. New York: Basic Books.

Ewing, K.P. 1990. The Illusion of Wholeness: Culture, Self, and the Experience of Inconsistency. *Ethos* 18:251–278.

Fairbairn, W.R.D. 1952. *Psychoanalytic Studies of the Personality*. London: Tavistock with Routledge and Kegan Paul.

Fingarette, H. 1969. *Self-Deception*. London: Routledge.

Guntrip, H. 1968. *Schizoid Phenomena, Object Relations, and the Self*. London: Hogarth Press.

Hacking, I. 1995. *Rewriting 1 He Soul: Multiple Personality and the Sciences of Memory*. Princeton: Princeton University Press.

Hallowell, A.I. 1955. *Culture and Experience*. Philadelphia: University of Pennsylvania Press.

Hallowell, A.I. 1959. Behavioral Evolution and the Emergence of the Self. In *Evolution and Anthropology*, edited by B.J. Meggars, pp. 36–60. Washington, DC: Anthropological Society of Washington.

Hegeman, E. 1995a. Transferential Issues in the Psychoanalytic Treatment of Incest Survivors. In *Sexual Abuse Recalled: Treating Trauma in the Era of Recovered Memory Debate*, edited by J. Alpert, pp. 185–213. Northvale, NJ: Jason Aronson.

Hegeman, E. 1995b. Resolution of Traumatic Transference: Two Class. *Contemporary Psychoanalysis* 31:409–422.

Herman, J.L. 1992. *Trauma and Recovery*. New York: Basic Books.

Hinton, A.L., ed., 1999. *Biocultural Approaches to the Emotions*. Cambridge: Cambridge University Press.

Hollan, D. 1988. Staying "Cool" in Toraja: Infornial Strategies for the Management of Anger and Hostility in a Nonviolent Society. *Ethos* 16:52–72.

Hollan, D. 1992a. Emotion Work and the Value of Emotional Equanimity Among the Toraja. *Ethnology* 31:45–56.

Hollan, D. 1992b. Cross-Cultural Differences in the Self. *Journal of Anthropological Research* 48:283–300.

Hollan, D. 1996 Cultural and Experiential Aspects of Spirit Beliefs Among the Toraja. In *Spirits in Culture, History, and Mind*, edited by J.M. Mageo and A. Howard, pp. 213–235. New York: Routledge.

Hollan, D. 1997. The Relevance of Person-Centered Ethnography to Cross-Cultural Psychiatry. *Transcultural Psychiatry* 34:219–234.

Hollan, D. 2001. Developments in Person-Centered Ethnography. In *The Psychology of Cultural Experience*, edited by H. Mathews and M. Carmella. New York: Cambridge University Press.

Hollan, D.W., and J.C. Wellenkamp. 1994. *Contentment and Suffering: Culture and Experience in Toraja*. New York: Columbia University Press.

Hollan, D.W., and J.C. Wellenkamp. 1996. *The Thread of Life: Toraja Reflections on the Life Cycle*. Honolulu: University of Hawaii Press.

Janet, P. 1890. *The Major Symptoms of Hysteria*. New York: Macmillan.

Johnson, A. 1998. Repression: A Reexamination of the Concept as Applied to Folktales. *Ethos* 26:295–313.

Johnson, A.W., and D. Price-Williams. 1996. *Oedipus Ubiquitous: The Family Complex in World Folk Literature*. Stanford: Stanford University Press.

Jung, C.G. 1964. *Man and His Symbols*. New York: Doubleday.

Kirmayer, L.J. 1994. Pacing the Void: Social and Cultural Dimensions of Dissociation. In *Dissociation: Culture, Mind, and Body*, edited by D. Spiegel, pp. 91–122. Washington, DC: American Psychiatric Press.

Kirmayer, L.J. 1996. Landscapes of Memory: Trauma, Narrative, and Dissociation. In *Tense Past: Cultural Essays in Trauma and Memory*, edited by P. Antze and M. Lambek, pp. 173–198. New York: Routledge.

Kleinman, A., and J. Kleinman. 1991. Suffering and Its Professional Transformation: Toward an Ethnography of Interpersonal Experience. *Culture, Medicine, and Psychiatry* 15:275–301.

Kohut, H. 1977. *The Restoration of the Self.* New York: International Universities Press.

Lambek, M. 1981. *Human Spirits: A Cultural Account of Trance in Mayotte.* Cambridge: Cambridge University Press.

Lambek, M. 1989. From Disease to Discourse: Remarks on the Conceptualization of Trance and Spirit Possession. In *Altered Stales of Consciousness and Mental Health: A Cross-Cultural Perspective,* edited by C.A. Ward, pp. 36–61. Newbury Park: Sage Publications.

Lambek, M. 1996. Afterword: Spirits and Their Histories. In *Spirits in Culture, History, and Mind,* edited by J.M. Mageo and H. Alan, pp. 237–249. New York: Routledge.

LeDoux, J. 1996. *The Emotional Brain: The Mysterious Underpinnings of Emotional Life.* New York: Simon and Schuster.

Levy, R.I. 1973. *Tahitians: Mind and Experience in the Society Islands.* Chicago: Chicago University Press.

Levy, R.I. 1984. Emotion, Knowing, and Culture. In *Culture Theory: Essays on Mind, Self, and Emotion,* edited by R.A Shweder and R.A. LeVine, pp. 214–237. Cambridge: Cambridge University Press.

Levy, R.I. 1990. *Mesocosm: Hinduism and the Organization of a Traditional Newar City in Nepal.* Berkeley: University of California Press.

Levy, R.I., and D.W. Hollan. 1998. Person-Centered Interviewing and Observation in Anthropology. In *Handbook of Methods in Cultural Anthropology* edited by H.R. Bernard, pp. 333–364. Walnut Creek, CA: Altamira Press.

Levy, R.I., J.M. Mageo, and A. Howard 1996 Gods, Spirits, and History: A Theoretical Perspective. In *Spirits in Culture, History, and Mind,* edited by J.M. Mageo and A. Howard, pp. 11–27. New York: Routledge.

LeVine, R.A. 1982. *Culture, Behavior, and Personality: An Introduction to the Comparative Study of Psychosocial Adaptation.* 2nd edition. New York: Aldine.

Linger, D.T. 1994. Has Culture Theory Lost Its Minds? *Ethos* 22:284–315.

Mageo, J.M., and A. Howard, eds., 1996. *Spirits in Culture, History, and Mind.* New York: Routledge.

Mead, G.H. 1934. *Mind, Self, and Society.* Chicago: University of Chicago Press.

Mitchell, S.A. 1988. *Relational Concepts in Psychoanalysis.* Cambridge, MA: Harvard University Press.

Mitchell, S.A. 1993. *Hope and Dread in Psychoanalysis.* New York: Basic Books.

Obeyesekere, G. 1981. *Medusa's Hair: An Essay on Personal Symbols and Religious Experience.* Chicago: University of Chicago Press.

Obeyesekere, G. 1990. *The Work of Culture.* Chicago: University of Chicago Press.

Parish, S.M. 1994. *Moral Knowing in a Hindu Sacred City: An Exploration of Mind, Emotion, and Self.* New York: Columbia University Press.

Parish, S.M. 1996. *Hierarchy and Its Discontents: Culture and the Politics of Consciousness in Caste Society.* Philadelphia: University of Pennsylvania Press.

Pinker, S. 1997. *How the Mind Works.* New York: W. W. Norton and Company.

Ramachandran, V.S. 1998. *Phantoms in the Brain: Probing the Mysteries of the Human Mind.* New York: William Morrow.

Schachtel, E.G. 1949 On Memory and Childhood Amnesia. In *A Study of Interpersonal Relations: New Contributions to Psychiatry,* edited by P. Mullahy, pp. 3–49. New York: Hermitage.

Schwartz, T. 1978. Where Is the Culture? Personality as the Distributive Locus of Culture. In *The Making of Psychological Anthropology,* edited by G.D. Spindler, pp. 419–441. Berkeley: University of California Press.

Shore, B. 1996. *Culture in Mind: Cognition, Culture, and the Problem of Meaning*. New York: Oxford University Press.

Slavin, M.O. 1990. The Dual Meaning of Repression and the Adaptive Design of the Human Psyche. *Journal of the American Academy of Psychoanalysis* 18:307–341.

Slavin, M.O, and D. Kriegman. 1992. *The Adaptive Design of the Human Psyche: Psycho-Analysis, Evolutionary Biology, and the Therapeutic Process*. New York: Guilford.

Spence, D.P. 1982. *Narrative Truth and Historical Truth: Meaning and Interpretation in Psychoanalysis*. New York: W. W. Norton.

Spiegel, D., ed., 1994. *Dissociation: Culture, Mind, and Body*. Washington, DC: American Psychiatric Press.

Spiro, M.E. 1951. Culture and Personality: The Natural History of a False Dichotomy. *Psychiatry* 14:19–46.

Spiro, M.E. 1993. Is the Western Conception of the Self "Peculiar" Within the Context of the World Cultures? *Ethos* 21:107–153.

Spiro, M.E. 1997. *Gender Ideology and Psychological Reality: An Essay on Cultural Reproduction*. New Haven, CT: Yale University Press.

Stem, D.N. 1985. *The Interpersonal World of the Infant: A View from Psychoanalysis and Developmental Psychology*. New York: Basic Books.

Stern, D.B. 1996. Dissociation and Constructivism. *Psychoanalytic Dialogues* 6:251–266.

Stern, D.B. 1997. *Unformulated Experience: From Dissociation to Imagination in Psychoanalysis*. Hillsdale, NJ: Analytic Press.

Strauss, C. 1992 Models and Motives. In *Human Motives and Cultural Models*, edited by R. D'Andrade and C. Strauss, pp. 1–20. New York: Cambridge University Press.

Strauss, C., and N. Quinn. 1997. *A Cognitive Theory of Cultural Meaning*. Cambridge: Cambridge University Press.

Sullivan, H.S. 1953. *The Interpersonal Theory of Psychiatry*. New York: Norton.

Sullivan, H.S. 1956. *Clinical Studies in Psychiatry*. New York: Norton.

Sulloway, F.J. 1996. *Bom to Rebel: Birth Order, Family Dynamics, and Creative Lives*. New York: Pantheon Books.

van der Kolk, B.A. 1987 The Psychological Consequences of Overwhelming Life Experiences. In *Psychological Trauma*, edited by B.A. van der Kolk, pp. 1–30. Washington, DC: American Psychiatric Press.

van der Kolk, B.A. 1989. The Compulsion to Repeat the Trauma. *Psychiatric Clinics of North America* 12:389–411.

van der Kolk, B.A., and O. van der Hart. 1989. Pierre Janet and the Breakdown of Adaptation in Psychological Trauma. *American Journal of Psychiatry* 146:1530–1540.

Volkman, T. 1985. *Feasts of Honor: Ritual and Change in the Toraja Highlands*. Urbana: University of Illinois Press.

Wallace, A.F.C. 1956. Revitalization Movements. *American Anthropologist* 58:264–281.

Wallace, A.F.C. 1970. *Culture and Personality*. 2nd edition. New York: Random House.

Wallace, A.F.C. 1972. *The Death and Rebirth of the Seneca*. New York: Vintage Books.

Weiss, J., and H. Sampson. 1986. *The Psychoanalytic Process: Theory, Clinical Observation, and Empirical Research*. New York: Guilford Press.

Wikan, U. 1990. *Managing Turbulent Hearts: A Balinese Formula for Living*. Chicago: University of Chicago Press.

Winnicott, D.W. 1965. Ego Distortion in Terms of True and False Self. In *The Maturational Processes and the Facilitating Environment: Studies in the Theory of Emotional Development*, pp. 140–152. New York: International Universities Press.

Young, A. 1995. *The Harmony of Illusions: Inventing Post-Traumatic Stress Disorder*. Princeton, NJ: Princeton University Press.

4 On the Varieties and Particularities of Cultural Experience

As someone who has spent more years than I care to remember trying to understand how people and the lifeworlds they inhabit fit together or not (cf. Levy 1973, 1990), I have always thought that phenomenology and psychoanalysis go hand in hand (cf. Devereux 1978; Csordas 2012; Throop 2012). After all, both are "phenomenological" in the sense of trying to understand how the world is felt and experienced from a first person point of view, and in relating awareness and behavior in the present moment to shadows of both the past and future. And each perspective, in my opinion, has strengths that help balance out the other's limitations. I confess at the outset, however, that my reading of this might be quite idiosyncratic, based at least partly on the fact that I am both practicing ethnographer and psychoanalyst. But if so, this personal stamp on my understanding of things will illustrate one of the points I want to make below. My comments flow from an historical perspective, suggesting how cultural phenomenology in American anthropology is, in part, a reaction against and correction of the classic psychoanalytical reductionism of the old "culture and personality" school. But I go on to suggest that more contemporary forms of psychoanalysis, heavily influenced by intersubjective, narrative, neuroscience, and even phenomenological perspectives, have much to offer a study of lived experience, especially in terms of helping understand how and why human attention and consciousness becomes captured and focused in the way it does.

The Legacy of Culture and Personality

When most of us think of the Culture and Personality school in anthropology, we immediately think of Ruth Benedict's classic, *Patterns of Culture* (1934), and her contention that culture is "personality writ large"; of Abram Kardiner's two books, the *Individual and His Society* (1939) and *The Psychological Frontiers of Society* (1945), in which he develops the "basic personality structure" concept; and of the "national character" studies of Gregory Bateson, Margaret Mead, Geoffrey Gorer, and others who attempted to describe and explain the psychology of whole societies and nation states. While Benedict's *Patterns of Culture* remains in print nearly 70 years after its original publication,

DOI: 10.4324/9781003529118-5

anthropologists now rarely reference this work. Critics have pointed out that nearly all of it ended up exaggerating the psychological similarities within cultures and the psychological differences among them while also arguing that many of its inferences about human psychology were derived from the collection and analysis of social, cultural, and institutional data alone, with little if any grounding in the lives and experience of actual people or the historical and political circumstances of the times (Hollan and Wellenkamp 1994: 3–7). One common mistake was to exaggerate the uniformity of childrearing practices within cultures and their impact on adult personality, a misapplication of psychoanalytic theory that unfortunately has led many cultural anthropologists and others to dismiss psychodynamic analysis altogether. These studies also tended to emphasize how cultures reproduce themselves, and so were not particularly helpful in explaining the dynamics of social and cultural change.

Elsewhere (Hollan 2002) I have argued that there is another line of research developing out of the early culture and personality school, one that I have referred to as the "subject-centered" approach,[1] which avoids many of the limitations noted above. But certainly much of the culture and personality school deserved the criticism leveled at it.

Although Irving Hallowell was well versed in culture and personality theory, and though he explicitly notes how a psychoanalytic approach could complement a cultural analysis of self and emotion (1955: 80), his own body of work, which he referred to as "phenomenological" in character (1955: 79), was a clear break from the psychoanalytic assumptions underlying many culture and personality studies. Rather than focus on personality dynamics per se, for example, he demonstrates how the subject becomes oriented and acts in a culturally constituted behavioral environment. While I agree with Csordas (2002: 58–59) that one of Hallowell's most widely cited articles, "The Self and Its Behavioral Environment" (1955: 75–110), presumes at the outset an already culturally objectified subject or self distinct from other objects in the world, much of his other work does reflect a more truly phenomenological account of behavior. For example, several of his chapters on Ojibwa ethnopsychology illustrate how people come to accept the reality of other-than-human beings not on faith, but through their own culturally mediated bodily and perceptual engagements with the lifeworld.

Hallowell's break with the culture and personality school was not an open or hostile one, though. He acknowledged how a psychoanalytic perspective could help develop a more accurate picture of self processes (Hallowell 1955: 80) and in such articles as "Fear and Anxiety as Cultural and Individual Variables in a Primitive Society" (Hallowell 1955: 250–265), he himself attempted to examine the way aspects of personal and emotional experience are shaped by both cultural and idiosyncratic factors. And yet his concerted and consistent move away from the psychoanalytic zeitgeist and toward a more full-blown phenomenological account of cultural behavior says as much or more than an explicit critique could. In effect, Hallowell was arguing that we must first get right what the lifeworld looks and feels like from the actor's point of view before we begin to speculate too extensively about their psychodynamics. If we fail in this, we risk misunderstanding or pathologizing behavior that is completely normal and "commonsensical" from a cultural or lifeworld perspective.

If Hallowell began the move to a more explicit phenomenological approach in American anthropology, it is of course Thomas Csordas (1994, 2002), Michael Jackson (1996, 2007), Vincent Crapanzano (1992, 2004), Byron Good (1994), Robert Desjarlais 1992, 1996), and Jason Throop (2003, 2010), among others, who have since continued that move and pushed it further, reacting not only to more psychoanalytically oriented work in anthropology, but also to the "culture as text," symbols and meanings, interpretive approach of Clifford Geertz (1973). I hesitate to attempt even a brief characterization of this collective body of work because as Michael Jackson has written (1996: vii–viii), quoting Roger Poole (1972: 81), "there is no definitive account of phenomenology, no general agreement on terms, nor could there ever be. It is a subject in development, everyone making of it what he [she] will for his [her] own work. The insight has been fruitful, the doctrine remains a challenge." Nevertheless, I think it would be fair to say that all of these authors cite Merleau-Ponty (1962) as a major source of inspiration and would agree with many of Jackson's own characterizations of the cultural phenomenology approach: that it is the scientific study of human consciousness in its lived immediacy (1996: 2); that consciousness and subjectivity are manifested in and through the body, such that embodiment "is a primordial aspect of human subjectivity" (1996: 32); that it is the Schutzian "life-world," the world as lived and experienced by the actor that is of interest, not the world as "objectively" given (1996: 18–19); that the distinction between subject and object is one that is lived and achieved, not given; that all people are always both subject and object to themselves (1996:21); and that "Meaning should not be reduced to that which can be thought or said, since meaning may exist simply in the doing and in what is manifestly accomplished by an action" (1996:32). And so, these authors demonstrate a strong interest in habitus and practice theory (Jackson 1996: 18–21) as well.

Of particular significance for my purposes here is the emphasis on a pragmatic analysis of actions and behaviors, one that focuses on their meanings and consequences, not their causes:

> For anthropology, this implies a practical relativism: the suspension of inquiry into the divine or objective truth of particular customs, beliefs, or worldviews in order to explore them as modalities or moments of experience, to trace out their implications and uses. . . The phenomenological method involves "placing in brackets" or "setting aside" questions concerning the rational, ontological, or objective status of ideas and beliefs in order to fully describe and do justice to the ways in which people actually live, experience, and use them—the ways in which they

appear in consciousness. Dewey calls this "the postulate of immediate empiricism," namely that "things are what they are experienced to be" (1905: 228). This phenomenological *epoche* or "bracketing" implies a rigorously empirical attitude, without being empiricist. *Empirie, nicht Empirismus,* declared Dilthey, in order to emphasize that though phenomenology focuses on the facts of consciousness it does not strive to explain those facts away by reducing them to antecedent conditions, biogenetic determinations, unconscious principles, or invisible causes.

(Jackson 1996: 10)

Such a perspective emphasizes that experience is situated *"within* relationships and *between* persons" and that the lifeworld should be "explored as a field of intersubjectivity and not reduced to objective structures *or* subjective intentions" (Jackson 1996: 26).

Here of course is one of the places where many phenomenologists take issue with psychoanalysis, arguing that as a discipline and system of interpretation psychoanalysis does in fact reduce complex intersubjectivity to unconscious principles, invisible causes, and subjective intentions.

The Legacy of Cultural Phenomenology

Much of the more recent work in cultural phenomenology cited above can be seen as a refinement and extension of Hallowell's notion of the "behavioral environment" (1955: 86–89), emphasizing that people act and live in the lifeworld that is psychologically, perceptually, and emotionally salient to them, not the world as objectively viewed from a third person point of view, and that this embodied lifeworld is culturally and intersubjectively mediated. These ideas have now become so central to so many scholars, especially to those in psychological anthropology, that they are like the air we breathe, completely taken for granted and commonsensical, in a phenomenological sort of way. They have become as much a part of our academic lifeworlds as the notion that anthropology must respect cultural variability and diversity. This is especially true of the notion that the body is the existential ground of culture (Csordas 1994, 2002), which has spawned an enormous literature on the cross-cultural study of the body and senses (see, e.g., Desjarlais 2003), and which, year by year, finds growing support in the neurosciences (see, e.g., Damasio 1994, 1999; Iacoboni 2008; LeDoux 1996, 2002).

In my opinion, so be it. Any theoretical or methodological strategy that helps "apprehend, in an integral fashion, the most significant and meaningful aspects of the world of the individual as experienced by him and in terms of which he thinks, is motivated to act, and satisfies his needs" (Hallowell 1955: 88) is a good one, especially when one considers the human tendency, cultural and personality theorists or otherwise, to "fill in the gaps" of one's limited knowledge of others by projecting onto them one's own parochial understandings of the world and people, whatever those might be.

For ethnographers, it is appropriate to resist the seduction of thinking one can know easily or in advance, without the hard work of ethnography and personal engagement, how and why people think and act in the ways they do—whether that seductive, reductive idea comes from psychoanalysis, practice theory, evolutionary psychology, folk wisdom, or anywhere else.

That psychoanalysts in particular are in need of this kind of interpretative restraint was brought close to home for me during my own training. One of my colleagues was presenting her ongoing work with an assistant professor at a local college. As was typical of case conferences, trainees and supervisors alike were not shy about jumping in and offering interpretations of why this young professor was struggling in the way he was. But very soon after the discussion began, I remember thinking to myself, "my colleagues here don't have a clue about what the tenure process is really like, how uncertain and stressful it can be, and how it might be affecting this man's behavior. Of course there is a psychodynamic side to how he is reacting, but there is a lifeworld side as well, and the lifeworld side seems to account for a lot of what this guy is up to." The fact that I was myself an untenured, assistant professor at the time made me squirm even more.

And yet. . .

But the descriptive and analytical challenge posed by phenomenology is a demanding one. Jackson writes, for example, that ideally we should be capturing not only the routine, habitual aspects of everyday life, but also "its crises, its vernacular and idiomatic character, its biographical particularities, its decisive events and indecisive strategies" (1996: 8), not only the typical and customary in life and experience, Dilthey's *Erfahrung*, but also what is "idiosyncratic, exceptional, and singular *(Erlebnis)*" (1996: 27) about it. We must remember that a human life "is seldom a blind recapitulation of givenness, but an active relationship with what has gone before and what is imagined to lie ahead" (Jackson 1996: 11). This is an exhortation to go beyond the study of how people conserve and perpetuate their lifeworlds, and, rather, to examine how they interpret, negotiate, reimagine, and endure these lifeworlds, as well as protest against them at times (Jackson 1996: 30).

In passages such as these, Jackson is reminding readers that people affect the world and other people as well as being affected by them. And yet my own reading of this emerging literature is that it is often more effective at describing the way life and experience are situated by the world than in capturing the crises, the idiomatic expressions, the biographical particularities, the indecisive strategies, the idiosyncrasies, the exceptions, the singularities, and the shadows of the past that Jackson refers to above (see also Linger 2010). This literature often reminds readers how essential bodies are to constructions of the world, but seldom details how differences in bodies—whether one is fat or thin, tall or short, beautiful or ugly—might affect that construction (for a notable exception, see Falgoust 2008). Readers learn how life is lived intersubjectively, in the spaces between people, but are rarely told what difference it might make to be interacting with such and such kind of person, with his or her own unique history of embodied relationships and memories, rather than another kind of person, with an equally complex and unique history. Readers are shown how people can be healed by opening up and expanding their imaginative worlds, but not often shown cases where that healing fails, or why it is that some people drop out of the healing or never show up in the first place (see Hollan 2004). Such phenomenologically inspired scholarship demonstrates how life as lived is an open-ended process and how the present is always giving way to the future, and yet leaves open whether certain forms of memory and embodiment really are more intractable and adhesive than others. This genre of work shows how habitual practices and engagements shape consciousness and experience, but more rarely shows how an actor's fantasy or dream or preoccupation or obsession may insinuate itself into a practice, thereby transforming it (cf. Good 2012).

My point here is similar to the one Thompson makes in pointing out the limitations of Husserl's classic example of listening to a melody to illustrate the threefold structure of time-consciousness:

> let us return to the point that we experience absorbed activity not as having a subject-object structure, but instead as an immediate coupling or dynamic attunement to our environment. From this perspective, Husserl's classic descriptions of listening to a melody seem disembodied and abstract. He does not tell us whether the experience is an absorbed listening to a familiar and cherished piece of music or a hearing of a new and unfamiliar work, whether the performance is live or a recording, whether the setting is a celebratory event in the company or others or a solitary and contemplative listening. Of course, Husserl is interested in precisely the invariant structure of time-consciousness, which presumably constitutes the listening experience as such in any possible situation. It is important to grant and recognize the force of this point. Nevertheless, in abstracting away from the concrete setting of the experience, we run the risk of objectifying the experience and thereby misdescribing it. Especially if the listening is an absorbed or immersed one, there will not be any explicit or thematic awareness of the melody as a distinct object, or any explicit or thematic awareness of our ongoing listening.
>
> (Thompson 2007: 326–327)

Ironically, then, what seems to be missing from some of this phenomenologically inspired work is how given individuals become dynamically "coupled with" or "attuned to" their "immediate" environments—that is, how they become marked by a particular set of historically specific interactions with others, and in turn, how historically specific individuals come to mark and infuse, in particular ways, the lives of others. It is this uniqueness and particularity of life experience that William James (1982) refers to as a person's "individual pinch of destiny," that subjective, "inner 'state'" in which all thinking, all consciousness, and all experiencing comes to pass. James does not make the mistake of reducing experience to this personal side of things, saying it consists of "A conscious field *plus* its objects felt or thought of *plus* an attitude towards the object *plus* the sense of a self to whom the attitude belongs" (1982: 499). But nor does he make the mistake of ignoring or minimizing its significance:

> —such a concrete bit of personal experience may be a small bit, but it is a solid bit as long as it lasts; not hollow, not a mere abstract element of experience, such as the "object" is when taken alone. It is a *full* fact, even though it be an insignificant fact; it is of the *kind* to which all realities whatsoever must belong; the motor currents of the world run through the like of it; it is on the line connecting real events with real events. That unsharable feeling which each of us has of the pinch of his individual destiny as he privately feels it rolling out on fortune's wheel may be disparaged for its egotism, may be sneered at as unscientific, but it is the one thing that fills up the measure of our concrete actuality, and any would-be existent that should lack such a feeling, or its analogue, would be a piece of reality only half made up.
>
> (James 1982: 499–500)

Contrary to what Geertz writes about this passage in *Available Light* (2000:167–186), James is not naively romanticizing the concept, philosophy, or psychology of "the individual" here, nor claiming that experience is locked away in the inner recesses of an isolated mind. He is merely attempting to capture the cross-cultural, existential fact that things happen to one person, even within the same local world, that do not happen to another, and that this difference in happenings or in developmental history, if you will, continues to leave its mark on the way people go on to interact with one another and experience and interpret the world.

I am not, by the way, arguing that the "individual pinch of destiny" lies outside the theory or method of cultural phenomenology, merely pointing out that to date it has not gained significant attention there. And from an historical perspective, this makes sense to me. If you are, in part, reacting against the reductionism and determinism of a narrowly conceived psychology or psychoanalysis, it makes sense that you would emphasize the "situated-ness" pole of the self-lifeworld dialectic loop. In some cases, this is implicit, as when Csordas writes that another's emotion is immediately familiar to us "insofar as we share the same habitus" (1994: 13). In others more explicit, as when Desjarlais answers his own question about how one can conduct a phenomenology of a group as diverse as his homeless shelter residents, each with their own "quite diverse backgrounds, concerns, and futures" by saying, "As it is, the ubiquity of regulations, the constancy of routines, and the commonality of afflictions (fear, hearing voices) lead shelter residents to lead quite similar lives" (Desjarlais 1996: 90 n. 9). What is evident is the tendency to smooth out the differences between people and their experiences by referring to their purportedly common habitus or routines or practices; in some cases to presume that they are thinking and feeling and imagining the same things simply because they are overtly acting in the same ways.

Parenthetically, Thompson notes a similar lack of attention to the "personal self" in the Husserlian tradition of phenomenology more generally:

> In phenomenology, this sense of a personal self corresponds to what Husserl called the "concrete ego." By this he means the "I" that is constituted by "habitualities"—dispositional tendencies to experience things one way rather than another—as a result of general capabilities and sedimented experiences through active striving. Yet although this conception of self is of great importance for Husserl, and although his phenomenology is rich in analyses of affect and association, empathy and intersubjectivity, the Husserlian "concrete ego" is strangely lacking in personality. Overall there has been regrettably little analysis of emotion at the level of personality in phenomenology (unlike the Freudian or psychoanalytic tradition).
>
> (2007: 381)

Reenter Psychoanalysis?

How then to give equal weight to the subject and object ends of the phenomenal field? How to capture the dynamic, looping, recursive, "autopoietic" interplay between both ends, in which self-generating processes lead to the development of a semipermeable boundary between self and other that though open to and dependent upon intersubjective influence, nevertheless produces and regulates its own internal topology and functional boundary (Thompson 2007: 97–107; see also Toren 2000, 2002, 2004)? How to acknowledge not only the situating effects of the complex, variegated worlds into which people are "thrown" and which their active engagements help co-constitute, but also the fact that the actors so thrown are not innocent blank slates to be written upon, but rather complexly evolved social animals, highly sensitive to their interpersonal behavioral environments, who throughout their lives formulate and revise a unique set of implicit and explicit memories of past engagements that feed-forward into their experience of future events and engagements? How to acknowledge the open-ended nature of this looping process, but also the phenomenal fact that some people experience themselves as being hopelessly "stuck" or unchanging or without a future? Or the fact that a person once stuck can become unstuck and then stuck again? Or that parts of a person's phenomenal field can be both stuck and unstuck, in a dissociative-like way, all at the same time?

It is here that I think contemporary psychoanalysis can be helpful. I use the term "contemporary" psychoanalysis deliberately since the field has developed considerably over the years—though you might never suspect this given the way psychoanalysis is often referenced in anthropology and the other social sciences, as if nothing has happened since Freud. Although there are many psychoanalysts today who would claim that the "classical" ideas of drive theory and repression still lie at the heart of the field, there are many others who would dispute that claim, especially many North American analysts trained in the post-Kohut era. Freud himself often struggled to reconcile drive theory (the so-called "one-person" psychology) and object relations theory (the so-called "two-person" or multiperson psychology), but today many analysts have fully embraced ideas and theories of attachment behavior (e.g., Bowlby 1969), developmental psychology (e.g., Stern 1985), object relations (e.g., Greenberg and Mitchell 1983), self psychology (e.g., Kohut 1971), intersubjectivity (e.g., Stolorow et al. 1987), narrative (Spence 1982), phenomenology (e.g., Loewald 2000; Stern 1997), and recent research in the neurosciences about memory and nonconscious emotional processing (e.g., Boston Change Process Study Group 2005; Rustin and Sekaer 2004; Stern 2004; Stern and The Boston Process of Change Study Group 1998).

Though there remain significant differences among these points of view, they are sometimes grouped together and referred to as "relational" theories or concepts in psychoanalysis (Mitchell 1988, 2000), and in many ways, they turn more traditional psychoanalysis on its head. For example, rather than presume that other people and objects in the phenomenal field gain their emotional significance and meaning for a subject to the extent they help that individual satisfy some of their deepest, self-contained and inherent wishes and desires, relational theorists presume that it is emotional attachments and identifications with other people and meanings, intersubjective fusions and interrelationships of one with others, that come to influence the very wishes and desires an individual experiences, and which of these do and do not become problematic. Experience of wishes and desires are understood as emergent from a specific history of interpersonal engagements, rather than relatively transparent expressions of underlying drives.

Note that I have not yet said much about "the unconscious" as an explanatory concept here, the overly quick, nonpragmatic resort to which is one of the things many anthropologists and others find most troubling about traditional psychoanalysis. As I have discussed at length elsewhere (Hollan 2000), psychoanalytic ideas about how unconscious and nonconscious processes are related to conscious ones have been developing over many years. Many relational analysts now hold the view that since consciousness must be actively constructed out of our myriad engagements with the world, there will be many such engagements that remain unconceptualized, unverbalized, and so outside conscious awareness, unless or until they gain representation through complex symbolic processes. This phenomenologically influenced take on consciousness leaves room for a theory of drives and active repression, but also recognizes that many things remain outside of awareness simply because attention, often culturally and intersubjectively shaped and influenced, has been diverted elsewhere.

For my purposes here, there are two things to note about this model. One is that it encourages not a speculative, haphazard search for "deep" repressed thoughts, memories, and desires, but rather a careful, almost moment-by-moment experience-near exploration of a person's stream of consciousness and sense of awareness, noting what draws attention and expression, either verbal or nonverbal, but also what seems not to be expressed, in much the way that Harry Stack Sullivan (1953) proposed many years ago (see also Fink 2007). This enables one to observe both self-reflective, "resting" or "substantive" states in the stream of consciousness, but also its more "moving," "flighty," "transitive" states as well (James 1962: 174–179). And notably, this is an enduring, long-term exploration that unfolds over weeks or months at a time, thereby diminishing the chance that one will mistake a fleeting interest or awareness for a more repetitive, emotionally significant one and vice versa. This is a far cry from the mistaken view some have that psychoanalysts are not interested in conscious or prereflective awareness or that they downplay its significance in human behavior. However, the model does encourage attention to the edges or horizons or shadows or fringes of consciousness (cf. Crapanzano 2004, 2006), or whatever the most appropriate metaphor might be, to help understand better why awareness is captured and flows in the way it does. The model promotes exploration of images or feelings at the margins of consciousness to enable an account of what can be spoken about or expressed in some other way and what cannot.

Although I have emphasized the relational school of psychoanalysis here because it suits my own analytic style and anthropological interests, I do not mean to privilege that perspective. One of my main points in this section is that much has changed in psychoanalysis over the last 80 years and that many of these newer perspectives, including Lacanian ones, may prove useful to anthropologists and their theorizing.

Even so, these contemporary perspectives alone will never resolve the analytic quandaries sketched out above, since even relational psychoanalysts remain hopelessly focused on a narrow range of the intersubjective and phenomenal field—essentially that which emerges between analyst and patient. But that narrow focus and control of context (the analyst's office) has allowed analysts to make detailed observations of how people engage and imagine the phenomenal field, capturing some of its complexity, its ebb and flow, its mood and state dependent-ness, its contradictions, its obsessive certainties and rigidities as well as its anxious and fearful uncertainties. Most especially for my purposes here, such observations offer a sense of how emotional memories develop over time, linking together different parts of the phenomenal field—people, objects, ideas, imaginings—in often surprising, idiosyncratic, nonhabitus-like ways. This in turn provides some insight into why people become oriented to the phenomenal field in the way they do, why they are open if not attracted to certain people, experiences, and ideas, but not so open to, even repelled by others. It is this kind of specificity, tied to the exploration of a person's "individual pinch of destiny," that can complement, I think, the findings and insights of cultural phenomenology as currently practiced.

Let me give a quick example of what I mean here. One of my psychotherapy clients is a white-collar employee, working for a large corporation. He is frustrated by his inability to get ahead at work. He is an extremely dedicated employee, is knowledgeable about how the corporate power and promotional structure works, and is acclaimed as an expert in his field, yet almost without fail, he finds himself becoming enraged with and alienated from his supervisors, whom he considers to be narrow-minded, overly conventional, and stubborn. My client knows he is constantly undermining himself with his displays of anger, yet he has only dawning awareness of how his descriptions of his supervisors mirror almost identically those of his deceased, working-class father, of whom he often dreams as a stubborn bully. A psychoanalytic-like perspective, and the kind of questioning and listening it entails, allows the analyst or anthropologist to explore how this man's frustrated ambitions are connected not only to the culture and hierarchical power structure of his work place, but also to his less than fully conscious tendency to engage authority figures through the veiled, embodied memories and images of his tough minded and tough acting father. Such a perspective helps in understanding how and why this particular man, as opposed to other employees in this corporation, engages with and reacts to the power structure in the way he does, and in turn, how his particular combination of technical expertise and interpersonal sensitivity shapes the culture and practice of his work place (see also Hollan 2007).

Obeyesekere's concept of the "personal symbol" (1981, 1990) comes close to capturing the articulation between individual emotional memory and aspects of the larger cultural or phenomenal field I have in mind (see also Parish 2008). But while I admire Obeyesekere's work, especially his presentation of rich life history materials, I argue here as I have elsewhere (Hollan 2000, 2004, 2006, 2014), that his personalization and particularization of cultural forms and the phenomenal field actually do not go far enough. Ironically, by identifying personal symbols as opposed to other kinds of symbols on which to focus, he leaves the impression there are purely conventional forms of behavior and belief that can escape the impingement of individual embodiment, memory, and imagination. As I have suggested above, I think it is a mistake to presume that people who enact similar behaviors, no matter how common or repetitive from a third person perspective, have the same experience of or motives for those enactments. The way in which a cultural model of behavior becomes a mental model with motivational force and salience is complicated (cf. Briggs 1998; Linger 2005; Shore 1996; Strauss and Quinn 1997). Humans learn behaviors in emotionally charged or flattened situations over time, epigenetically. The past, sometimes highly idiosyncratic experiences of a behavior, partially shape the way one enacts and experiences the future while current enactments reshape memories and schemas of past behavior. Physical, overt enactments of most public behavior can receive relatively direct feedback and socialization, and so can be brought into conformity with cultural standards or ideals fairly easily. One can be told, "do it this way" or "don't do it that way." But emotions and imaginings surrounding an enactment are not so easily socialized and corralled. One can be taught that some form of behavior communicates respect but experience it as humiliating to others or to one's self. One can be taught that some form of behavior should be joyful but experience it as unimaginably poignant or tragic. And all of this can change over time. The richness and variegated nature of personal experience, made possible by the creative and generative capacities of human minds and brains and the differences in life situations, will always overflow the conventional, cultural forms into which experience is poured or within which it is instantiated.

Elsewhere (Hollan 2000) I have referred to this overflow as the experiential or subjectivity potential of a population. Because no two individuals, even within the same family or small community, ever experience instituted cultural forms in exactly the same way (cf. Schwartz 1978; Spiro 1951), the reproduction of these forms necessarily must be a highly dynamic process subject to constant, even if subtle, modification and change. To paraphrase a William James comment about the stream of consciousness (1962: 169), no cultural form once gone can recur and be identical with what it was before. Ironically, this is almost exactly the way Obeyesekere describes what he refers to as "subjectification," the process whereby received cultural forms are refashioned through the cauldron of individual fantasy and imagination. But Obeyesekere limits this interplay of form and imagination to behaviors and symbols that are nonobligatory, whereas I argue it is characteristic of the cultural process per se. No enactment, whether conventional and obligatory or not, is performed outside of the body–mind, with its highly particularized residues of past experience. Indeed, I think this is why James was so insistent about including "the individual pinch of destiny" in his concept of experience and why he wrote that "To describe the world with all the various feelings of the individual pinch of destiny … left out of the description—they being as describable as anything else—would be like offering a printed bill of fare as the equivalent of a solid meal…. A bill of fare with one real raisin on it instead of the word 'raisin,' with one real egg instead of the word 'egg,' might be an inadequate meal, but it would at least be a commencement of reality" (James 1982: 499–500).

So while I appreciate Obeyesekere's discussion of personal symbols, I think he is wrong, in the end, to preserve the person–culture divide in his typology of symbols and behavior. People and the cultural forms they live in and through are mutually constitutive, as Melford Spiro (1951) pointed out over 50 years ago. By acknowledging the "individual pinch of destiny" that infuses all cultural forms, we not only avoid the serious error of mistaking the menu for real food, but we set the table for a much more satisfying discussion of the role of feeling and imagination in human life.

Before concluding, let me note that my emphasis on the varieties and particularities of experience and the personalization of cultural forms in no way undermines or trivializes attempts to generalize about human behavior or to make valid claims of an applied, engaged, or activist intent. It is merely to argue that such efforts must come to terms with and actively theorize the great diversity at the experiential level, as Anthony Wallace first did many years ago (Wallace 1961). When this is done, patterns emerge, but they will be different from the ones that would be predicted when not factoring in such diversity (Hollan 2005), as when Brown and colleagues (2009) observe that among both white and Cherokee Appalachian youth, "varieties of intimate individual experience in formative years are more powerful predictors of life choices than broad social categories like ethnicity, age, and gender" (Wallace 2009: 254). This should serve as a reminder of Wallace's important and incisive observation that cultures do not eliminate experiential differences among people, but rather find creative ways for ignoring them or organizing and coordinating them (1961, 2009).

Conclusion

From my perspective, cultural phenomenologists and psychoanalysts, at least certain varieties of them,[2] are not as antithetical in approach as they are sometimes made out to be. In particular, both groups are concerned with understanding how the world is conceptualized, felt, and experienced from the first person point of view. However in practice each community does carve out its own piece of the phenomenal world to focus on, and each has developed their own methodologies to illuminate that focus. Cultural phenomenologists have tended to focus on how experience is situated in the lifeworld, how it is enabled or constrained by the imaginative and perceptual possibilities emergent in that world. And they have pursued their studies largely through detailed ethnography and engaged, committed participant observation, including long-term apprenticeships (Desjarlais 1992). They have emphasized, implicitly if not explicitly, the "protentional" aspects of experience, how the present moment is always unfolding into the future, going beyond itself in an indeterminate way.

Psychoanalysts, on the other, by deliberately holding the world at bay through the use of a single observational setting, have focused on how specific emerging subjects accrete emotional experiences and meanings over time, and how those accretions affect present and future engagements in the life world, including those between subject and analyst in the here and now. The emphasis here has been on emotional memory and the "retentional" aspects of experience, how the present moment is affected by carry over from the past and "the continuous holding onto the present as slipping away and sinking into the past" (Thompson 2007: 319).

In my view, these foci and their respective methodologies are complementary. Many psychoanalysts need reminding that the lifeworld really does extend beyond the confines of their offices, while cultural phenomenologists need occasional reminders that experiences accrete, and that these accretions, while certainly shaped, constrained, and revised through engagement and practice, never fully escape an individual's "pinch of destiny." Put more strongly, the two perspectives need one another. Experience should not be reduced to solipsism, but nor should specific individuals and their experiential "heaviness" be lost in the haze of ever-receding future horizons. The unfolding of self-awareness is indeed an autopoietic, recursive process the complexities of which surely escape any single perspective.

Again, I admit this may be an idiosyncratic view of things, given my own peculiar history as self-identified, person-centered ethnographer and relational-style psychoanalyst. But if so, I am not the only one whose pinch of destiny has left its mark. In a recent analysis and appreciation of Clifford Geertz's life work, Richard Shweder (2007) has written about Geertz's "resolute irresolution" regarding many of the major debates in the social sciences, including "positioning himself between any variety of relativism (which he claimed 'disables judgment') and any variety of absolutism (which he claimed removes judgment from history)" (Shweder 2007: 200). In developing this discussion, Shweder quotes from Geertz himself, who writes of his earlier life:

> So it is hardly to wonder that my work looks like a grasping for patterns in a swirl of change. I was preadapted. My parents were divorced when I was three, and I was dispatched (the verb is appropriate) to live alone with an older woman, a nonrelative, amid the sylvan beauties of the Northern California countryside (a "nonvillage" of three or four hundred farmers, shopkeepers, and summer visitors) in the plumb depths of the Great Depression. I was well cared for, and that's about it, and I was pretty much left to put my life together (not without real help from the schoolteachers responding to a bright kid, and, later on, the U.S. Navy, responding to a callow klutz) by myself. Without going on…all this predisposed me to becoming, in both life and work, the seeker after a pattern, however fragmentary, amid a swirl of accident, however pervasive... It has never occurred to me, not really being a deep thinker, just a nervous one, to try to resolve this "binary." I have just sought to live with it. Pitched early into things, I assumed, still assume, that what you are supposed to do is keep going with whatever you can find lying about to keep going with: to get from yesterday to today without foreclosing tomorrow. And it does, that resolute irresolution, indeed show in my work.
>
> (Geertz 2005: 123)[3]

Interestingly, although Geertz spent much of his career cautioning against an overly psychological perspective on the human condition, here he is explicitly using a life history and developmental approach to help make sense of his own life and work. Of course, there are many other examples of the effects of earlier life experiences on academic work, as when Jackson alludes to his own separation anxiety (2007: 172) in a discussion of the "liminal" phase of fieldwork, the period "after separation from one's familiar lifeworld, but before one finds one's feet and feels at home in one's new environment."

The point is that no one escapes the epigenetic unfolding of experience, and that it matters for understanding the human condition not only how that unfolding opens and continues into the future, but also where, when, and how it begins and assumes its unique character and quality.

Acknowledgments

I am grateful to Don Seeman and Sarah Willen for inviting me to the Lemelson SPA conference, "What's at Stake in the Ethnography of Human Experience?"(Emory University, September 2008) at which I presented an earlier version of this article. The conference was funded, in part, by a generous gift from Robert Lemelson. My thanks as well to Janet Keller for her excellent editorial suggestions and to my three anonymous reviewers.

Notes

1 This is a more "person-centered" body of work running from Sapir through the early Spiro (1951) and Wallace (1961) and on to Levy (1973), Schwartz (1978), and Obeyesekere (1981, 1990).

2 Both schools of thought are broad and varied, as I have suggested. It is clear to me that "relational" style psychoanalysts and cultural phenomenologists have much in common. Indeed, in many respects, they have more in common with each other than relational analysts have with other, more "classical" style analysts. One difference in these schools, however, is that the analysts have a long history of articulating the differences among themselves, in terms of perspectives and methodologies, in a fairly direct and explicit way, while such differences among the cultural phenomenologists remain rather muted. This may be because the cultural phenomenologists agree on most things or because their commonalities far outweigh their differences. But I think it would be an interesting project for someone to analyze more thoroughly not only how the cultural phenomenologists resemble one another, but also how they differ among themselves.

3 Those familiar with Spiro's work will know that "preadaptation" is a concept he uses to indicate how someone's prior experiences can lead them to be more or less receptive to cultural notions and practices in later life (see, e.g., Spiro 1997). It would be interesting to know whether Geertz was familiar with Spiro's views on preadaptation or whether this is his own language and thinking.

References

Benedict, R. 1934. *Patterns of Culture*. New York: Houghton Mifflin.

Boston Change Process Study Group. 2005. The "Something More" than Interpretation Revisited: Sloppiness and Co-Creativity in the Psychoanalytic Encounter. *Journal of the American Psychoanalytic Association* 53(3):693–729.

Bowlby, J. 1969. *Attachment*. New York: Basic Books.

Briggs, J. 1998. *Innuit Morality Play: The Emotional Education of a Three Year Old*. New Haven: Yale University Press.

Brown, R.A., D.H. Rehkopf, W.E. Copeland, E.J. Costello, and C.M. Worthman. 2009. Lifecourse Priorities Among Appalachian Emerging Adults: Revisiting Wallace's Organization of Diversity. *Ethos* 37(2):225–250.

Crapanzano, V. 1992. *Hermes' Dilemma and Hamlet's Desire*. Cambridge: Harvard University Press.

Crapanzano, V. 2004. *Imaginative Horizons: An Essay in Literary-Philosophical Anthropology*. Chicago: University of Chicago Press.

Crapanzano, V. 2006. The Scene: Shadowing the Real. *Anthropological Theory* 6:387–405.

Csordas, T.J. 1994. *The Sacred Self: A Cultural Phenomenology of Charismatic Healing*. Berkeley: University of California Press.

Csordas, T J. 2002. *Body/Meaning/Healing*. New York: Palgrave.

Csordas, T.J. 2012. Psychoanalysis and Phenomenology. *Ethos* 40(1):54–74.

Damasio, A.R. 1994. *Descartes' Error: Emotion, Reason, and the Human Brain*. New York: Avon Books.

Damasio, A.R. 1999. *The Feeling of What Happens: Body and Emotion in the Making of Consciousness*. New York: Harcourt Brace.

Desjarlais, R.R. 1992. *Body and Emotion: The Aesthetics of Illness and Healing in the Nepal Highlands*. Philadelphia: University of Pennsylvania Press.

Desjarlais, R.R. 1996 Struggling Along. In *Things as They Are: New Directions in Phenomenological Anthropology*, edited by M. Jackson, pp. 70–93. Bloomington: Indiana University Press.

Desjarlais, R.R. 2003. *Sensory Biographies: Lives and Deaths Among Nepal's Yolmo Buddhists*. Berkeley: University of California Press.

Devereux, G. 1978. *Ethnopsychoanalysis: Psychoanalysis and Anthropology as Complementary Frames of Reference*. Berkeley: University of California Press.

Dewey, J. 1905. Immediate Empiricism. *The Journal of Philosophy* 2:597–599.

Falgoust, N.A. 2008. Body Portraits of Spiritual Selves: Culture Working Through Relationships in an Afro-Brazilian Community. Unpublished Doctoral Dissertation. University of California, Los Angeles.

Fink, B. 2007. *Fundamentals of Psychoanalytic Technique: A Lacanian Approach for Practitioners*. New York: W. W. Norton.

Geertz, C. 1973. *Interpretation of Cultures*. New York: Basic Books.

Geertz, C. 2000. *Available Light: Anthropological Reflections on Philosophical Topics*. Princeton: Princeton University Press.

Geertz, C. 2005 Commentary. In *Clifford Geertz by His Colleagues*, edited by R.A. Shweder and B. Good, pp. 108–124. Chicago: University of Chicago Press.

Good, B.J. 1994. *Medicine, Rationality, and Experience*. Cambridge: Cambridge University Press.

Good, B.J. 2012. Phenomenology, Psychoanalysis, and Subjectivity in Java. *Ethos* 40(1):24–36.

Greenberg, J., and S. Mitchell. 1983. *Object Relations in Psychoanalytic Theory*. Cambridge: Harvard University Press.

Hallowell, A.I. 1955. *Culture and Experience*. Philadelphia: University of Pennsylvania Press.

Hollan, D. 2000. Constructivist Models of Mind, Contemporary Psychoanalysis, and the Development of Culture Theory. *American Anthropologist* 102(3):538–550.

Hollan, D. 2002. Varieties of Cultural Experience. Paper presented in the panel, "Culture and Personality: Renewal and Revision in Contemporary Research," Annual meetings of the American Anthropological Association, New Orleans, LA. November 20–24.

Hollan, D. 2004. Self Systems, Cultural Idioms of Distress, and the Psycho-Bodily Consequences of Childhood Suffering. *Transcultural Psychiatry* 4(1):62–79.

Hollan, D. 2005. Dreaming in a Global World. In *A Companion to Psychological Anthropology: Modernity and Psychocultural Change*, edited by C. Casey and R. Edgerton, pp. 90–102. Oxford: Blackwell.

Hollan, D. 2006. Is a Handshake Ever Just a Handshake?: On the Embodiment and Enactment of Cultural Forms and Meanings. Paper presented in the panel, "Experiential Horizons: On the Intermingling of Imagination, Fantasy, Memory, and Emotion
in the Practice of Everyday Life," Annual Meetings of the Canadian Anthropological
Association. Montreal, Canada, May 9–14.

Hollan, D. 2014. From Ghosts to Ancestors (and Back Again): On the Cultural and
Psychodynamic Mediation of Selfscapes. *Ethos* 42(2):175–197.

Hollan, D.W., and J.C. Wellenkamp. 1994. *Contentment and Suffering: Culture and
Experience in Toraja*. New York: Iacoboni, Marco.

Iacoboni, M. 2008. *Mirroring People: The New Science of How We Connect With
Others*. New York: Farrar, Straus and Giroux.

Jackson, M., ed., 1996. *Things as They Are: New Directions in Phenomenological
Anthropology*. Bloomington: Indiana University Press.

Jackson, M., ed., 2007. *Excursions*. Durham: Duke University Press.

James, W. 1962. *Psychology: Briefer Course*. New York: Collier Books.

James, W. 1982 [1902]. *The Varieties of Religious Experience*. New York: Penguin Books.

Kardiner, A. 1939. *The Individual and His Society*. New York: Columbia University Press.

Kardiner, A. 1945. *The Psychological Frontiers of Society*. New York: Columbia University Press.

Kohut, H. 1971. *The Analysis of Self*. New York: International Universities Press.

LeDoux, J. 1996. *The Emotional Brain*. New York: Simon and Schuster.

LeDoux, J. 2002. *Synaptic Self: How Our Brains Become Who We Are*. New York:
Penguin Books.

Levy, R.I. 1973. *Tahitians: Mind and Experience in the Society Islands*. Chicago: University of Chicago Press.

Levy, R.I. 1990. *Mesocosm: Hinduism and the Organization of a Traditional Newar
City in Nepal*. Berkeley: University of California Press.

Linger, D. 2005. *Anthropology Through a Double Lens: Public and Personal Worlds in
Human Theory*. University of Pennsylvania Press.

Linger, D. 2010. What Is It Like to Be Someone Else? *Ethos* 38(2):205–229.

Loewald, H.W. 2000. *The Essential Loewald: Collected Papers and Monographs*. Hagerstown, MD: University Publishing Group.

Merleau-Ponty, M. 1962. *Phenomenology of Perception*. London: Routledge.

Mitchell, S.A. 1988. *Relational Concepts in Psychoanalysis: An Integration*. Cambridge: Harvard University Press.

Mitchell, S.A. 2000. *Relationality: From Attachment to Intersubjectivity*. Hillsdale, NJ:
The Analytic Press.

Obeyesekere, G. 1981. *Medusa's Hair: An Essay on Personal Symbols and Religious
Experience*. Chicago: University of Chicago Press.

Obeyesekere, G. 1990. *The Work of Culture*. Chicago: University of Chicago Press.

Parish, S.M. 2008. *Subjectivity and Suffering in American Culture*. New York:
Palgrave.

Poole, R. 1972. *Towards Deep Subjectivity*. London: Allen Lane.

Rustin, J, and C. Sekaer. 2004. From the Neuroscience of Memory to Psychoanalytic
Interaction: Clinical Implications. *Psychoanalytic Psychology* 21(1):70–82.

Schwartz, T. 1978. Where Is the Culture? Personality as the Distributive Locus of Culture. In *The Making of Psychological Anthropology*, edited by G. Spindler, pp. 419–
441. Berkeley, CA: University of California Press.

Shore, B. 1996. *Culture in Mind: Cognition, Culture, and the Problem of Meaning*.
New York: Oxford University Press.

Shweder, R.A. 2007. The Resolute Irresolution of Clifford Geertz. *Common Knowledge* 13:191–205.

Spence, D.P. 1982. *Narrative Truth and Historical Truth: Meaning and Interpretation in
Psychoanalysis*. New York: W. W. Norton.

Spiro, M.E. 1951. Culture and Personality: The Natural History of a False Dichotomy. *Psychiatry* 14:19–46.

Spiro, M.E. 1997. *Gender Ideology and Psychological Reality: An Essay on Cultural Reproduction*. New Haven, CT: Yale University Press.

Stern, D. 1985. *The Interpersonal World of the Infant*. New York: Basic Books.

Stern, D. 2004. *The Present Moment in Psychotherapy and Everyday Life*. New York: W. W. Norton.

Stern, D.B. 1997. *Unformulated Experience: From Dissociation to Imagination in Psychoanalysis*. Hillsdale, NJ: Analytic Press.

Stern, D., and The Boston Process of Change Study Group. 1998. The Process of Therapeutic Change Involving Implicit Knowledge: Some Implications of Developmental Observations for Adult Psychotherapy. *Infant Mental Health Journal* 19(3):300–308.

Stolorow, R., B. Brandchaft, and G.E. Atwood. 1987. *Psychoanalytic Treatment: An Intersubjective Approach*. Hillsdale, NJ: Analytic Press.

Strauss, C., and N. Quinn. 1997. *A Cognitive Theory of Cultural Meaning*. Cambridge: Cambridge University Press.

Sullivan, H.S. 1953. *The Interpersonal Theory of Psychiatry*. New York: Norton.

Thompson, E. 2007. *Mind in Life: Biology, Phenomenology, and the Sciences of Mind*. Cambridge: Harvard University Press.

Throop, C.J. 2003. Articulating Experience. *Anthropological Theory* 3:219–241.

Throop, C.J. 2010. *Suffering and Sentiment: Exploring the Vicissitudes of Experience and Pain in Yap*. Berkeley: University of California Press.

Throop, C.J. 2012. On Inaccessibility and Vulnerability: Some Horizons of Compatibility between Phenomenology and Psychoanalysis. *Ethos* 40(1):75–96.

Toren, C. 2000. Mind and Inter-Subjectivity: An Anthropological Perspective. *Journal of Intelligent Systems* 10(1):1–25.

Toren, C. 2002 Anthropology as the Whole Science of What It Is to Be Human. In *Anthropology Beyond Culture*, edited by R. Fox and B. King, pp. 105–124. London: Berg.

Toren, C. 2004. Becoming a Christian in Fiji: An Ethnographic Study of Ontogeny. *Journal of the Royal Anthropological Institute* 10(1):222–240.

Wallace, A.F.C. 1961. *Culture and Personality*. New York: Random House.

Wallace, A.F.C. 2009. Epilogue: On the Organization of Diversity. *Ethos* 37(2):251–255.

5   Emotional Entrainment in Crowds and Other Social Formations

The sociologist, Randall Collins (2004, 2009), has recently argued that emotional entrainment—the process whereby interacting human nervous systems can become physiologically and rhythmically attuned to one another—is a primary element of all social formations, including crowds. Collins uses and endorses recent research from a variety of disciplines suggesting that biologically based, embodied forms of imitation and mutual attunement, including empathy, mirror neurons, and sensitivity to facial expressions, are far more central to human social and cultural behavior than previously imagined. In this chapter, I use ethnographic and clinical material from rural Indonesia and the urban United States, respectively, to critically examine some of Collins's claims about the role of emotional entrainment in crowds and other social formations.

I argue that while Collins is certainly correct in drawing our attention back to the ways in which social formations are embodied in deeply emotional and intersubjective ways, he errs in suggesting that people entrain to other bodies in fairly uniform ways, under the influence of a mutual focus of attention. People in crowds and other groups entrain to one another, but they entrain to particular bodies in particular historical and cultural moments. These histories of mutual encounter leave particularized emotional residues in people that loop into future engagements in complex and emergent ways that cannot be predicted from a person's habitus alone. Because Collins overgeneralizes the way emotions become entrained for people—a key part of his theory—he is unable to account for the *various* ways in which people's emotional ghosts and memories are aroused to new life by social interaction.

I begin by reviewing Collins's theory of the centrality of emotions and emotional entrainment in human sociality and then use some of the psychoanalyst Hans Loewald's observations about the fluidity and contingent emergence of unconscious or preconscious thoughts, feelings, and images to suggest the limits of his theory. I illustrate and discuss these theoretical points by analyzing clinical and ethnographic case material from Toraja, Indonesia, and the greater Los Angeles area of southern California. I conclude by suggesting that the "crowd" of emotional ghosts circulating within any group of people always far exceeds the number of concrete bodies present per se, which is

DOI: 10.4324/9781003529118-6

why many social formations, whether highly organized and scripted or not, remain as emergent and unpredictable as they do.

My critique of Collins's entrainment theory is based on data gathered through an ethnographic and clinical approach that Robert I. Levy and I have referred to as person-centered ethnography and observation (Levy and Hollan 2014). Person-centered ethnography attempts to represent human behavior and subjective experience from the point of view of the acting, intending, and attentive subject and to actively explore, rather than to assume, the emotional and motivational saliency of social, cultural, political, and economic forces. The focus is not only on the behavioral environment in which a person acts, but also on how individual persons are reacting to, embodying, internalizing, and transforming that environment. This includes investigating—often through open-ended interviewing techniques—what a person might be thinking, feeling, sensing, imagining, fantasizing, and dreaming as well as what they might be enacting through more overt forms of expression and behavior. Such a fine-grained ethnographic approach is well suited, indeed even necessary, to evaluate the kind of broad claims Collins makes about the role of emotional entrainment in the formation and reproduction of social groupings, including crowds.

Collins's Theory of Interaction Rituals

In two recent books, *Interaction Ritual Chains* (2004) and *Violence: A Micro-Sociological Theory* (2009), Collins develops a theory of interactions rituals as central to human life. Collins uses the concept of a "ritual" very broadly to include nearly any type of social interaction imaginable, including what are often referred to as "crowds," though he focuses primarily on face-to-face interactions in real time. The physical presence of human bodies interacting with one another is critical to his theory, since it is the emotional entrainment these bodies generate in one another that drives and explains much of social life. According to Collins, "Interaction rituals in general are processes that take place as human bodies come close enough to each other that their nervous systems become mutually attuned in rhythms and anticipations of each other, and the physiological substratum that produces emotions in one individual's body becomes stimulated in feedback loops that run through the other person's" (2004: xix). Here, Collins uses and endorses recent research from a variety of disciplines suggesting that biologically based, embodied forms of imitation and mutual attunement—including empathy, mirror neurons, and recognition of facial expressions—are far more central and critical to human social and cultural behavior than previously imagined. Nevertheless, he argues forcefully, in good sociological fashion, that it is social interaction that drives these chains of emotional and physiological arousal and entrainment, not the other way around.

According to Collins, then, emotional entrainment does not happen in a social vacuum. It primes and is primed by common actions or events or by a mutual focus of attention, separating out those people who are part of the interaction from those who are not. Bodies can be drawn near by a mutual focus of attention, or the emotional arousal caused by nearby bodies can facilitate a mutual focus of attention, but both must be present for a "successful" ritual to occur, and both processes are mutually reinforcing. As feedback and reinforcement between emotions and mutual focus intensify through rhythmic entrainment, the interaction ritual generates, when successful, a collective effervescence leading to a sense of collective solidarity, to symbols of social relationship, and to common standards of morality, such that participants in the ritual feel righteous anger and indignation when the ritual frame or sense of solidarity is violated in some way.

Successful rituals also generate positive emotional energy—collective effervescence—in participants, so that they feel confidence, elation, strength, enthusiasm, and initiative, much of which is carried away from the ritual and into other arenas of life. Collins argues that people tend to seek out, consciously and very much unconsciously, gatherings, crowds, and rituals that give them a sense of emotional energy and social solidarity while avoiding those that do not. "We operate," he says, "through an emotional magnetism toward and repulsion from particular thoughts and situations in the flow of everyday life; we are seldom reflective about this, and are often grossly inaccurate in our assessments when we are reflective" (Collins 2004: 97).

Collins is a sociologist and so of course he cites primarily sociological work in the development of what he refers to as his "radical microsociology" theory of "mutual focus/emotional-entrainment" mechanisms and processes, drawing on and integrating especially some of the classical ideas and concepts of Emile Durkheim and Erving Goffman. Yet his theory resonates deeply with some earlier anthropological work as well. The emphasis on complex feedback and feedforward loops among dynamically related and mutually sensitive bodies leading to predictable types of interactional patterns closely resembles Gregory Bateson's (1972) identification of what he referred to as "schismogenic" patterns of social interaction and his ideas about an "ecology of mind." The idea that people are unconsciously drawn to certain kinds of interactions, roles, meanings, and symbols while unconsciously avoidant of or repelled by others, overlaps considerably with Gananath Obeyesekere's (1981, 1990) concept of "personal symbols," nonobligatory aspects of culture that can acquire deep, usually unconscious, significance and expressive capacity for some people but not for others. According to Obeyesekere, it is the unconscious differential emotional investment in certain kinds of symbols and meanings, but not in others, that distinguishes personal symbols from all other types of meanings in the cultural and social world.

The Limits of Collins's Theory

Collins theorizes that the "emotional magnetism" driving social circulation and interactional participation can be explained in fairly straightforward sociological terms: as people participate in the interactional rituals that are available to them, they find themselves attracted, usually in a less than conscious way, to those interactions that enhance their emotional energy and sense of social solidarity while avoiding those that do not. Over time, this pattern of social participation becomes internalized, such that people's thoughts, dreams, fantasies, and internal dialogs begin to mirror and reproduce the meanings and emotions of the interactions they have participated in, which sustains their emotional energy between rituals and which, in turn, inclines people back toward social gatherings where those meanings and emotions can be evoked and enacted with others.

Collins acknowledges that many attempted rituals, crowds, and social gatherings fail, leaving participants feeling flat or even drained of energy, and that even in successful interactions, the emotional energy field is often unevenly distributed among the participants, so that some people are deeply engaged and energized while others may remain on the margins. He argues that some of this interactional failure and emotional inequality can be explained by structural variables such as power or status differentials, but I think it is exactly here where his model of emotional entrainment begins to fail him. This is because the model's basic assumptions—bodies entrain, people mutually focus, leading to a common emotional experience and sense of solidarity—do not capture the kind of emotional complexities and ambivalences, whether for structural reasons of power and status or otherwise, that can haunt people in even the most successful of interactions. Indeed it is such emotional complexity and variability that helps to explain why so many social formations, including many types of crowds, can be as messy, unpredictable, and emergent as they are. I turn now to the work of the psychoanalyst Hans Loewald to help illuminate some of these emotional complexities.

Ghosts of the Unconscious

In one of Loewald's most widely cited articles, "On the Therapeutic Action of Psychoanalysis" (2000), he discusses the centrality and importance of "transference" in human life. By transference he means not only the unwitting transfer of emotional reactions and expectations developed in interaction with known intimates onto others who are less well known and with whom one is less intimate—the traditional psychoanalytic sense—but also the way unconscious memories and emotions come to infuse and animate consciousness and experience more generally and, in turn, how more conscious and organized parts of mind come to give form, meaning, and expression to thoughts, feelings, and perceptions that otherwise remain latent and unformulated. Such transference or communication among different parts of the self-system and between the self and other people and objects is critical, he argues, for the linking of past to present and future, of memory to perception, and of emotion and motivation to action and behavior. When such linkage breaks down, people can become haunted by the "ghosts" of the less conscious parts of mind, which may press for recognition in the form of recurring dreams and memories, somatic and emotional sensations, and symptoms of various kinds.

Loewald borrows the idea of ghosts of the unconscious from Freud, who in Chapter 7 of *The Interpretation of Dreams* likens the persistence of unconscious thoughts and wishes to the ghosts of the underworld in the Odyssey: "If I may use a simile, they [unconscious thoughts and wishes] are only capable of annihilation in the same sense as the ghosts in the underworld of the Odyssey—ghosts which awoke to new life as soon as they tasted blood" (Freud 1965: 592n1). Loewald uses this metaphor of unconscious ghosts to discuss how psychoanalysts use the transference between analyst and client to evoke the client's most troubling but unconscious thoughts and feelings, so that they can be brought into the light of conscious awareness and given new meaning and conscious articulation:

> Transference is pathological insofar as the unconscious is a crowd of ghosts, and this is the beginning of the transference neurosis in analysis: ghosts of the unconscious, imprisoned by defenses and symptoms, are allowed to taste blood, are let loose. In the daylight of analysis the ghosts of the unconscious are laid and led to rest as ancestors whose power is taken over and transformed into the newer intensity of present life, of the secondary process and contemporary objects.
>
> (Loewald 2000: 249)

The concept and image of a person's inner world and unconscious that we get from Loewald (and many other psychoanalysts) is very different than the one we get from Collins. Collins focuses on the social aspects of this inner world: how over time, through a process of internalization, a person's thoughts, dreams, fantasies, and inner dialogs begin to mirror and reproduce the meanings and emotions of the interactions they have participated in. He suggests, for example:

> If we had a large enough collection of chains of thoughts from people in particular situations, it may well turn out that they think many of the same elements, even arranged in many of the same combinations. With greater theoretical abstraction, examining the formative conditions of inner IR [interaction ritual] chains, the commonality we find must be still greater.
>
> (Collins 2004: 220)

And indeed this is a key aspect of his entrainment theory: that through rhythmic entrainment of emotion and attention, successful interaction rituals produce common and collective thoughts and sensations of solidarity and effervescence that, in turn, motivate people to seek out similar interactions and rituals in the future and to avoid those that do not reinforce such emotionally gratifying thoughts and sensations.

Loewald's unconscious "crowd of ghosts," on the other hand, is the emotional, cognitive, and fantasy residues of a person's past interactions with others that have either been pushed out of awareness for defensive purposes or which have simply remained out of conscious thought because attention and symbolic and linguistic elaboration have been drawn elsewhere (Hollan 2000). While some of these ghosts become socialized and reflective of collective thought and sensation in just the way Collins suggests, many of them remain highly particular to the individual, resulting from a person's unique history of interaction with other people in which emotionally related thoughts and feelings become associated to one another in a nonlinear looping way (Hollan 2012, 2014). Such associations of emotionally connected thoughts and memories, linking past interactional experiences to each other and to those occurring in the here and now, may "haunt" present interactions with thoughts or sensations that, from a third person point of view, often seem to undermine, contradict, or be inconsistent with the most readily observable and apparent aspects of the interaction. For example, a person's apparently joyful interactions might be haunted by the sense that the joy cannot possibly last for more than a moment. A person about to receive some form of social recognition or appreciation might be haunted by the sense that they are really a fraud, deserving of nothing more than contempt. Expressions of love for another might be haunted by feelings of anger and disappointment, and so on.

From a Loewaldian perspective, such emotional hauntings reflect the ambivalence and ambiguity that are a part of almost all social interactions. Although overt enactments of most public behavior can receive relatively direct feedback and socialization from others, and so can be brought into conformity with cultural expectations or ideals fairly easily, the emotions and imaginings accompanying many enactments are not so easily socialized and controlled. People can and do experience thoughts, emotions, and fantasies during an interaction that are at odds with its ostensible meanings and purposes. Such contrary thoughts and feelings can be left unattended or pushed out of conscious awareness, but they remain labile and can be stirred back into consciousness if they are allowed to taste new blood; that is, if present or future interactions present emotional stimuli to which the unattended or repressed thoughts and feelings can be associated.

Loewald notes that psychoanalysts inevitably and deliberately evoke the transference of these unattended and repressed thoughts and feelings during the course of analytic treatment, but of course they are inevitably stirred and evoked by other types of interactions as well, including crowd formation. And indeed, this is where Loewald's model of emotional evocation and entrainment differs considerably from Collins's. Rather than assume that emotional entrainment and common focus lead to the development of common and collective inner worlds, Loewald would maintain that people may respond to social interactions in various and unique ways—depending on past relationship experience—and that some of these less common thoughts and feelings will remain durable, susceptible to being reignited and expressed if presented

with the right emotional stimuli. From this perspective, the crowd of unconscious ghosts that people bring into social interactions always far exceeds the
number of actual participants present, and the range of ways in which these
unattended or repressed thoughts and memories may be stirred (or further
repressed) by an interaction will also remain broad and contingent, depending on who the other participants are and on how the interaction unfolds.
There is emotional action and reaction here, but of a kind that is much more
emergent and unpredictable than Collins suggests. Let me now present some
ethnographic and clinical "hauntings" that illustrate some of these points and
which allow me to develop the discussion further.

Hauntings

Nene'na Limbong, Toraja, South Sulawesi, Indonesia

Nene'na Limblong was one of the men I knew well during the time I was
doing fieldwork in a mountain village in Toraja on the island of Sulawesi in
Indonesia in the 1980s and 1990s (Hollan and Wellenkamp 1994, 1996).
Nene'na Limbong was a high-status man, and a relatively wealthy one by
local standards, meaning only that he and his family could afford to eat rice
throughout the year rather than needing to supplement their diet with sweet
potatoes, cassava, or other foods that were considered inferior to rice. Most
Toraja at that time were wet rice farmers, living in small, widely scattered
hamlets across high valleys and mountainsides, though many of the younger
people were beginning to migrate to other parts of Sulawesi and Indonesia for
employment and education.

In part because Nene'na Limbong had the social means and position to
do so, he was an active participant in community feasts, especially feasts
at funerals,[1] at which he would slaughter as many water buffalo, pigs, and
chickens as he could afford and thought appropriate, so that meat could
be distributed throughout the community according to people's relative
social position, and so that he himself could gain prestige through this
contribution of animals. These funeral feasts were often large and lively
events, drawing not only the immediate and extended family of the deceased, but also many of the deceased family's friends, neighbors, and
feasting partners. People were excited to see how many and what kind of
animals were being contributed by whom and to whom the slaughtered
meat of those animals would be distributed. Meat was supposed to be distributed according to relative social status, but determinations of relative
social status were always in play, given that people could enhance their
status by donating and slaughtering more animals. This made the meat
division at a funeral a highly charged event, and one that could be quite
contentious at times, as people argued about who deserved what kind of
meat and how much. Indeed, by the 1980s, such disputes and the great
expense of many funerals had led some Toraja, especially younger and

more educated ones, to think that funerals had become a waste of time and resources.

Nevertheless, the Toraja feast remains, in many ways, the classic effervescence-generating social gathering that is central to Collins's theory: bodies come together in close proximity with a heightened mutual focus, in this case, an intense focus on the kind and number of animals to be slaughtered and on to whom the animals' meat will be distributed. Nene'na Limbong certainly gained emotional energy and a sense of satisfaction from these feasts, since as long as he continued to contribute animals to them, they reasserted and maintained his social position. He was considered a "big" and important man in large part because he was known for having donated many animals to feasts over the years and it was assumed that his own funeral would be an important event, to which many people, in turn, would contribute large numbers of animals for feasting. Yet even such an obvious beneficiary of feasting activities as Nene'na Limbong was ambivalent about his participation. This was not obvious from his public behavior, much of which was reinforcing of the feasting culture, just as Collins might predict. But when we were once talking about his past and present nighttime dreams,[2] he told me one in which he had seen his body being cut up and distributed to people in just the way a buffalo is butchered and distributed at a feast.[3] He had been frightened by this image of himself as a sacrificial animal, in part because such dreams were thought to be prophetic, and the memory of the dream from several years prior was still fresh in his mind and easily and vividly narrated to me.

Loewald would probably argue that the dream captured Nene'na Limbong's implicit awareness that his life-sustaining interdependencies with others, as epitomized on feasting occasions, were also at some level overwhelming and even murderous to him. The dream captured this awareness graphically and dramatically and drew Nene'na Limbong's focused attention in a way that his day to-day complaints about lower-status people using the local rules of reciprocity to take advantage of him did not. His wariness and fear of others' needs and demands had been pushed out of his everyday consciousness for the most part, but they were not absorbed and replaced by collective focus and effervescence as a result of his participation in feasting. Rather, his wariness had remained durable and could be stirred into dream consciousness, and then into waking consciousness, by his chance encounters in everyday life in a transference-like way. So while Nene'na Limbong's participation in feasts and other communal gatherings elevated his mood and energy in some ways, it also aroused and entrained contrary emotions and images that were far from promoting solidarity, trust, or confidence. The same kind of interactional ritual not only attracted, but also repulsed, and left behind a distinctive emotional residue of wariness and fear. While many people knew that Nene'na Limbong often complained that others' were taking advantage of his obligation to share his relative wealth, few could imagine that such a fortunate and high-status person could actually envision himself to be as helpless and vulnerable as a sacrificial animal.

George, Southern California, USA

Let me now move to a psychotherapeutic consulting room in southern California where George, a white, middle-aged, middle-class, unemployed man I have known for several years, described to me what it feels like to have the possibility of being hired back for contract work by the same corporation that fired him only the year before to downsize payroll and pension obligations. I am turning to this example to illustrate the broad range of social rituals and interactions that Collins's theory is meant to cover and explicate. Work interactions and rituals are less crowdlike than the Toraja funeral feast since they usually involve fewer people, are more scripted, and occur on a regular and routine basis, but they too involve the mutual focus of attention and rhythmic entrainment that optimally lead workers to a sense of collective solidarity and achievement. The issue once again is, does rhythmic entrainment and a mutual focus of attention, which are common to many social formations (including work rituals), lead to the kind of common, collective feelings and inner dialogs and to the kind of predictable future social behavior as a result of emotional magnetism, as Collins claims? Or, as someone like Loewald would no doubt argue, must things inevitably be more complicated than this, given the significance and ubiquity of transference in human life?

George began by telling me how torn he was about the idea of returning to work. On the one hand, he needed the money. But he also enjoyed his work, and he was very proud of the long and successful career he had had with his previous employer. He had also enjoyed the collegial relations he had developed with some of his co-workers and the opportunities they had given him for learning new skills and new approaches to his work. Collins would probably argue that George's strong urge to return to work illustrates that his previous work rituals and interactions had been successful ones, and that the positive emotional energy and sense of collective solidarity they had developed in him were now impelling him back to work, just as his theory would predict.

However, George's self-esteem had been deeply wounded by his laying off, this despite the fact that he "knew" rationally that his managers were just responding to corporate orders and to the changing world economy. The job he was being asked to return to, including salary, was nearly identical to the one he had left, but now that his bureaucratic and legal status had changed from regular employee to contract worker, he felt differently about things. He felt ashamed about returning to the same job with a diminished status, and he worried what others would think of him if he did such a thing. Would they think he had no shame or that he had no better prospects, even though from the point of view of Collins's theory, he is being offered an opportunity to reestablish gratifying rituals with people?

While George was telling me about these mixed feelings and motivations, he began to remember a disturbing dream from the previous night in which a gang of men had been pulling him into the darkness to assault him. This then led to a number of recollections about how he was often bullied as a child, and how ashamed he was then and now that he was never able to stand up for himself.

A week later, George decided to accept the temporary contract work, feeling that he had no choice, given his financial situation. While at first glance the level of coercion or ambivalence that George feels about returning to work would seem to indicate a different kind of interaction ritual than the ones Collins is concerned with—those in which participation is determined more by emotional attraction or repulsion than by structural or other deterministic variables—I want to suggest just the opposite: that many interaction rituals, including everyday work rituals and other types of crowd formations, generate more ambivalence in people than Collins's model would indicate. Very few social interactions involve complete "choice" or "free" emotional magnetism or repulsion on the part of participants. If people do not feel constrained or pressured to participate in social interactions by financial or economic necessity, as does George, they may feel constrained by cultural or political expectation, or by fear of hurting people, or by fear of loss of status or esteem, or by fear of ostracism, and so on. George's case may be a strong example of how a social interaction may engender or entail emotions that run counter to its most explicitly communicated goals and purposes, but it is by no means unusual in this regard. And while people may be fully conscious of some aspect of their ambivalence toward a certain type of social interaction, other aspects only become more conscious as repressed or unconscious thoughts and emotions become stirred or triggered by immersion in the interaction, exactly as someone like Loewald would hypothesize.

When George eventually learned that he would have to undergo a standard background and financial check before he was given access back to the same offices where he had worked for over 20 years as a full-time employee, he was angered and humiliated yet again, and his ambivalence about returning to work grew even stronger. In this context, he remembered another recent dream: "I am in a classroom of some kind, towards the back, feeling distant from the teacher and other students up front." As he is recounting this dream, he tells me it reminds him of the second-grade teacher he told me about before, one who once pulled him out of class to tell him how disappointed she was in him. "You are smart enough to be in the front of the class with the other good students, if you would just put your mind to it," she told him.

While George is consciously aware of how humiliating it is for him to return to work under the circumstances that were presented to him, he is mostly unaware of his own implicit tendency to emotionally link together actual and imagined episodes of humiliation from throughout his life: his feelings of humiliation about returning to work precipitate dreams about being assaulted and about sitting in the back of a classroom feeling alienated and ashamed, which in turn stir up memories of never being able to defend or stand up for himself and of being reprimanded by his second-grade teacher for not working hard enough. These linkages become more conscious and recognizable for George, and for myself, as he spontaneously verbalizes his thoughts, feelings, and dreams in a stream of consciousness sort of way. Prior to this, however, there is no awareness, only the sense that the thoughts and emotions flood over him in an unbidden way.

Of course the flip side of this from a social interactional point of view is that George's interlocutors are also not likely to be aware of his tendency to re-experience emotions and memories in this way. George's manager, for example, may know that George might feel embarrassed about coming back to work as a contract worker, but of course he has no way of knowing that George actually dreams of it as a kind of assault. As with Nene'na Limbong, there is a haunting entrainment of emotion going on here, but it is a nonlinear, looping one, linking together emotional resonances from the past and present in ways that would elude Collins's model of relatively smooth social participation and reproduction.

Toward a Specificity of Emotional Entrainment

Collins's theory of interactional rituals does us a service by drawing our attention back to the ways in which social formations, including crowds of all kinds, are embodied in deeply emotional ways. I think he is also right in his efforts to acknowledge and attempt to integrate new biological and neuroscience research about emotional entrainment into social theory. As Collins notes, to acknowledge this research is not to give it a privileged position, but rather to acknowledge and understand better some of the mechanisms through which social formations may affect and shape emotions, bodies, and physiology in very concrete, identifiable ways. I have also suggested, however, that Collins's model of emotional entrainment can be misleading, implying as it does that a mutual focus of attention, coupled with close bodily interaction, will lead to a fairly uniform emotional experience for members of a group that will in turn, incline those same people back toward similar interactions and emotional experiences in the future, or conversely will lead them to avoid interactions that are less gratifying. In contrast, my ethnographic and clinical examples illustrate that the overt meanings of an interaction ritual, no matter to what extent attention is focused or constrained, do not necessarily coincide with the implicit emotional meanings for the participants involved, which may be varied and contradictory (cf. Obeyesekere 1981, 1990; Spiro 1984). That is why someone like Nene'na Limbong can be haunted by dreams and images of himself as a sacrificial animal, even though the Toraja feast reinforces and enhances his social position in many ways.

George's case is also problematic for Collins's theory: the theory of emotional magnetism implies that people will either gain emotional energy and a sense of solidarity from participating in a certain kind of interaction or they will not. If they do, they will be drawn back to similar interactions in the future. If they do not, they will learn to avoid those kinds of interactions in the future. But George both did and did not want to return to work, for very particular reasons. He wanted an opportunity to work and to learn, he wanted a chance to reestablish collegial ties with his former workmates, and he wanted and needed a chance to earn money. In many of these ways, he is just like any other person who has had gratifying work experiences and wants the chance to have them again—just as Collins's theory would predict. What the theory would miss, however, is that George's previous work gratifications were also different from other workers. As a single and relatively solitary man, George used work more than anything else to provide a structure to his time and activities. Without that work structure, he felt lost and disoriented, unlike many of his co-workers who had preferred to work from home in order to be closer to their families.

But it is not only George's attractions to work that differ, but also his aversions, and it is these complicated emotional ambivalences about so-cial interactions that Collins's theory has the most trouble accounting for. While some people would not think twice about returning to work under George's circumstances—always preferring to work rather than not work—others, like George, would likely feel embarrassed or ashamed to return to the same job but with a diminished legal and bureaucratic status. But what would set George apart from these others is that his sense of humilia-tion is quite specific, linking together his treatment at work with memories of a castigating second-grade teacher and with dream images of assault. Such particular memories and images are noteworthy because they mean that while George may not be the only unhappy and disgruntled employee at his place of work, he is unhappy and disgruntled in his own particular way. The persistence of George's emotionally associated memories and dream images, as punctuated, looping, and nonlinear as they may be, illustrate that past emotional experiences are not as easily smoothed out and revised by present-day interactions as Collins's social imprint model would imply. They can be smoothed out and revised in light of present-day interactions, but they can also remain quite inert, strongly influenc-ing the way a person experiences an interaction, even when attention is otherwise mutually and communally oriented, linking together different parts of the phenomenal field—people, objects, ideas, imaginings, past, and present—in ways that can be surprisingly idiosyncratic and contrary to the prevailing habitus.

The larger point here is that while people in groups, including crowds, do emotionally entrain to one another, they do not do so in uniform ways. Rather, they entrain to particular bodies in particular historical moments, and these histories of encounter leave particularized emotional residues that loop into future engagements in unpredictable ways. The crowd of emotional ghosts circulating within any group of people always far exceeds the number of concrete bodies present per se, which is why, I would argue, that many social formations, whether highly organized and scripted or not, remain as emergent and unpredictable as they do. During social situations of almost any kind, these latent emotional ghosts are often stirred to new life in divergent, transference-like ways, not uniformly. What triggers one emotional ghost—a sight, a smell, a touch, a focus of attention—will not necessarily stir another. The complex emotional effervescence produced by any social formation, including crowds, is certainly constrained by such variables as number and proximity of bodies and by the extent and kind of mutual focus and attention, but its emergent, dynamical properties, related in part to the contingent way latent emotional meanings associate to one another and are aroused by social interaction, will always exceed and overflow those parameters.

Notes

1 The Toraja are well-known in Indonesia and elsewhere for their elaborate and expensive funeral feasts. See, for example, Volkman (1985) and Adams (2006).
2 Many Toraja believed that certain types of dreams were prophetic, which made them of great interest to people, and one of the topics I raised in my person-centered interviews with people (Levy and Hollan 2014).
3 He mentioned this dream while talking about a number of other disturbing dreams that had to do with the many social, political, and existential problems he had overcome in his life. For further discussion of these dreams, see Hollan (2003).

References

Adams, K. 2006. *Art as Politics: Re-Crafting Identities, Tourism, and Power in Tana Toraja, Indonesia*. Honolulu: University of Hawaii Press.
Bateson, G. 1972. *Steps to An Ecology of Mind*. Chicago: University of Chicago Press.
Collins, R. 2004. *Interaction Ritual Chains*. Princeton, NJ: Princeton University Press.
Collins, R. 2009. *Violence: A Micro-sociological Theory*. Princeton, NJ: Princeton University Press.
Freud, S. 1965. *The Interpretation of Dreams*. New York: Avon Books.
Hollan, D. 2000. Constructivist Models of Mind, Contemporary Psychoanalysis, and the Development of Culture Theory. *American Anthropologist* 102:538–550.
Hollan, D. 2003. The Cultural and Intersubjective Context of Dream Remembrance and Reporting: Dreaming, Aging, and the Anthropological Encounter in Toraja, Indonesia. In *Dream Travelers: Sleep Experiences and Culture in the Western Pacific*, edited by R.I. Lohmann, pp. 168–187. New York: Palgrave.
Hollan, D. 2012. On the Varieties and Particularities of Cultural Experience. Ethos 40:37–53.
Hollan, D. 2014. From Ghosts to Ancestors (and Back Again): On the Cultural and Psychodynamic Mediation of Selfscapes. Ethos 42:175–197.
Hollan, D.W., and J.C. Wellenkamp. 1994. *Contentment and Suffering: Culture and Experience in Toraja*. New York, NY: Columbia University Press.
Hollan, D.W., and J.C. Wellenkamp. 1996. *The Thread of Life: Toraja Reflections on the Life Cycle*. Honolulu, HI: University of Hawaii Press.
Levy, R.I., and D.W. Hollan 2014 Person-Centered Interviewing and Observation. In *Handbook of Methods in Cultural Anthropology*, 2nd ed. edited by H. Russell Barnard and C.C. Gravlee, pp. 313–342. Lanham, MD: Rowman & Littlefield.

Loewald, H.W. 2000. *The Essential Loewald: Collected Papers and Monographs*. Hagerstown, MD: University Publishing Group.

Obeyesekere, G. 1981. *Medusa's Hair: An Essay on Personal Symbols and Religious Experience*. Chicago: University of Chicago Press.

Obeyesekere, G. 1990. *The Work of Culture*. Chicago: University of Chicago Press.

Spiro, M.E. 1984. Some Reflections on Cultural Determinism and Relativism With Special Reference to Emotion and Reason. In *Culture Theory: Essays on Mind, Self, and Emotion*, edited by R.A. Shweder and R.A. LeVine. Cambridge, UK: Cambridge University Press.

Volkman, T. 1985. *Feasts of Honor: Ritual and Change in the Toraja Highlands*. Urbana: University of Illinois Press.

Part II

Varieties and Particularities of Selfscapes

6   Selfscape Dreams

Dreams appear to serve many biological, psychological, and communicative functions.[1] These include the imaginary fulfillment of unconscious wishes, the solving of problems, the integration of new experience into emerging schemas of self, the working through and mastery of traumatic experiences and other types of intrapsychic conflict, and the representation and expression of family and community relations. In this chapter, I explore the possibility that some types of dreams—those that are imagistically and emotionally vivid and easy to recall—serve yet another purpose. Some dreams reflect back to the dreamer how their current organization of self relates various parts of itself to its body, and to other people and the world. I call these "selfscape" dreams. They provide the mind with a continuously updated map of the self's current state of affairs: its relative vitality or decrepitude, its relative wholeness or division, its relative closeness or estrangement from others, its perturbation by conscious and unconscious streams of emotions, and so on. They are one of the ways in which the mind/body seems to assess itself.

Selfscape dreams, I suggest, will be found everywhere in the world because they serve a basic psychological function. Their content, on the other hand, varies considerably because the relationships of part-self to part-self and of self to world they map and represent will vary considerably from culture to culture and from person to person even within the same culture. My examples of dreams from Sulawesi and the United States will illustrate this variation in how the self is constituted and represented to itself in different cultures, but also suggest the similarity in psychological function I have outlined here.

I focus on dreams that are vivid, both emotionally and imagistically, and easy to recall—at least in the short term. Cultures vary in the extent to which they encourage the remembering of dreams. And we will find much variation in the ability of individuals to remember dreams even within given cultures. Nevertheless, my work in Sulawesi and the United States suggests that most people experience dreams that cry out for their attention, at least occasionally. These are the dreams that awaken people in the middle of the night or the emotional residues of which carry over into waking life of the following days, weeks, or years. In both Sulawesi and the United States, I have been struck by

DOI: 10.4324/9781003529118-8

how often the manifest content and imagery of such dreams can be related to the dreamer's life circumstances and to their current conscious or unconscious state of mind, body, self, and emotion.[2] In this chapter, I illustrate how selfscape dreams in two very different parts of the world map out the relations of self to body and to other objects and people.

I begin by reviewing work that has influenced my thinking about selfscape dreams. I then discuss how and why I collected the dreams I present here, before turning to an analysis of the dreams of two particular men: one from Sulawesi (Nene'na Limbong) and one from the United States (Steve). I conclude with a summary of my argument and a discussion of its implications.

Background

My perspective on dreams has been influenced by a number of researchers. Following Pinchas Noy (1969, 1979) and a number of other scholars who share similar ideas,[3] I assume that the nondiscursive, emotional, and imaginal processes characteristic of dreaming are not necessarily more primitive than nor inferior to the cognitive, conceptual, and discursive mental activities characteristic of waking thought and consciousness. Further, I assume that while dreaming may come to represent, and be implicated in, processes of psychological regression, they also may play a central role in psychological growth and development. As Noy points out, processes such as displacement, condensation, and symbolization may be especially well suited to represent similarity and difference in the construction and modification of self-related schemas, and they capture well the timeless nature of the experience of self-continuity. Noy also points out that the nonverbal and imaginal processes characteristic of dreaming seem to develop, mature, and become more complex over time, like other cognitive and perceptual processes.

My thinking about dreams also has been influenced by recent work in the neurosciences. In *Descartes' Error* (1994) and in *The Feeling of What Happens* (1999), Antonio Damasio reminds us just how deeply the mind is rooted in the body and its biological processes. Perceptions and cognitions of the world are always influenced by emotional states that mediate between neural representations of the body as it acts on the physical and sociocultural environment and as that environment, in turn, impinges upon the body. In effect, emotions are the glue that hold together representations of the body and the world.

Dasmasio emphasizes how dependent the mind is upon continuously updated representations of the body and how these representations qualify our perceptions of the world. In the later stages of the first book and throughout the second, he begins to speculate about the origins and maintenance of the self and consciousness. He suggests that neural representations of the self must be continuously updated and modified in a manner similar to that of bodily processes. Further, he speculates that the earliest representations of the self very likely emerge from, or coincide with, representations of the body as it interacts with the world. Thus, according to Damasio, neural representations of the body, self, and world are inextricably tied together through complex emotional states and processes, all of which must be continuously updated and modified as they stimulate and impinge upon one another.

Interestingly, Damasio barely mentions dreams in either of his books,[4] even though dreaming clearly involves many of the emotional processes and representations of body, self, and world that are his central concern. My contention here is that dreams may provide a vantage point from which we can observe how the mind continuously updates and maps out the self's current state of affairs.

That this mapping out does indeed include the self's relation to its own body is supported by Oliver Sacks, who in a recent paper entitled "Neurological Dreams" (1996), reports how people may dream of damage or repair to their brains or bodies long before such injury or repair becomes manifest in physical or behavioral symptoms. He presents cases of migraine, sensory and motor seizures, lesions of the visual cortex, blindness, encephalitis lethargica, acute sensory neuronopathy, motor-neural reorganization, disturbances of body-image from limb and spinal injury, parkinsonism, Tourette's syndrome, and psychosis, all of which were foreshadowed in dreams before becoming manifest in symptoms. He comments, "One must assume in such cases that the disease was already affecting neural function, and that the unconscious mind, the dreaming mind, was more sensitive to this than the waking mind. Such premonitory or, rather, precursory dreams may be happy in content, and in outcome, as well. Patients with multiple sclerosis may dream of remissions a few hours before they occur, and patients recovering from strokes or neurological injuries may have striking dreams of improvement before such improvement is "objectively" manifest. Here again, the dreaming mind maybe a more sensitive indicator of neural function than examination with a reflex hammer and a pin" (1996: 214).

Finally, my thinking about selfscape dreams has been influenced by the work of the psychoanalysts Heinz Kohut and W. R. D. Fairbairn. In *The Restoration of the Self* (1977), Kohut distinguished "self-state" dreams from those whose latent contents are rooted in repressed wishes, desires, fantasies, and drives. The latter dreams, those that Freud ([1900] 1956 described and analyzed, can be deciphered and talked about through the process of free association.

In contrast, self-state dreams are characterized by visual imagery that is not easily associated to or talked about. Rather, it can be manifestly and directly related to the dreamer's current life situation and to alterations in their conscious and unconscious sense of self-esteem and well-being. Such dreams and imagery, according to Kohut, usually involve unconscious efforts to cover over dramatic shifts in self-organization: "Dreams of this ... type portray the dreamer's dread vis-à-vis some uncontrollable tension-increase or his dread of the dissolution of the self. The very act of portraying these vicissitudes in the dream constitutes an attempt to deal with the psychological danger by covering frightening nameless processes with nameable visual imagery... Free associations do not lead to unconscious hidden layers of mind; at best they provide us with further imagery which remains at the same level as the manifest content of the dream" (Kohut 1977: 109).

The meanings of self-state dreams are on the surface, so to speak. Thus, people who unconsciously sense a disruption or dissolution of self-organiza- tion may dream of themselves in a rocketship shooting off into empty space or sitting precariously on a swing that is swinging ever higher and higher, and faster and faster (cf. Kohut 1971: 4–5).

Kohut thought self-state dreams are linked to dramatic and ominous shifts in the dreamer's self-esteem and overall psychological balance. However, later self psychologists, including Paul Tolpin (1983), believe they are related to less ominous shifts in the condition of the self as well. Many contemporary self psychologists now take self-state dreams to be more common than Ko- hut imagined, and suggest that such dreams may be used to express shifts in self-organization of all kinds—not just potentially traumatic or perilous ones. Tolpin and others also argue, in contrast to Kohut, that free associations may indeed be helpful in interpreting self-state dreams, though primary emphasis is still placed on how the manifest imagery can be related to the dreamer's current life situation.

Long before Kohut, Fairbairn (1952) was struck by the manifest content of dreams and their relation to the dreamer's self. After analyzing a woman who spontaneously described her dreams as "state of affairs" dreams, he came to view dreams as "dramatizations or 'shorts' (in the cinematographic sense) of situations existing in inner reality" (1952: 99). The manifest contents of dreams did not disguise the fulfillment of repressed wishes and drives. Rather, they accurately depicted the unconscious relationships among part-selves and of part-selves to the internalized representations of other people.

Both Kohut and Fairbairn came to believe that the manifest content of dreams could be related in a fairly direct way to the state of the dreamer's self. However, Kohut emphasized how dreams could illuminate the self's response to its relations with real people and objects in the world,[5] while Fairbairn em- phasized how they could shed light on a dreamer's internal organization of self. In my view, both may be right: the manifest content of dreams often can be related either to the self's perturbation from the outside, or to its internal- ized state of affairs, or to both at the same time.

I use the concept of selfscape dreams to integrate some of these ideas about dreams and psychological processes, as well as to highlight both simi- larities and differences I have with particular researchers. The term obviously is a play on those used by Kohut and Fairbairn, which emphasize the manifest content of dreams and their relationship to self-organization. But along the lines of Damasio's work, I also wish to emphasize how dreams may provide a current map or update of the self's contours and affective resonances relative to its own body, as well as to other objects and people in the world. The self emerges and maintains itself in the biological and imaginal space between body and world. Selfscape dreams map this terrain. Thus, the "scape" part of the term.

To summarize briefly, selfscape dreams involve complex, developmentally sensitive imaginal, emotional, and cognitive processes that reflect back to the dreamer how their current organization of self relates various parts of itself to itself, its body, and to other people and objects in the world.

How and Why the Dreams Were Collected

The dreams I discuss here were collected for different reasons and under different conditions. Nene'na Lirnbong's dreams were collected while I was conducting long-term fieldwork among the Toraja from 1981 to 1983. The Toraja are wet rice farmers who live in scattered villages and hamlets throughout the central highlands of the province of south Sulawesi in Indonesia.[6] They are famous throughout Indonesia, and now throughout much of the world, for their elaborate and complex funeral ceremonies.

Most Toraja currently consider themselves to be Christians. However, their religious and existential beliefs are still influenced by traditional ideas about the power and significance of ancestral figures, *nenè*, and spiritual beings referred to as *deata* (see Hollan 1996). Many Christian Toraja still encounter *nenè* and *deata* in their dreams, and many still believe that such entities intervene directly in human affairs. For most Toraja villagers, the question is not, which spiritual beings, including the Christian God, actually exist and which do not? But rather, which of these beings, at any given moment in one's life, has the power to influence the course of one's fate and fortune?

Toraja society is organized hierarchically, and social position and status are reckoned through both heredity and the competitive slaughter of buffalo, pigs, and chickens at community feasts (Volkman 1985). Many younger Toraja now leave the highlands to find work in the urban areas of Indonesia. But it is not uncommon for them to send much of their cash income back to the highlands, where it is used by their families in the competitive staging of ever larger and more elaborate feasts. These large and spectacular community feasts have, in turn, attracted ever larger numbers of international tourists in recent years, and tourism has now become a major industry in certain parts of the highlands.

My fieldwork in Toraja involved extensive participant observation of everyday lives and activities. However, it was focused around the collection of loosely structured, open-ended interviews in which Jane Wellenkamp and I asked people to describe and reflect upon their life experiences (see Hollan and Wellenkamp 1994, 1996).

As part of these interviews, we asked people to report current or past dreams to us. Our respondents were not surprised by our interest in dreams because the Toraja are one of those groups of people who believe that certain types of dreams can foretell the future. In fact, prophetic dreams—those that are vivid, emotionally charged, and easy to remember—are marked with a special term (*tindo*). They are clearly distinguished from other dream and sleep experiences in which the dreamer merely continues to have fragmentary thoughts about the previous day's activities or those in which they are attacked by spirits (*tauan*) (Hollan and Wellenkamp 1994: 101–107; Hollan 1989, 1995). The Toraja share dreams with one another, and they may consult people who are thought astute at interpreting dreams if they have a dream they find especially puzzling or upsetting. They are less likely to report or share dreams thought to portend good fortune, however, fearing that such good omens may be stolen by others.

Steve's dreams, on the other hand, were collected during a psychoanalytic encounter in Southern California begun in the 1990s. A white, a-religious man in his early 40s, Steve is a high tech specialist who came to therapy complaining of depression and of feeling weak, incompetent, and broken inside. As part of a therapeutic process stretching over several years, Steve has reported scores of dreams to me.

In both samples of dreams, I examine the dream as narrated, not the dream as experienced, which, of course, we can never know directly (see Crapanzano 1980). And in both cases, the dreams as narrated are influenced by cultural and transferential factors, which I discuss below.

The samples of dreams I present here are selective. In the case of Nene'na Limbong, they are selective because I have access only to a small number of dreams he narrated to me during our interviews together, most of which share a common theme. And of these, I have space to discuss only three. Steve's case presents the opposite problem. Steve has told me a great number of dreams over the time I have worked with him, the themes of which fall into several genres or subtypes. I select only one of these themes to discuss here.

Thus, the two samples of dreams are different in important ways. Nevertheless, they are both comprised of dreams that had great emotional significance for the dreamers involved, and were easily remembered and narrated.

The Dreams of a Toraja Elder

As part of an open-ended interview process I conducted with seven Toraja men, I asked Nene'na ("Grandfather of") Limbong, a high-status, wealthy elder, to discuss some of his dreams with me. In the last of our interviews together, Nene'na Limbong reported nine dreams from different stages of his life, eight of which he considered highly meaningful and prophetic, and one of which was a spirit attack nightmare.

In another paper (Hollan 2003), I discuss at length why I think Nene'na Limbong reported these nine dreams and not others, reasons that are related to transferential, intersubjective, and stage-of-life issues. To summarize that argument very briefly, Nene'na Limbong was preoccupied with old age and his approaching death at the time I interviewed him. Eight of the nine dreams he reported expressed a concern with status enactment or loss and the threat of death or bodily disintegration—the very issues he was most concerned with near the end of his life, as he was struggling to maintain his social position and influence. Further, the kind of person I was (white North American, male, relatively young and "wealthy," by Toraja standards) and the kind of questions I was asked only intensified Nene'na Limbong's awareness of these issues, since my presence in the community was perceived by him as an implicit threat to his own status and position.

In any case, in the space I have here I must focus on the manifest content of only three of Nene'na Limbong's dream narratives and suggest how they are related to his life circumstances and organization of self. I begin by presenting the three dreams, and Nene'na Limbong's own interpretations of them. The dream narratives are taken from the interview transcripts. I have edited them for clarity, and I have inserted explanatory comments in brackets.

Dream 1: When I was still young [around 17 or 18, before he was married], I dreamed that there were many people, like at a feast. I sat on a mat while the people swarmed about me, petitioning me. Then my stomach started coming out of my mouth, pouring onto the mat in front of me. It didn't stop until it was all out on the mat. I awoke, startled and afraid.

Meaning of Dream 1: It meant that when I became an adult, I would become an *adat* expert [an expert on traditional custom] and divider of meat at feasts [a very important position, given that the quality and amount of meat a person receives is symbolic of his of her status]. When I divide meat at a feast, words come out of my mouth just like my stomach does in the dream: "Here is the piece for A, here is the piece for B, here is the piece for C."

Dream 2: I was already an adult and had children when I had this dream. I dreamed that I was in an open field with many other people, and we saw a plane approaching that was carrying bombs. Then the plane dropped its bombs and I was hit and fell to the ground! Many of the people I had been standing with were also hit, but some were not. Those who survived began to say, "Nene'na Limbong is surely dead." But an hour after I had been hit and fallen, I stood up! I stood up and I said, "I am not wounded. I am not hurt. You can see for yourselves!" And then I was just like normal.

Meaning of Dream 2: It foreshadowed the deaths of my parents and first wife, all three of whom died within a period of seven years. During that time, I had to sacrifice many buffalo at their funerals. But I was able to survive financially without having to sell off my land. The dream predicted that I would survive that hard time without losing my wealth or position.

Dream 3: One time I dreamed that my throat had been cut! There was a man who cut my throat. I fell down! And I was frightened. I woke up frightened thinking, "I'm dead!" A man cut me with a machete and I fell down dead and my eyes went dark. Then my body was cut up and distributed to A and B and C [He then whispers in a low, terrified tone of voice]. "Oh, this is my body being cut up!" But I could see it happen! I was cut up and distributed [his voice continues low, quiet, horrified]. I was very frightened.

Meaning of Dream 3: The dream really meant that I would eventually slaughter many buffalo and become an important man.

Focusing for a moment on the actual imagery and content of these three dreams, and using Nene'na Limbong's interpretations as commentaries on them, we see a common theme emerge: in all of these dreams Nene'na Limbong suffers some kind of bodily assault, if not death, in the context of status enactment. In dream 1, he loses his entrails as he attempts to respond to his clients' petitions. In Dream 2, expectations that he fulfill his ritual obligations become as destructive and damaging as an aerial bombardment. And in Dream 3, his achievement of status through the sacrifice of buffalo is linked to his own bodily disintegration and death. The dreams depict the social and ritual demands of others as a type of predation or attack. They liken the risk of the loss of status to dismemberment, disembowelment, and death.

Elsewhere (Hollan and Wellenkamp 1994, 1996) I have suggested that the Toraja pay a psychological price for their participation in family and social networks that emphasize status competition and the extensive use of reciprocity to maintain relatedness. Nene'na Limbong's dreams offer a window onto some of these widespread social anxieties, anxieties that for the most part are culturally hypocognized (Levy 1984) and suppressed, if not repressed, in daily life. But the intensity of the anxiety that we find in these dreams, and the graphic nature in which it is depicted, is also related more specifically to Nene'na Limbong's social position. Born to an aristocratic family and subject to innumerable social obligations and responsibilities, Nene'na Limbong has been struggling even more than most, and throughout his life, to assert and hold onto his status and sense of self-worth, even as the hereditary privileges to which he clings come under increasing attack in the political economy of modem-day Indonesia.

These dreams illustrate a part of Nene'na Limbong's self responding to a part of his environment with dread and fear. They depict a part of himself experiencing the boundaries among body, self, and other as fluid, permeable, and breachable—in fact, dangerously so. Even one's own guts are not really one's own, and are up for grabs. And one's image blends into that of a sacrificial animal. But the dreams also show his underlying resilience and defensiveness. In Dream 2, he miraculously arises from the dead, showing that a part of himself refuses to succumb to the assaults upon himself. And his interpretations of Dreams 1 and 3, based on widely shared assumptions about the symbolic meanings of dreams, enable him to shore up his conscious sense of perseverance and transcendence (see Kracke 1987 for another example of how cultural idioms of dream interpretation can be used to defend against anxiety generated by distressing dreams).

The Dreams of a Southern California Professional

Steve lives in a large metropolitan area of southern California, works in a highly technical field, and commutes long distances to and from his work and social activities. Although he has lived in his own apartment since he was in his late 20s (he is now in his 40s), he has never left the psychological grip of his parents, who conceived him late in their own lives and raised him as an only child in almost complete social and emotional isolation.

Steve is extremely ambivalent about his relationship with his parents: on the one hand he loves them and cannot imagine how he will live without them (both are quite old and in ill health). But on the other hand, he realizes that his inability to separate himself from them has been the root cause of much of his misery. He complains that it is as if he and his parents are stuck together in a huge pool of honey, unable or unwilling to free or separate themselves.

Unlike Nene'na Limbong, Steve does not remember and ponder his dreams because the larger, dominant culture of which he is a part holds them to be significant. Rather, he does so because he and I are engaged in a therapeutic endeavor in which dreams are thought to illuminate psychological problems and conflicts. He ponders his dreams because he believes that by doing so, he will understand himself better, and eventually change his behavior. But he reports his dreams also, at least in part, because he thinks I expect this of him, and because he wants to be perceived by me as a cooperative client. In other words, transference factors influence the way in which Steve reports his dreams, just as they influence Nene'na Limbong's dream narratives.

The content and frequency of the many dreams Steve has reported to me have varied. He has repeatedly dreamed of himself as an animal or as a mere speck of dust. And he has had dreams in which he is trying to avoid or escape the attention of others. But the most frequent and emotionally salient type of dream has been car dreams, dreams in which the car he is riding in or driving becomes blocked, stalled, broken down, involved in a crash, or in some other way impeded in its path.

The car is a ubiquitous, highly salient symbol of the self in North American culture. It is used by people to express their status aspirations, their sense of fashion, their sexuality, their wish for freedom, mobility, and autonomy, and so on. The identification between self and auto is promoted by huge advertising budgets, and it is reinforced day in and day out by the amount of time most North Americans spend in their cars.

What kind of cultural understandings might the image "self as auto" entail? Perhaps the notion that life and people should run smoothly and without interruption; that when life and people do break down, they should be repairable; that life is a journey involving constant movement and progress, and that one is in trouble if one is stopped too long by the side of the road; that big, strong, fast, powerful cars are better than small, weak, slow, broken-down cars; that it is better to be the driver of a car than a passive passenger; that it is better to own a car than not; that one's car is one's castle and its boundaries are sacred; and so on.

Let me now present three of Steve's dreams that illustrate some of these cultural understandings (and others, no doubt). I choose the following three because they illustrate so well Steve's sense of being stalled and damaged, and the depth of his despair. The narratives are reconstructed from my notes, which I jotted down at the end of therapy sessions.

Dream 1: He's driving towards work but as he approaches, he notices other employees driving away. They seem to be headed in the opposite direction. He begins to hurry wanting to find out where everyone is going. But by the time he finally gets to work, almost everyone is gone As he drives off to find the others, two huge, dark locomotives cross the street in front of him, blocking his path. He must decide whether to race around them and then worry about running into other locomotives as he goes, or to just give up and stay where he is. He decides to give up and just stay where he is.

Dream 2: He's driving with his parents. He sits in the back while his mother drives and his father rides in the front passenger seat. He needs or wants to stop, but his mother is oblivious. He cautiously leans over the driver's seat to take the wheel from her and steer towards the curb. At first, his mother seems to be cooperating, but as they approach the curb, she fails to brake and they run into the rear of a parked car. He is greatly concerned about how much damage has been done to his car, which he thinks must be in the thousands of dollars. But his father downplays the whole incident, claiming that the damage couldn't be more than a few hundred dollars at most, which infuriates and disappoints him.

Dream 3: He's driving down the road past a long line of parked cars. He suddenly realizes how easy it would be to turn into the cars and kill himself. And then he does crash his car. He wakes up in a hospital, barely conscious. His father or someone is there. He says to this person, "Kill me or put me out of my misery."

The manifest content of these dreams represents well the utter frustration and misery that a part of Steve's self experiences in relation to his parents, to me (on occasion), and to his current situation in life. In Dream 1, he is moving in the opposite direction from that of his peers, and when he finally seems to be getting back on track, he is blocked by impassable locomotives. Steve immediately related the two locomotives to his parents when he first reported this dream. In Dream 2, he is shown taking the back seat to his parents, even in his own car. Once again, his efforts to change directions and exert more control prove fruitless: his mother is oblivious to his need to stop, and her failure to brake results in a crash. And then to make matters worse, his father severely underestimates the extent of his car's damage and incapacity. In Dream 3, he seems to exert more control, but only that necessary to kill himself. And even here, he fails in his attempt and must plead with his father (or someone?) to put him out of his misery. Steve's character in the dreams is hopelessly blocked at every turn, is incapable of action, suffers great misery which is only exacerbated by the indifference of others, and longs for an end to it all.

The dreams illustrate in a remarkably revealing and accurate way the manner in which Steve struggles in his current relationships and situation in life. However, from a Fairbairnian perspective, they also reveal how Steve's internal representations of part-self and other have come to be organized and experienced. Having internalized as part of himself parental-like images who prevent his growth and development, are oblivious to his incapacitation, and from whom he cannot escape, Steve engages the world from a position of entrenched paralysis and passivity. He is a man who experiences himself to be profoundly unfree, shackled, and dependent, despite his culture's valorization of self-sufficiency and autonomy.

Discussion and Conclusion

I have argued that certain types of dreams—those that engage the emotional and imaginal underpinnings of self-organization—reflect back to the dreamer how their current organization of self relates various parts of itself to itself, its body, and to other people and objects in the world. Both sets of dreams I have presented here illustrate this function, though in different ways. In Nene'na Limbong's dreams, we see a self organizing itself around the need to enact status and the risks that such enactment entails. By fulfilling status obligations, one risks social effacement and death, which is depicted in the dreams quite literally as the dissolution or destruction of the body. Images of the permeability of the body's boundaries, accompanied by the emotions of fear and dread, illustrate as well how the demands and expectations of others can be experienced as an annihilation of self, even in a society where the culture encourages a strong, conscious identification between self and other in many contexts.

In Steve's dreams, we see a self-organization depicted with reference to the possibilities for mobility, directionality, autonomy, and self-control. Threats to these possibilities evoke images of broken down, damaged, or immobilized cars that are no longer capable of moving. Loss of control over the course of one's journey, resulting from either extrapersonal or intrapersonal obstacles, can be experienced as so painful and unpleasant that a part of oneself might prefer death.

Steve's dreams illustrate as well the extent to which internalized representations of self and other can become intermingled and fused, even in a culture that valorizes independence and autonomy. Indeed, they demonstrate the special danger such fusings can pose for people who place a strong value on the integrity of the self, and who fear its violation or influence from without. Steve seems unable to gain control over his own "car" (meaning "self") without the presence of a parental image there to thwart him, even though this internal control is what is demanded of him by his culture. Although Steve's struggle for self-control is particularly intense, could not many North Americans identify with the pain and difficulty of his effort to exorcise outside influence?

Following from this, selfscape dreams provide evidence that self-organization may be much more fluid and less unitary than we had once imagined, as emerging constructivist models of mind suggest (see Hollan 2000). According to these models, the self is not a seamless, unfractionated whole; but rather the end product of a complicated series of feedforward and feedback loops within a broad and open system of information exchange. This self system encompasses the synaptic structure of the brain, intrapersonal processes of memory and symbol formation, and interpersonal, self-other configurations as organized and shaped through familial, social, and historical processes.

Thus, the self system is organized hierarchically, dynamically, and temporally. Lower-level subsystems may or may not come together to form a superordinate self (or selves) that is aware of its constituent parts. Lower-level subsystems may or may not remain separate from other parts of self-organization and function relatively independently and autonomously. In any or all of these cases, the organization of the self system, and the border between what is conscious and unconscious, is highly responsive to both the intrapersonal and extrapersonal processes within which it is embedded. Selfscape dreams illustrate some of this complexity of self-organization.

Although selfscape dreams can probably be found everywhere, only some cultures seem to recognize them and take advantage of the feedback they provide. Cultures that focus attention on dreams, categorize them, and label them—especially those that identify some types of dreams as prophetic—recognize that some dreams can be related, either directly or indirectly, to the fate and well-being of the dreamer. In Toraja, what I am calling selfscape dreams (and what the Toraja refer to as *tindo*) may motivate a person to initiate or terminate some type of behavior that significantly alters how he or she experiences the world or parts of themselves, such as the making of amends to family, neighbors, or ancestral spirits. For example, when Nene'na Limbong once dreamed of his deceased father attempting to drag him off to the afterworld (and so to certain death), he consulted a dream expert who told him to acknowledge his father's angry and hungry spirit by sacrificing a pig to him (Hollan 1989). From a cultural point of view, Nene'na Limbong's sacrifice repaired and reestablished his relationship with the spirit of his dead father. From a psychological point of view, it allowed him to acknowledge and work through a sense of guilt.

The dreams I have presented here are dreams of affliction: they depict the self in fear and dread, and under assault. Although selfscape dreams may, in fact, represent the self in states of health, pleasure, and elation (see Sacks 1996), my anecdotal evidence from both the United States and Indonesia suggests that dreams of the self in states of pain are more common than those in which the self is experiencing pleasure. Damasio reminds us that the human brain "handles positive and negative varieties of emotion with different systems" and that there "seem to be far more varieties of negative than positive emotions" (1994: 267). Further, he suggests that as a species, we seem to utilize the avoidance of pain more than the attraction to pleasure as a determinate of behavior, or as a source of feedback affecting our behavior (1994: 267).

Perhaps selfscape dreams, entwined as they are with emotional processes, have come to be weighted in the same direction. Perhaps it has become more important for us to know when the self is in pain than when it is in pleasure. Perhaps the self in pleasure is not, from an evolutionary point of view, a problem in the same way that the self in pain is. In any case, selfscape dreams offer us a unique vantage point from which to observe how self-organization is affected by its interactions with other people and with the world.

Notes

1 See, for example, Barrett (1996), Breger (1977), D'Andrade (1961), Fishbein (1981), Fosshage (1983), Freud [1900] (1956), Lohmann (2003), Noy (1969, 1979), and Tedlock (1987, 1994).
2 For another much-cited work on the manifest content of dreams, see Hall and Van de Castle (1966).
3 See for example Kracke (1987), Tedlock (1987, 1994, and this volume), Price-Williams (1987), and Stephen (1995 and this volume).
4 There are no index entries for dreams in *Descartes' Error* and only six minor ones in *The Feeling of What Happens*.
5 More accurately, Kohut was interested in how the self experienced its relationships with other people, which he referred to as "selfobject" relationships. Self-state dreams, according to Kohut, illustrated how the self responded to changes in its selfobject relations.
6 There are only two large market and administrative towns in Toraja–Makale in the south and Rantepao in the north. As I have noted, the vast majority of Toraja still live in relatively isolated villages and hamlets.

References

Barrett, D., ed., 1996. *Trauma and Dreams*. Cambridge: Harvard University Press.
Breger, L. 1977. Function of Dreams. *Journal of Abnormal Psychology* 72:1–28.
Crapanzano, V. 1980. *Tuhami*. Chicago: University of Chicago Press.
D'Andrade, R.G. 1961. Anthropological Study of Dreams. In *Psychological Anthropology*, edited by F.L.K. Hsu. Homewood, IL: Dorsey.
Damasio, A. 1994. *Descartes' Error*. New York: Avon Books.
Damasio, A. 1999. *The Feeling of What Happens*. New York: Harcourt Brace.
Fairbairn, W.R.D. 1952. Endopsychic Structure Considered in Terms of Object-Relationships. In *Psychoanalytic Studies of Personality*. London: Tavistock Publications.

Fishbein, W., ed., 1981. *Sleep, Dreams, and Memory*. New York: SP Medical and Technical Books.

Fosshage, J.L. 1983. The Psychological Function of Dreams. *Psychoanalysis and Contemporary Thought* 6:641–669.

Freud, S. [1900]1956. *The Interpretation of Dreams*. New York: Basic Books.

Hall, C.S., and R. Van de Castle. 1966. *The Content Analysis of Dreams*. New York: Appleton-Century-Crofts.

Hollan, D. 1989. The Personal Use of Dream Beliefs in the Toraja Highlands. *Ethos* 17:166–186.

Hollan, D. 1995. To the Afterworld and Back: Mourning and Dreams of the Dead Among the Toraja. *Ethos* 23:424–436.

Hollan, D. 1996. Cultural and Experiential Aspects of Spirit Beliefs Among the Toraja. In *Spirits in Culture, History, and Mind*, edited by J. Mageo and A. Howard. New York: Routledge.

Hollan, D. 2000. Constructivist Models of Mind, Contemporary Psychoanalysis, and the Development of Culture Theory. *American Anthropologist* 102:538–550.

Hollan, D. 2003. The Intersubjective Context of Dream Remembrance and Reporting: Dreams, Aging, and the Anthropological Encounter in Toraja, Indonesia. In *Dream Travelers: Sleep Experiences and Culture in the Western Pacific*, edited by R.I. Lohmann. New York: Palgrave.

Hollan, D.W., and J.C. Wellenkamp. 1994. *Contentment and Suffering: Culture and Experience in Toraja*. New York: Columbia University Press.

Hollan, D.W., and J.C. Wellenkamp. 1996. *The Thread of Life: Toraja Reflections on the Life Cycle*. Honolulu: University of Hawaii Press.

Kohut, H. 1971. *The Analysis of the Self*. New York: International Universities Press.

Kohut, H. 1977. *The Restoration of the Self*. Madison, CN: International Universities Press.

Kracke, W. 1987. Myths in Dreams, Thought in Images. In *Dreaming*, edited by B. Tedlock. Cambridge: Cambridge University Press.

Levy, R.I. 1984. Emotion, Knowing, and Culture. In *Culture Theory: Essays on Mind, Self, and Emotion*, edited by R.A. Shweder and R.A. LeVine. Cambridge: Cambridge University Press.

Lohmann, R.I., ed., 2003. *Dream Travelers: Sleep Experiences and Culture in the Western Pacific*. New York: Palgrave.

Noy, P. 1969. A Revision of the Psychoanalytic Theory of Primary Process. *International Journal of Psychoanalysis* 50:155–178.

Noy, P. 1979. The Psychoanalytic Theory of Cognitive Development. *Psychoanalytic Study of the Child* 34:169–216.

Price-Williams, D. 1987. The Waking Dream in Ethnographic Perspective. In *Dreaming*, edited by B. Tedlock. Cambridge: Cambridge University Press.

Sacks, O. 1996. Neurological Dreams. In *Trauma and Dreams*, edited by D. Barrett. Cambridge, MA: Harvard University Press.

Stephen, M. 1995. *A'aisa's Gifts*. Berkeley: University of California Press.

Tedlock, B., ed., 1987. *Dreaming*. Cambridge: Cambridge University Press.

Tedlock, B. 1994. The Evidence from Dreams. In *Handbook of Psychological Anthropology*, edited by P.K. Bock. Westport, CN: Greenwood Press.

Tolpin, P. 1983. Self Psychology and the Interpretation of Dreams. In *The Future of Psychoanalysis*, edited by A. Goldberg. New York: International Universities Press.

Volkman, T. 1985. *Feasts of Honor*. Urbana: University of Illinois Press.

7 Selfscapes of Well-Being in a Rural Indonesian Village

Many would agree that the state of being well has certain biological and so-cial correlates. It is hard to be well if one is starving, if one is in chronic pain, or if one is the victim of assault or lives in constant fear of assault. But people who are not starving, who are not in chronic pain, and who do not live in fear of assault can tell us how miserable they are. So whatever well-being is, it entails more than the fulfillment of basic biological and social needs.

In this chapter, I argue that at the individual level, being well is inher-ently a contingent, subjective state that varies through space and time. To admit that well-being is subjective does not mean that it cannot be studied using traditional methods of participant observation and interviewing, nor to deny the prospects for comparative analysis. But it does demand that our investigations take a person-centered perspective (see Hollan 2000, 2001; Levy and Hollan 2015); that is, that they attempt to understand how the world is felt and experienced from the subject's point of view. I begin by explaining why well-being is so subjective and contingent, and I intro-duce the concept of a "selfscape." I then present the idea that despite this contingency, all societies establish gradients of well-being in which certain kinds of routines or activities are given positive valence and encouraged while others are given negative valence and discouraged. In the following two sections, I analyze the contingency and variability of well-being in a rural Toraja community in the mountains of south Sulawesi, Indonesia. I conclude by summarizing the argument and offering suggestions for future research.

Why Well-Being Is Subjective

Well-being is subjective and contingent because, in my view, it is related to the evolution of a human self-system that is constantly evaluating its condi-tion, for survival purposes, relative to its own body, to other people, and to the world. All humans possess this basic biological ability to evaluate and moni-tor themselves (Hallowell 1955), but because self-systems only emerge and develop in interaction with particular social and physical worlds, they will differ from one another in both predictable and idiosyncratic ways.

DOI: 10.4324/9781003529118-9

In *Descartes' Error* (1994) and in The *Feeling of What Happens* (1999), the neuroscientist Antonio Damasio reminds us just how deeply the mind is rooted in the body and its biological processes. He emphasizes how dependent the mind and survival are upon continuously updated representations of the body and its relative health or illness, and how these representations "qualify" our perceptions of the world. For example, sick or hungry people are likely to act differently, to engage the environment differently, and to experience and perceive the behaviors and intentions of others differently than those who are healthy and satiated. In the later chapters of the first book and throughout the second, Damasio begins to speculate about the origins and maintenance of the self and consciousness. He suggests that neural representations of the self must be continuously updated and modified in a manner similar to that of bodily processes, and he speculates that the earliest representation of the self very likely emerge from, or coincide with, representations of the body as it interacts with the world. Thus, neural representations of the body, self, and world are inextricably tied together through complex emotional states and processes, all of which must be continuously updated and modified as they stimulate and impinge upon one another. The brain creates the phenomenological *illusion* of an ongoing, unified self as it represents fluctuating body and emotional states in interaction with a constantly changing environment, but it really is only an illusion, since the self-system itself, and its sensing of pleasure and pain, wellness and unwellness, is never static but is always dynamically related to the changing states of body and world it monitors.

Thus, the self-system, and by implication one's awareness of one's own state of wellness or unwellness, is a dynamic and ever-changing product of the interaction of body/brain and experience. Without a body/brain, there is no experience. Without experience, without engagement in the culturally constituted and variable world, there is no emergence of self-processes, and consequently, no awareness of wellness or lack of wellness (Hollan 2004).

Implications for the Study of Well-Being

There are important implications in all of this for the study of well-being. One is that well-being must be highly contingent, depending on how the self-system is mapping itself at any given moment relative to changing states of body and environment and the interactions between the two. This mapping process is complex. In part, it is constrained by biological "values" of the body that have evolved in our species over an extended period of time, such as sensitivity to particular kinds of pleasures and pains and the physiological limits of cellular homeostasis (see Hinton 1999). As Damasio has suggested, the brain's moment-to-moment mapping of the body's internal dynamics is itself a hugely complicated process. But the body does not exist in a physical, social, or cultural vacuum. Indeed, the self-system maps the body as it moves through a culturally constituted world, which, like the internal dynamics of the body, is characterized by dynamic states of both stasis and change and is sensed and perceived through a cultural lens. Moreover, the culture through which the self-system senses and evaluates itself is not uniformly given, but is distributed across the social landscape (see Schwartz 1978) and is internalized to varying degrees by any given person. For example, as we shall see in a later section, not all Toraja internalize the belief in supernatural retribution to the same degree, and those who do, do not always embody or enact the belief in the same way.

But the complexities do not end here. As the self-system maps and evaluates the body as it moves through the culturally constituted landscape, it simultaneously maps a memoryscape of the body and self interacting with the world. Some of this mapping is conscious. A person thinks, "these artifacts or activities or people are familiar or unfamiliar; they have made me happy or unhappy or healthy or sick in the past." But much of it is nonconscious or unconscious. Psychoanalysis and the cognitive and neurosciences have taught us that consciousness captures but a small part of what the self and body/brain "know" about people and objects in the world. Implicitly and nonconsciously, we are always relating or associating these current experiences to our representations and constructions of past experiences.

Sometimes these associations are relatively direct and straightforward: without being consciously aware, we avoid or act aggressively towards artifacts or activities or people who have made us sick or unhappy in the past; we approach or actively embrace those that have made us happy or healthy. But other times, our nonconscious associations to the culturally constituted landscape are more convoluted and obscure, as psychoanalysis suggests. Without conscious awareness, people may attempt to dominate or control or even embrace those artifacts or activities or people that have frightened or hurt them in the past, in a compensatory way. For example, someone may become a soldier or police officer or football player to compensate for an inner sense of weakness or vulnerability. On the other hand, people may flee or avoid or ignore artifacts or activities or people that pose no "objective" threat to them because they have nonconsciously and erroneously associated them to actual or imagined experiences of the past that *have* posed some threat. For example, a person may be prone to criticize or avoid present-day authority figures, regardless of their actual behavior, because of negative experiences with such authority figures in the past. As Freud suggested, the self-system can become divided against itself, and its interactions with the world characterized by emotional states of ambivalence and conflict.

Thus, the self-system is constantly mapping its own representations of its own past experiences onto the space and time of the contemporary culturally constituted world. I refer to these moment-by-moment mappings as *selfscapes*. The complexity and contingency of selfscapes pose daunting analytical challenges for the study of well-being. Because they develop in worlds that are saturated with multiple and conflicting values, they themselves are inevitably value-laden; people can only be well or unwell relative to some set of internalized values. Because they occur through time and across culturally constituted space, they themselves may conflict and contradict one another: for example, what promotes happiness and well-being at one moment, in one context, at one stage of life may not do so at another moment, in another context, at another stage of life. And because self-systems grow and develop epigenetically—that is, because their earlier experiences partially shape the way they respond to later experiences—people's selfscapes must differ from one another even in relatively small, monocultural communities, since people's life experiences will vary along dimensions of age, gender, status, birth order, idiosyncratic experience, and so on.

From this perspective, being well has a lot to do with the relative "fit" between a person's mind/body and the physical and social world. It is hard to be well if one's basic biological needs are not being satisfied, but one can be equally "unwell" if one is alienated from one's family or community or too often experiences humiliation, shame, fear, or anxiety—even if one is otherwise biologically fit. It is important to note that the poorness of fit between people and their social worlds can come about for several reasons. One can be excluded from the activities or routines that one finds most appealing or meaningful. One may exclude oneself from such appealing activities and routines, due to excessive shyness, shame, or inner conflict. Or, the activities or routines one *has* become embedded in are experienced as painful, unpleasant, or unfulfilling. Either lack of involvement or overinvolvement in the social world can become a problem for people.

Social and Cultural Gradients of Well-Being

While individual selfscapes are variable and contingent, in all communities they unfold in worlds that are socially and culturally organized in particular ways, no matter how swiftly these patterns of organized life might be changing as a result of larger-scale political and economic forces. Intentionally or not, all communities establish zones or gradients of well-being in which certain kinds of routines or activities are given positive valence and encouraged, while others are given negative valence and discouraged. Of course from the individual's point of view, the valence of some activities is mixed. Communities attempt to reward participation in some activities or routines, thought to benefit the individual or group over the long-term, even though they may bring some short-term frustration or pain from the individual's point of view. Schools and other forms of formal education are good examples of activities that evoke ambivalent reactions from people in many parts of the world. Some activities or routines acquire a negative valence not because they are actively discouraged, but simply because they are not positively valued or encouraged. For example, teaching in the United States is not actively disparaged per se, but because its prestige is not as high as many other professions, many people will avoid it or prefer to work in some other way.

Thus, all communities create zones of activities and engagements for people that affect their sense of well-being in relatively positive or negative ways. As people move through the course of a day and traverse the socialscapes around them, as they move from one location to another and engage with various types of people and activities, they feel more or less safe and secure, more or less stimulated and engaged, more or less well or unwell. Almost all communities attempt to establish some form of "safe haven" for people—areas or activities in which people's basic social and emotional needs are fulfilled and in which they are protected from too much stress and anxiety. Households and family and friendship groups often serve this function. Conversely, there are zones or activities in all communities in which livelihoods and reputations are at stake, in which egos, if not bodies, can get bloodied and bruised, such as in the very public, and often-contentious, division of sacrificial meat at a Toraja funeral. The contours of these socialscapes and the rules for navigating them will vary from culture to culture. Although individuals may, and often do, respond to these zones in different ways (as I suggest in a later section), the zones themselves have a certain stability for the simple reason that many of them are institutionalized through custom or law and so persist beyond the life span of individuals.

Gradients of Well-Being in a Toraja Village

Despite rapid growth and change in the market towns of Rantepao and Makele, rural Toraja hamlets in highland Sulawesi, Indonesia, remain scattered among steeply terraced rice fields and patches of forest and gardens, much as they did when I conducted extended field work there in the 1980s and 1990s (see Hollan and Wellenkamp 1994, 1996). As one walks through these mountains or drives along one of the handful of rough, unpaved roads that slice through them, one sees that hamlets consisting of two or three to up to a dozen households, most without running water or electricity, are strategically placed to accommodate the back-breaking cultivation of rice. Such cultivation remains the primary means of livelihood for those who have stayed in the countryside and have been unwilling or unable to migrate to city and town.

As throughout much of rural Indonesia (and indeed throughout much of rural Asia as a whole), the cultivation of rice in Toraja establishes a certain rhythm and direction to life. In most areas, there is not enough accessible river flow to ensure year-round cultivation, as in Bali and parts of Java. Instead, cultivation is dependent on the annual monsoon rains, which usually begin around October and continue through March or April. During the months that rains are saturating and filling the terraced fields, women grow rice seedlings and then laboriously transplant them by hand to the surrounding fields. Men by hand and with buffalo plow the fields in preparation for planting, and they spend hours weeding and protecting seedlings from birds and other pests once they have taken root. They also spend countless hours and days repairing and maintaining the terracing of the fields. Both men and women hand cut and harvest the rice once it begins to mature, towards the end of the rainy season and the beginning of the dry. While children in these areas now spend a good portion of their day in school, they too are often engaged in agricultural activities of one kind or another or in the household activities that either support or result from agricultural work.

Toraja households tend to be nuclear in structure, consisting of married or unmarried couples and their children. As households mature and develop, children leave to marry and form their own household units. The older couples or single parents left behind may then begin to adopt or foster some of their grandchildren or other children to provide household labor and companionship. Or, if they are old enough or infirm enough, they may themselves be folded into a child's household. From the point of view of a person's sense of well-being, it is the household unit that provides many of the good things in life: relative safety and nurturance, relatively relaxed intimacy, and refuge from the demands and uncertainties of life outside the household. Indeed, traditional ancestral houses, called *tongkonan*, are symbolically constituted as womblike structures that are thought to be founts of fertility and prosperity. Activities outside the household, on the other hand, nearly always have a more mixed valence. For example, the people Jane Wellenkamp and I worked with in the 1980s were very accomplished farmers and gardeners, but they were also quick to note that manual labor was exhausting, could cause lasting injury or premature aging, and was a primary cause of personal and social suffering. Life outside the household also exposed people to potential social dangers, such as unwanted or unfair requests for aid and assistance and black magic. Of course relations with "outside" people could also be pleasurable, as when groups of men or women or children gather to gossip and joke, or when people are able to enhance their pride and prestige by slaughtering animals at communal feasts. But even these enjoyable activities could turn sour.

One of the reasons the social terrain outside the household can be so treacherous to navigate is that it is organized hierarchically. As throughout much of Indonesia, in Toraja, social rank is inherited through one's family as well as achieved through one's own accomplishments, such as completing higher levels of education, holding certain kinds of jobs, or slaughtering animals at community feasts. Distinctions are drawn among traditional nobles, the newly wealthy, and commoners, and there is an elaborate etiquette to ensure that each group receives the deference and respect it deserves. Crosscutting this pronounced social hierarchy is an ethos of reciprocity in which those with more are expected to nurture and come to the assistance of those with less. In practice, higher-status and wealthy people are expected to help those of lower status and the poor with their material needs, and in return, the lower status and the poor are expected to shower the high-status people with deference and labor. If people misjudge the social terrain in some way, if they fail to give deference when deference is expected, if they fail to give assistance when it is warranted or if they ask for assistance when it is not, they may shame or anger others and so open themselves to retaliation in the form of reciprocal disrespect or magical attack.

The fine-balancing act between giving to others what they deserve and getting from others what is one's own due comes to a high-stakes head in the meat division at community feasts. It is there when a family's rank becomes most visible and obvious to others, symbolized in a very concrete way by the amount and kind of meat it receives. It is a site where if all goes well and one receives the meat that is one's due, one leaves feeling proud, respected, and acknowledged by the community. But if not, one can feel shamed and humiliated in front of the whole community.

Navigation of the social terrain varies by gender as well. Generally speaking, the status of women in Toraja is high: the kinship system is bilateral; women can inherit land and property; there is no preference for male children; women's work (gardening, planting, harvesting, cooking, childcare) is valued; and, from a cross-cultural point of view, gender differences are not given much cultural elaboration. For example, the Toraja language does not have separate pronouns for males and females, and the terms for siblings and grandparents are gender neutral. Further, adolescent initiation practices are relatively unelaborated, and they do not serve to highlight dramatic differences between males and females. Indeed, some prominent male roles are closely identified with feminine functions and characteristics; for example, the traditional male leader and coordinator of rice-growing activities and rituals is called the *Indo' Pandang,* literally, "Mother of the Ground" (Hollan and Wellenkamp 1994: 88–91).

Yet there is nearly complete segregation by gender in public places such as feasts and rituals, where men are given preferred food, drink, and seating. Beginning in childhood, males are given more freedom to explore the social terrain. Boys are more often encouraged to tend buffalo, gardens, and rice fields that take them away from the village, whereas girls are more often encouraged to stay closer to home to help out with childcare and other household work. By adolescence, boys are free to wander in search of romance and adventure, whereas girls are expected to travel in groups or with chaperons, especially at night. Women who try to evade these restraints on their behavior are said to deserve whatever might befall them, including rape.

While expectations for men and women vary, their roles and responsibilities are thought to be complementary. A well-functioning, prosperous household is one in which both male and female work is being performed. From a Toraja perspective, men and women need one another. Unmarried or unattached people are anomalous and are thought worthy of pity or compassion.

Age is another factor that affects how one navigates the social terrain in Toraja. Generally speaking, children and old people are given more freedom and behavioral license than young and middle-aged adults (Hollan and Wellenkamp 1996). Although people remember times as children when they were overwhelmed by learning or mastering new skills and responsibilities, most say childhood is one of the happiest periods of life, a time when other people are responsible for feeding them and they are relatively free to go to school and play with their friends. Adulthood, on the other hand, is considered to be one of the most difficult, stressful periods of life. Adults are ultimately responsible for feeding and caring for themselves *and* everyone else in the village, including their children and older, infirm parents. They also shoulder primary responsibility for maintaining the family's status and prestige by slaughtering animals at community feasts and for paying for their children's education—demands that are often at odds with one another. Given all the stresses and burdens of adulthood, many people say they look forward to old age when, like children, other people assume more responsibility for them and they have less work and worries. Older people are also freer to challenge or defy accepted rules of conduct, for example, by becoming more openly ill-tempered or impatient.

Spiritual and religious beliefs and practices not only constitute an important part of the social terrain in Toraja but also affect how one maneuvers through it. Before the Dutch introduced Christianity to the highlands in the early 1900s, the Toraja followed a number of prescriptions, prohibitions, and ritual practices meant to keep them on good terms with a variety of gods, spirits, and ancestral figures. These numinous beings were thought to reward proper behavior with prosperity while punishing improper behavior with illness and misfortune. Although the vast majority of the Toraja now consider themselves to be Christian and no longer follow many of the rituals and prohibitions of their forebears, many still adhere to the general idea that spiritual beings, including God, Jesus, and ancestral figures, punish misbehavior and reward good. For the Toraja, part of being well is knowing that one has not done anything to warrant spiritual retribution.

Thus, the socialscape of well-being in the Toraja countryside is not flat or uniform. One is not merely well or unwell. Rather, one moves through a dense, contoured set of culturally structured, though constantly changing, relationships and activities with both positive and negative valences. How one encounters and reacts to this socialscape will vary depending upon one's age, gender, social and marital status, wealth, occupation, level of education, type and degree of religious belief, and so on, but also by the nature of one's past experiences. To illustrate this, let us consider a day in the life of Nene'na Tandi, one of my primary informants and collaborators.

A Toraja Selfscape

At the time I knew Nene'na Tandi in the 1980s, he was approximately 60 years old and lived in a two-room bamboo thatched house with his wife and a young, adopted son. In his youth, he had attended school through grade six and had traveled as far as the west coast of New Guinea in search of employment, but had eventually returned to Toraja when he failed to acquire the wealth and prosperity he had hoped for. Since then, he had lived as a farmer and gardener in the village. Though of commoner birth, he was wickedly witty and intelligent, and his oratory skills gave him far more influence in the village than he otherwise deserved, given his middle-level family status and limited wealth.

Nene'na Tandi began most of his days by getting up at dawn and eating leftover rice and hot tea or coffee with his wife and son. As I have suggested, most Toraja enjoy these moments with family. Away from the prying eyes of neighbors and nonfamily, they can slip out of some of the etiquette that binds them in other contexts, and they are free not to worry so much about where they fit into the pronounced social hierarchy of the village. But Nene'na Tandi enjoyed these moments, particularly with his wife, even more than most because his two previous marriages had been loveless and contentious. His present wife, on the other hand, was one of his favorite companions, although such intimacy between spouses was considered highly unusual. Thus, Nene'na Tandi's sense of domestic well-being derived part of its emotional force and saliency from its implicit and explicit comparison to similar but unhappy experiences in his past.

Nene'na Tandi also enjoyed being with his adopted son, one of several children he had fostered over the years, who performed much of the household's work. But the boy's presence was also a daily reminder that he himself had never been able to have children, which was embarrassing for him, because it implied that he was probably infertile, and frightening, since childlessness was thought to be one of the signs that a person was being punished by spiritual forces. Nene'na Tandi took seriously the idea that he might be worthy of retribution since he had often defied his parents and elders during his youth. Thus, the same cultural and emotional space that afforded Nene'na Tandi's moments of safety and intimacy also led him to worry about the state of his spiritual health and well-being.

Even at age 60, Nene'na Tandi would leave his house early in the morning to work in his gardens and rice fields. Whether or not he enjoyed these movements through the village and surrounding countryside depended very much on whom he encountered there. When Nene'na Tandi was with close family or friends, I often found him regaling them with his wit and charm. He could be a highly sociable man and loved to brag that since he was not wealthy, his true gifts to people were his "sweet words" and sage advice.

But as a long-time leader in the community and as someone who was concerned with maintaining his own status and prestige, he had also gotten himself involved, or had been drawn into, several disputes with people. As one of the first committed Christians in the community, he sometimes criticized more traditional people for their backward, superstitious ways. As a community leader, he had strong ideas about how the community should invest its resources and how it should deal with the local and national governments. As a commoner, he was resentful of those who had inherited their wealth and prestige and the advantages it gave them in acquiring even more renown through the competitive slaughter. of animals at feasts. And as a former adjudicator of disputes, he had upset and alienated as many petitioners as he had rewarded or made happy.

This history of contentious relationships put Nene'na Tandi at risk, or so he thought, since it was common knowledge that people who believe themselves shamed or mistreated might use magic to retaliate. Indeed, he claimed that he had already been the victim of magic twice before in his life: once when someone from a neighboring village poisoned his palm wine in retaliation for his involvement in a divorce case, and once when a stranger, for some unknown reason, cast a spell on him as he was returning home from the market town of Rantepao. As a result of such experiences, Nene'na Tandi had acquired special medicine to protect himself from magical attack, and he would attempt to avoid unexpected meetings with strangers or people with whom he had had disagreements with, although such chance, unexpected meetings did sometimes occur. Thus, encounters with people outside the household could undermine Nene'na Tandi's sense of well-being as well as enhance it, depending on who the people were and the nature of the encounter.

Once out in the fields or gardens, Nene'na Tandi felt relatively safe and secure, though he often complained about how exhausting the work was. If people were around, they were almost always his friends or neighbors. By late morning or midday, his son or wife would bring him a meal, and he would eat, chew betel nut, and relax for a while. If his meal and rest strengthened him, he would continue working in the fields for the remainder of the day. If, on the other hand, his food exacerbated his stomach ailments, as it sometimes did, he would return to the village at midday, forced to consider yet again whether the spirits or ancestors might have found reason to make him sick.

The return to the village at the end of the day was the reverse of the journey out: Nene'na Tandi exposed himself to possible insult or injury when away from his house or fields, but assured himself of relative safety and security once he had returned home. Once home, he usually ate his evening meal with his wife and son, and then slept with them on the floor of the back room. Sleep and dreaming could itself be eventful and expose one to yet other adventures and potential risks and dangers, since the Toraja believe that a dreamer's soul may wander away from the body during sleep and encounter other souls and spirits. Some of these encounters in dreams are thought to be prophetic: a spirit or ancestor figure gives something or takes something away, presaging either fortune or misfortune in waking life. Nene'na Tandi has had several dreams in which his deceased parents came to him offering advice and guidance, foreshadowing a positive turn of events for him. He converted to Christianity permanently only after his wife's aunt had had a dream suggesting he would die unless he immediately became a Christian.

One of the reasons Nene'na Tandi felt very paternal towards one of the boys in his hamlet was because he and the spirit of the boy's mother had had frequent sexual encounters in his dreams. Because of that, he had become convinced that he was the boy's true father. Such a conviction, and the dreams upon which it is based, allow Nene'na Tandi to believe that at least his dream spirit is capable of having children, which is comforting to him. For the Toraja, waking and dreaming consciousnesses are woven together. Events and concerns of the day can find their way into dreams. But just as certainly, dream experiences at night affect how one interprets daily events, and so one's conscious sense of well-being.

Nene'na Tandi's selfscape does and does not resemble others in Toraja. In some ways, his concerns about magical retaliation are similar to those of other wealthy and high-status people, afraid of the envy and malice of those less well to do, even though he was not particularly wealthy or high status himself. This is because his charisma and oratory skills give him an influence and social position he did not otherwise deserve. But note how the same gift both enhances his well-being, by improving his social status, and undermines it, by presenting him with worries and concerns other people do not have. Like other commoners, he embraces Christianity, in part, to develop a source of pride and dignity for himself apart from those controlled by the elite. And as a male, he enjoys freedom of movement throughout the socialscape and preferential consumption of valued commodities, such as meat, alcohol, and tobacco, especially in public.

His relationship with his wife, his adopted son, and the dream spirit of a neighboring woman are more unique, however. And here too, the emotional valence is mixed. On the one hand, these relationships remind him of his possible infertility, and stir up guilt about his misbehavior as a youth and concerns that he is worthy of spiritual retribution. Yet the same misfortune is partially responsible for his deep (and unusual) love of his present wife, who has remained faithful and loyal to him despite the lack of children, for the satisfaction he has received from fostering a number of children over the years, and for the pleasure he derives from imagining himself as the spiritual father of a beautiful young woman's son. This illustrates that well-being or its lack for any particular individual is influenced both by that person's placement within a culturally structured social world (their status, gender, age, religion, and so on) and by the way their earlier life experiences and memoryscapes come to affect how later life events are interpreted and reacted to. For example, Tominaa Sattu, a man who shared many of Nene'na Tandi's social characteristics, often dreamed not of having sex with the spirits of beautiful young women, but of the spirits of his beloved and much-missed parents, both of whom died while he was still a boy. Now a father and grandfather himself, he often still refers to himself as an "orphan." Here is a man whose sense of well-being was deeply shaken by the loss of his parents in childhood, never to be regained completely. And Indo'na Sapan endures the embarrassment and disadvantages of being a single mother, not because she has not had the opportunity to remarry (several men have asked her), but because she refuses ever to be hurt again in the way her former husband hurt her by having affairs with other women. Her singleness compromises the well-being of her and her children in very real, significant ways, but in her mind, not so much as it would be compromised by having a husband cheat on her again.

Discussion and Conclusion

Even this abbreviated description of a day in the life of Nene'na Tandi illustrates that the ebb and flow of his sense of well-being is a function of his location in a specific cultural space, the time of day or night, his proximity or distance from specific individuals with whom he shares specific relationship histories, the degree to which he has internalized certain cultural beliefs and practices (and not others), and his memoryscapes of past experiences. And he is not unique in this regard. Other Toraja experience similar ebbs and flows in their well-being, as do all people.

We could, of course, attempt to average out this emotional flow and say, "on balance, these cultural beliefs, practices, and artifacts promote well-being while these do not." But that would be an artificial and problematic exercise. For one thing, it would ignore the very thing the self-system has evolved to capture: the flow, particularity, and epigenetic nature of life experience for a given individual. For another, it would obscure the fact that states of wellness and unwellness are always in dynamic relationship to one another, and it is this dynamic interplay that should be the focus of our studies. By virtue of valuing and rewarding certain kinds of routines and activities, all communities necessarily disvalue other kinds, thereby creating gradients of well-being that are inescapable. Ruth Benedict (1934) pointed this out long ago when she noted that what is considered "abnormal" is always relative to what is considered normal. While some communities, no doubt, are much better about minimizing states of unwellness than others, no community can eliminate them altogether. No group of people can be completely well or unwell.

I have argued that being well is a contingent, dynamic state of being that is related to fluctuating states of body and world and the interactions between the two. This dynamism should make us wary of too quickly assessing the costs and benefits of the mere existence of particular cultural beliefs and practices without first understanding when and to what degree they are enacted, with whom, under what circumstances, and the nature of their historical development. For example, because of a rebellious youth, Nene'na Tandi takes ideas about spiritual punishment more seriously than many other Toraja do, and the relatively deep internalization of these beliefs has affected his well-being in complicated ways. On the one hand it has engendered considerable fear and anxiety in him, and very likely has contributed to or exacerbated his lifelong stomach ailments. Yet it is also one of the reasons he has now become a mature, thoughtful adult who commands the respect of many of his fellow villagers. Thus current states of well-being actually may depend on having passed through previous periods of not being well, and conversely, current states of unwellness may have less to do with contemporary practices than with those that shaped earlier life experiences and memoryscapes.

Here again, Nene'na Tandi is not alone. We cannot assess how routines and practices affect the wellness or lack of wellness for people without also assessing how they are encountered and experienced by specific individuals· over time. People do not encounter the world as blank slates; rather, their experience of the world unfolds epigenetically. What they have experienced in the past affects how they experience things in the present and future, for good or ill, for wellness or unwellness. This is an area of study that deserves much more cross-cultural research. How do societies and communities around the world "prime" people for wellness or unwellness in childhood and then later in life? Are all forms of resilience culturally specific or are there certain kinds of activities and engagements that seem to promote well-being everywhere? And how and why do activities or engagements that promote well-being for most people tum sour for others? Why is it that some Americans use competitive strategies learned and embraced in childhood to further their sense of well-being throughout the life course, whereas others learn to shun such strategies or use them in ways that alienate them from others or undermine their happiness?

I argue that studies of well-being should embrace these complexities rather than deny them or sweep them into overly static analytical categories. To admit that states of well-being are subjective and both temporally and spatially dependent does not prevent them from being studied using traditional anthropological methods. As I have suggested, we can use participant observation and perhaps certain neurological and physiological tests to examine how selfscapes ebb and flow through the course of the day and night and other culturally relevant cycles of experience. For example, we could measure stress hormone flows throughout the course of a day and night. Eventually, we might be able to collect brain scan images throughout the course of a naturally occurring day and night.

And we can use person-centered, open-ended interviews (Levy and Hollan 2015) to examine how these fluctuating states of the self-system are related to people's representations and constructions of their past experience. Such engagement is essential. At bottom, wellness and unwellness are what they are felt and experienced to be, not what they appear to be from a third-person point of view. Overt behaviors and routines alone can be misleading. A routine or behavior that looks "healthy" from the outside might be practiced to avoid shame or to expiate a conscious or nonconscious sense of guilt, either one of which, over the long run, could produce depression, anxiety, and other forms of unwellness. Conversely, a behavior that appears to be unhealthy, painful, or overly taxing might be a person's way, either consciously or nonconsciously, of attempting to identify with a beloved or respected parent, mentor, or hero figure, thereby, over the long run, promoting resilience and well-being. We can know these things only by asking people about their life experiences and by exploring with them how they have learned to link and associate past and present.

By collecting and mapping the selfscapes of representative samples of people through both space and time, we can begin to build up an empirically grounded understanding of how states of well-being and dysphoria are distributed within and across culturally constituted worlds. We might then begin a comparative analysis of such mappings, looking for similarities in the ways people construct well-being as well as taking note of the ways these constructions differ. This would lead to much better understandings of what kinds of early life experiences are most likely to promote or undermine well-being at later stages of life; how variables such as gender, age, ethnicity, and religious belief and practice intersect to promote or undermine well-being; and how states of wellness and unwellness can be related to one another. Almost all societies, for example, use shame, anxiety, fear, and other unpleasant emotional states to motivate the performance of socially valued roles and behaviors (Spiro 1965). How do different societies manage the trade-off between short-term pain and long-term gain? At what point does the short-term pain, carried forward through memory and emotional association into the future, undermine the possibility of being well, and how do societies assess (or not assess) this?

Such empirically grounded work is painstaking and difficult, but it is one of the ways we can assure ourselves that our assessments of others' well-being tell us more about *them* than about our own values and moral commitments.

References

Benedict, R. 1934. *Patterns of Culture*. Boston, MA: Houghton Mifflin.

Damasio, A.R. 1994. *Descartes' Error: Emotion, Reason, and the Human Brain*. New York: Avon Books.

Damasio, A.R. 1999. *The Feeling of What Happens: Body and Emotion in the Making of Consciousness*. New York: Harcourt Brace.

Hallowell, A.I. 1955. *Culture and Experience*. Philadelphia: University of Pennsylvania Press.

Hinton, A, ed., 1999. *Biocultural Approaches to the Emotions*. Cambridge: Cambridge University Press.

Hollan, D. 2000. Constructivist Models of Mind, Contemporary Psychoanalysis, and the Development of Culture Theory. *American Anthropologist* 102:538–550.

Hollan, D. 2001. "Developments in Person-Centered Ethnography." In *The Psychology of Cultural Experience*, edited by H. Mathews and C. Moore, pp. 48–67. New York: Cambridge University.

Hollan, D. 2004. Self Systems, Cultural Idioms of Distress, and the Psycho-Bodily Consequences of Childhood Suffering. *Transcultural Psychiatry* 41:62–79.

Hollan, D.W., and J.C. Wellenkamp. 1994. *Contentment and Suffering: Culture and Experience in Toraja*. New York: Columbia University Press.

Hollan, D.W., and J.C. Wellenkamp. 1996. *The Thread of Life: Toraja Reflections on the Life Cycle*. Honolulu: University of Hawaii Press.

Levy, R.I., and D.W. Hollan. 2015. "Person-Centered Interviewing and Observation in Anthropology." In *Handbook of Methods in Cultural Anthropology*, edited by H. Russell Bernard and C.C. Gravlee, 2nd edition, pp. 313–342. Walnut Creek, CA: Altamira Press.

Schwartz, T. 1978. "Where Is the Culture? Personality as the Distributive Locus of Culture." In *The Making of Psychological Anthropology*, edited by George D. Spindler, pp. 419–441. Berkeley: University of California Press.

Spiro, M.E. 1965. "Religious Systems as Culturally-Constituted Defense Mechanisms." In *Context and Meaning in Anthropology*, pp. 100–113. New York: Free Press.

8 From Ghosts to Ancestors (and Back Again)

On the Cultural and Psychodynamic Mediation of Selfscapes

This article focuses on an emotional encounter I once had with a Toraja (south Sulawesi, Indonesia) elder in which this man began to reenact and re-experience a dream from many years prior to our involvement. I use this encounter to illustrate how cultural and psychodynamic factors combine and intertwine to mediate self-other and intraself relationships. In developing this argument, I use the concept of "selfscapes" (Hollan 2003b, 2004, 2005a, 2008, 2009) to suggest how dynamic, fluid, and contingent self-other distinctions often are, but also to capture the persisting aspects of memory and self-organization that are sometimes lost or underemphasized by the strong focus on intersubjectivity in the social sciences today. Because this article builds on some of A. Irving Hallowell's seminal ideas about how psychodynamic theories and concepts might be used to enrich and extend cultural phenomenological analysis, I begin by reviewing some of those ideas, especially as Hallowell came to articulate them in his widely cited article, "The Self and Its Behavioral Environment" (Hallowell 1955).

From this review of Hallowell, I then move on to discuss some psychoanalytic assumptions about how interactions with other people are thought to affect the development of self-processes, focusing especially on Hans Loewald's idea that an integrated phenomenal field connecting self-processes and other people and objects exists throughout life. I also discuss Loewald's views on "transference" and on how less conscious, more emotionally charged and imaginal parts of self-organization come to infuse the more highly organized, conscious parts of self and vice versa. I then use some of Loewald's ideas, a cultural phenomenology of Toraja dream and spirit notions, and the concept of a selfscape to analyze the interaction between Nene'na Limbong and myself. I argue that the particularities of people's socially, culturally, and politically influenced encounters with others help determine which "ghosts" haunt their lives and which cultural forms are used to manifest and articulate them. But I also suggest the way in which the stirrings of latent mind and memory lead people to embody, enact, animate, and ultimately transform social and cultural processes and other people in the way they do.

DOI: 10.4324/9781003529118-10

Hallowell's View of Culture and Psychodynamics

Hallowell notes in his widely cited article, "The Self and Its Behavioral Environment," that while self-awareness, the ability to distinguish oneself and one's actions from all other people and objects in the world, is a "generic human trait" (1955: 75), the boundary between what is considered part of the self and what not-self is a fluid one (1955: 84) determined at least in part by both social and cultural processes. When discussing self-awareness as a "social product," Hallowell quotes from the psychologist, Gardner Murphy, who writes,

> Like all other objects of experience, the self grows out of a matrix of indefiniteness which exists at the first perceptual level. It comes gradually into being as the process of differentiation goes on within the perceptual field ... There is considerable evidence to show that the body in all its forms is at first as strange, as unfamiliar, as unorganized as are any other perceived objects. For many months, much of it is not recognized as self.
>
> (1955: 81)

Hallowell is emphasizing here, following Murphy, that the ability to distinguish self from not-self is a developmental achievement that occurs gradually and incrementally, over time. While contemporary developmental psychologists and others would take issue with the idea that human perceptual capacities are actually this undeveloped and disorganized at birth,[1] such a notion was widespread at the time Hallowell was writing. Indeed, it is one of the reasons why he thought it was so important to study socialization and enculturation processes, because he assumed that the self grows and develops only in relation to other people, objects, and concepts.

Prior to this quote from Murphy, Hallowell also refers (1955: 79) to the work of J. M. Baldwin, C. H. Cooley, and G. H. Mead, all of whom were known for developing the idea that a person's sense of self is greatly influenced by what is reflected back to them by the evaluations and expectations of others and that all people become the repositories of such reflections.

While acknowledging these basic, "generic" social processes in the development of self-awareness, Hallowell's actual goal is to demonstrate how much the self is shaped by *culture*, which provides the symbolic means of representation and reference—linguistic, conceptual, aesthetic, and otherwise—by which the self comes to articulate itself, and is articulated, as distinct from other objects in the world (1955: 81–82). Because the symbolic and conceptual resources that orient the self to time, space, objects, motives, and norms vary cross-culturally, so too must the content and the qualities of the selves so oriented, including their boundaries with other people and objects.

In making the case for a cultural analysis of self, Hallowell distinguishes his project not only from those that have focused on the "social" constituents of self found everywhere, but also from those with a more directly psychological or psychodynamic perspective. He writes:

> Since the major purpose of this paper is to clear the ground for a more effective handling of cross-cultural data that seem relevant to a deeper understanding of the role of self-awareness in man as *culturally constituted* in different societies, I am not directly concerned with questions of personality dynamics as such. The discussion is deliberately couched at another level which, for want of a better term but without implying too many theoretical implications, might best be called "phenomenological."
>
> (1955: 79; emphasis in original)

A paragraph later, however, Hallowell acknowledges the limits of such an approach, saying, "It is quite true, of course, that the self as known to the individual may not represent a 'true' picture from an objective point of view," but this more complete picture would require "another perspective and indicates the point at which technical constructs such as ego or superego are necessary in order to help make analysis intelligible in *psychodynamic* terms" (1955: 80; emphasis in original). While carving out an analytical space for the cultural phenomenological analysis of self-awareness, Hallowell is at the same time reminding us that this is but a partial perspective that must be complemented by study of actual interpersonal relations and the psychodynamics they engender and are engendered by. And indeed, in articles such as "Fear and Anxiety as Cultural and Individual Variables in a Primitive Society," Hallowell himself attempts to examine the way aspects of personal and emotional experience are shaped by both shared and idiosyncratic factors, writing that "a comprehensive account of the determining factors in the affective experience of individuals must include on the one hand an analysis of the influence of culture patterns and, on the other, an investigation of the factors that determine quantitative or qualitative individual variations from a given cultural norm" (1955: 265).

In this article, I adopt and underscore Hallowell's suggestion that we draw from both cultural phenomenological and psychodynamic approaches to gain a fuller understanding of self-other relationships and their dynamics. As I have discussed elsewhere (Hollan 2012a), while it is evident that much of Hallowell's own work is a clear break from and reaction to the psychoanalytic reductionism found in the culture and personality school of his time, it is also apparent that this break was not an open or hostile one. Hallowell was simply arguing that we must first understand what the world looks and feels like from the actor's point of view before we speculate too extensively about his or her psychodynamics. Otherwise, we risk misunderstanding or pathologizing behavior that is completely normal or commonsensical from a cultural perspective.

Until recently, some of the leading self-identified cultural phenomenologists following in the wake of Hallowell (e.g., Csordas 1994; Desjarlais 1992; Good 1994; Jackson 1996; Throop 2010) have not explicitly picked up on this suggestion that we use psychodynamic theories and concepts to complement or round out cultural phenomenological analysis, preferring instead to follow Hallowell's emphasis on a "pragmatic" analysis of actions and behaviors, one that explicitly focuses on their meanings and consequences. But this might now be changing. In a recent special issue of *Ethos* (2012) subtitled, "Reinvigorating Dialogue between Phenomenological and Psychoanalytic Anthropologists," a number of anthropologists noted for their contributions to cultural phenomenology are beginning to imagine how some combination of cultural phenomenological and psychodynamic approaches might enrich the study of human behavior and experience (e.g., see Csordas 2012; Jackson 2012; Throop 2012; Willen and Seeman 2012). Byron Good (2012a: 26) in particular is now suggesting that some form of psychodynamic theorizing is critical for capturing and comprehending aspects of contemporary psychological and political subjectivity, especially of the kind he has been examining in Indonesia recently.

Psychoanalytic Models of Self-Other Relationships

Freud (1965) was particularly interested in dreams because he thought they told us something important about how we relate ourselves to various parts of our own minds and to other people and objects in the world. In dreams, he argued, one can see more clearly than at other times how the self-system imaginatively projects some of its thoughts, wishes, and desires into the world but also how different aspects of the surrounding world become subsumed and made a part of self-processes. Freud's elucidation of dreaming processes such as projection, condensation, displacement, incorporation, identification, and so on—all characteristic of what he referred to as primary process thinking—suggest that he was well aware of how dynamic and malleable the self-system is and how difficult it is for people under certain conditions to identify or maintain firm boundaries between themselves and the world. And yet he also underscored the importance of "reality testing" in waking life, the idea that after a certain age, people generally do begin to distinguish clearly between fantasy and objective reality, between hallucinatory gratification of wishes and actual satisfaction of needs and desires, between self and not-self. This is one of the tensions, if not contradictions, in Freud's work that has fueled decades of debate in psychoanalysis: Do other objects and people in the world gain their emotional significance and meaning for people only to the extent they help them satisfy some of their deepest, *self-contained* wishes and desires? Or do people's emotional attachments and identifications with other people and meanings, their fusions and intermingling with them, come to influence the very wishes and desires they come to experience within themselves and which they do not?

The early Freud and many advocates of "classical" psychoanalysis posit a relatively early developmental separation between self and other in waking life. Once rational, logical, discursive thought develops, which Freud referred to as secondary process thinking, most primary process ways of relating self to other are "banished into the night," into dream experiences (1965: 606). Apart from dreams, boundaries may blur again in transference reactions and neuroses and in states of love and distress, such as melancholy or psychosis, but under normal waking circumstances, secondary process thinking is maintained, and the integrity of the self-system is preserved.[2]

Object-relations theorists complicate this picture considerably (Greenberg and Mitchell 1983).[3] Melanie Klein, W. R. D. Fairbairn, D. W. Winnicott, and Heinz Kohut, among others, all presume a more fluid boundary between self and other, and they all emphasize the extent to which our internalized representations of ourselves in interaction with others—whether based on actual interactions or imagined ones—influence our actions in, and reactions to, the world. Yet even Winnicott (1996), with his notions of "transitional" objects and spaces, seems to assume that there are in fact self-other boundaries that become established between people, which then allow for or require the development of transitional spaces between them.

In contrast to these perspectives, Hans Loewald (2000), who studied philosophy with Martin Heidegger before becoming a physician and psychoanalyst, takes a more phenomenological approach to the self-other conundrum: rather than posit that a relatively firm boundary between self and other becomes established at some point in life which we must then imagine becoming occasionally blurred or broken later on, he presumes an integrated phenomenal field that exists throughout life. Loewald's ideas about the self-other relationship are scattered throughout his many writings, and I cannot do justice to them in a short chapter. But many of them are especially clear and prominent in his paper, "Ego and Reality" (2000). Like many psychoanalysts prior to the writings of Heinz Kohut, Loewald adopts Freud's use of the term "ego" to refer to reality-oriented aspects of personality organization, many of which are conscious but some of which, such as the deployment of defense mechanisms, are unconscious. While there are differences in the way psychoanalytic writers use the terms "ego" and "self," there is much overlap in their usage as well, especially in contemporary psychoanalysis. For my purposes here, I think it is fair for readers to substitute "self" for "ego" in the passages from Loewald I quote below. With regard to the earliest stages of self-development, Loewald writes:

> … we know from considering the development of the ego [read self] as a development away from primary narcissism, that to start with, reality is not outside, but is contained in the pre-ego of primary narcissism, and becomes as Freud says, detached from the ego. So that reality,

understood genetically, is not primarily outside and hostile, alien to ego, but intimately connected with and originally not even distinguished from it.

(2000: 8)

Put another way:

...This state of affairs can be expressed either by saying that "the ego detaches itself from the external world," or, more correctly: the ego detaches from itself an outer world. Originally the ego contains everything.... In other words, the psychological constitution of ego and outer world go hand in hand....

(2000: 5)

Thus far, these ideas are very close to the ones Freud sketches out in the early pages of *Civilization and Its Discontents*, where he notes that the earliest stages of self development may be characterized by "oceanic" feelings deriving from the incomplete separation of self from surrounding world (Freud 1961: 11–20). But it is Loewald's view that the self-other relationship remains highly dynamic and mutually constitutive throughout life and that its earliest stages of development may coexist with later stages that distinguishes him from many other psychoanalytic observers, including Freud, and that links him to the phenomenological tradition:

I mentioned earlier that Freud has raised the problem of psychological survival of earlier ego stages side by side with later stages of ego development, a problem he says has as yet hardly been investigated. If we look closely at people we can see that it is not merely a question of survival of former stages of ego-reality integration, but that people shift considerably, from day to day, at different periods in their lives, in different moods and situations, from one such level to other levels. In fact, it would seem that the more alive people are (though not necessarily more stable), the broader their range of ego-reality levels is. Perhaps the so-called fully developed, mature ego is not one that has become fixated at the presumably highest level or latest stage of development, having left the others behind it, but is an ego that integrates its reality in such a way that the earlier and deeper levels of ego-reality integration remain alive as dynamic sources of higher organization.

(2000: 20)

Loewald is arguing here that what has usually been thought of as "ego" or "self" is an active construction that can only become articulated or meaningful in relation to something that is organized as not-self. Initially we *are* our objects, and they *are* us (cf. Mitchell 2000: 39–44). As we interact with other people and objects and become more familiar with them, and in the case of other people, become actively socialized by them, we become more so-phisticated at differentiating the phenomenal field, at distinguishing ourselves from other people and things and other things and people from ourselves. But these separations and distinctions are only temporal reorganizations of an integrated field (cf. Throop 2003) and so may become less differentiated at times, reverting back to previous organizations or shift to other differenti-ated states. From this perspective, identifications and internalizations are not a "taking inside" of that which is outside and projections a "throwing out" of that which is inside, but a temporary relaxing or stiffening of differentiation of the phenomenal field linking self and not-self brought about by situational events and by emotionally charged interactions with particular others. This is reminiscent of Devereux's reminder that "since it [ego] is defined as *being* a boundary, it cannot, at the same time, also *have* a boundary and especially not a boundary that can be 'ruptured'" (Devereux 1967: 321; emphasis in original). Rather, "One must stress once more that [ego], when defined in this manner, is not simply 'mobile.' It is *actually* created at each instant. It can, therefore, have no a priori locus nor genuine 'metrical' properties" (324; emphasis in original).

What is especially notable here is Loewald's claim that such fluidity of self-other organization throughout life is not necessarily regressive or deleterious, though of course it may be, but rather that it may actually be an indication of emotional health and maturity.

From Ghosts to Ancestors

In one of Loewald's most widely cited articles (2000),[4] "On the Therapuetic Action of Psychoanalysis," he discusses the centrality and importance of trans-ference in human life. By transference he means not only the way self-bound-aries are relaxed and reorganized in interaction with others, the conventional psychoanalytic sense, but also the way the less conscious or unconscious, less organized, more emotionally charged, imaginal, and atemporal parts of self-organization come to infuse and animate the more highly organized, conscious parts of self. And in turn, how more highly organized parts of self-organization come to give form, meaning, and articulation to parts that are less well organized. Such "transference" or communication among different parts of the self-system and between the self and other people and objects is critical, he argues, for the linking of past to present and future, of memory to perception, and of emotion and motivation to action and behavior. When such linkage or communication breaks down, we can become haunted by the "ghosts" of the less conscious parts of our minds pressing for recognition and articulation, in the form of recurring memories and dreams, somatic symp-toms, anxiety, depression, and so on.

Loewald borrows the idea of the ghosts of the unconscious from Freud who in Chapter 7 of *The Interpretation of Dreams* likens the persistence of unconscious wishes to the ghosts of the underworld in the Odyssey: "If I may use a simile, they [unconscious wishes] are only capable of annihilation in the same sense as the ghosts in the underworld of the Odyssey—ghosts which awoke to new life as soon as they tasted blood" (Freud 1965: 592n1). Indeed, as Loewald suggests below, psychoanalysis as a form of therapy is predicated upon evoking the ghosts of the unconscious so that they may be brought into the light of day; that is, integrated with higher levels of self-organization:

> The transference neurosis, in the technical sense of the establishment and resolution of it in the analytic process, is due to the blood of recognition, which the patient's unconscious is given to taste so that the old ghosts may reawaken to life. Those who know ghosts tell us that they long to be released from their ghost life and led to rest as ancestors. As ancestors, they live forth in the present generation, while as ghosts they are compelled to haunt the present generation with their shadow life. Transference is pathological insofar as the unconscious is a crowd of ghosts, and this is the beginning of the transference neurosis in analysis: ghosts of the unconscious, imprisoned by defenses and symptoms, are allowed to taste blood, are let loose. In the daylight of analysis the ghosts of the unconscious are laid and led to rest as ancestors whose power is taken over and transformed into the newer intensity of present life, of the secondary process and contemporary objects.
>
> (2000: 249)

Selfscapes: The Interface of Embodied Memories and Social Contingency

Loewald's use of the term "transference" to refer to aspects of both self-other interactions and to intraself organization and communication is meant to suggest the overall fluidity and complexity of self-other organization throughout life. It points to a sense of self-awareness that arises at the interface of self-system-worldly interactions and embodied memories and emotions and that is contingent upon contexts of both space and time. This conceptualization of transference and self-awareness is more fluid and context-dependent than was Freud's, and yet like Freud, given Loewald's primary focus on psychoanalytic interests and concerns, it is a conceptualization that tips on the side of intraself organization and so undertheorizes the variability and contingency of the social world that interacts with and partially shapes the intraself organization of memory and emotion.

Elsewhere (Hollan 2003b, 2004, 2005a, 2008, 2009), I have used the term "selfscapes" in an attempt to right this balance (cf. Ewing 1990).[5] A selfscape, in my terminology, drawing on Damasio's (1994, 1999, 2010) work on embodied mind and emotion, is the self system's implicit moment by moment mapping of its own representations of its own past embodied experiences onto the space and time of the contemporary culturally constituted world. The "-scape" part of the term refers to both the intraself and extraself terrains that the self system simultaneously maps and represents during the course of a day and night—the mapping continues at night during sleep, especially in the form of dreams[6]—and from which a contingent and dynamic sense of self emerges moment by moment. It gives due weight to the influence of embodied emotion and memory on an emerging sense of self-awareness but also due weight to the varieties and contingencies of the social, cultural, and political scapes (cf. Appadurai 1996) within which the body and self-system are deeply embedded and which are constantly perturbing and influencing aspects of self-organization.

The "self" part of the term is meant to underscore that though the body-mind is highly dependent on its transactions with the world, a distinction between one's own bodily organism and body-mind and all other objects in the world, however variable and contingent, is a given throughout life. At a time in the social sciences when intersubjectivities and boundary cross-ings of all kinds are being emphasized, it is important to remember that the dynamic, looping, recursive, autopoietic interplay of the phenomenal field maintains distinctions between self and other that though open to and dependent upon intersubjective influence, nevertheless produces and regu-lates an internal typology and organization (Thompson 2007). It is these persisting, even if highly variable and dynamic, distinctions between self and other that enable all humans everywhere to develop moral societies in which actors can be and are held accountable for at least some of their behaviors (Hallowell 1955). And it is these persisting distinctions between self and other that may eventuate in what I will later refer to as states of "cosubjectivity," in which the copresence of people stimulate a cascade of memories and emotions in those copresent, but when these subjective stir-rings, both conscious and unconscious, remain largely invisible, hidden, or obscure from one coparticipant to another. Such states remind us, I will argue, that basic intersubjective processes such as joint attention, mutual eye gaze, and emotional attunement may eventuate not only in overlapping aspects of experience and subjectivity among those copresent, but also in people *mis*perceiving and *mis*understanding one another, even in the ab-sence of overt conflict.

The concept of selfscapes is, then, a bridging and integrating concept that is meant to capture both the integrity of self-systems and their experiential accretions over time and also their contingency and looping dynamism in relation to their transactions with the world (Hollan 2012a). In what follows, I use it and Loewald's ideas about transference to specify why and how a particular Toraja man comes to reexperience a dream in a particular way at a particular moment in time. Through this exercise, I also demonstrate in a more general way the mutual relevance of phenomenological and psycho-dynamic ideas for anthropological analysis (cf. Good 2012a; Hollan 2012a; Jackson 2012).

Ghosts and Ancestors in Toraja, South Sulawesi, Indonesia

In "On the Therapeutic Action of Psychoanalysis," Loewald alludes to cultures he has experienced or read about that distinguish between ghosts and ancestral spirits as two different types of numinous beings, though he gives no hint of which cultures he actually has in mind. He implies that such beliefs reflect something important about how various parts of the mind come to be organized and related to one another, and yet, given his particular interests and objectives, he does not explore the converse: the way these very same cultural beliefs and practices not only reflect but also shape and mediate the self-other relationship and the psychodynamic processes that are related to it—issues that I examine in the following sections.

Loewald could easily have been referring to the Toraja of the highlands of South Sulawesi, Indonesia, when discussing "those who know" ghosts and ancestors. Although the vast majority of Toraja now consider themselves to be Christians, at the time of my primary fieldwork there in the 1980s and 1990s, many of their ideas about how the human soul or spirit passes through life and into death and the afterlife were influenced by beliefs and practices that long predated the arrival of the first Dutch missionaries in the early 1900s. For example, most of the rural villagers that Wellenkamp and I came to know intimately (Hollan 1996; Hollan and Wellenkamp 1994, 1996) believed that people were born with a spirit or soul, most often referred to as *bombo*, that remains with a person throughout life, becoming detached from the body only occasionally in dreams or as a result of severe startle or shock, and then finally and completely at death. Like the cultures that Loewald alludes to, there was a notion that the spirit of a recently deceased person hovered near its corpse, remaining restless and potentially harmful to the living, until it was ushered into the afterworld through the performance of appropriate mortuary rites, usually including the sacrifice of chickens, pigs, and buffalo. Once these rites had been completed, people could begin to refer to the spirit as an "ancestral" spirit or *nene'*, which is also the term used to refer to people who have become grandparents or great-grandparents. Nene' were thought to watch over their living descendants, occasionally visiting them in their dreams, delivering blessings or misfortunes, depending upon whether the living had been fulfilling their obligations to family and ancestors or neglecting them. Thus the living slowly socialized and domesticated the bombo into their proper role as ancestral spirits who were entitled to certain rights and offerings vis-à-vis the living while ancestral spirits, in turn, encouraged the living to honor their obligations toward the recently deceased and other ancestral and numinous beings. Through this mutual socialization process, bombo were transformed from the restless, mysterious, haunting, and uncontrollable "ghosts" that Loewald refers to into "ancestral" figures, the nene', with whom the living had a more conventionalized and predictable relationship.

Culture, Experience, and Psychodynamics

But how were such ideas about bombo and nene' actually lived and experienced by people, and what can that tell us about the actualization and variability of human selfscapes? To consider this, let me now turn to an encounter I once had with Nene'na Limbong, a relatively wealthy,[7] high-status elder in the village where Jane Wellenkamp and I worked in Toraja in the 1980s. Near the end of a series of person-centered interviews[8] with Nene'na Limbong, I am asking him about his dream experiences (see Hollan 2003a), knowing that many Toraja consider certain types of dreams to be prophetic. He tells me about a number of these prophetic-type dreams he has had, many of which, according to his interpretations, that have foretold his ability to survive serious threats to his social, political, or physical well-being, including a threat of violence during a period of political unrest in Sulawesi, the serious challenges of maintaining his social reputation through the hosting and financing of large and expensive community feasts, and a prolonged and life-threatening illness. I then get more pointed and ask if he has ever dreamed of his parents or any other deceased relatives, knowing that such dreams are supposed to be a common experience. He responds immediately with a very detailed and emotionally charged account of a dream in which his father attacks him and attempts to drag him off to the afterworld. He recalls how terrified he was, since he knew the living cannot survive in the afterworld and how he struggled to escape.

> One time I dreamed that my dead father came and tried to take me away with him! He came to me and said that he wanted to take me because my time in the village was up and I had to go. I said, "I don't want to go!" But he grabbed my arms and tried to take me. He said, "I must take you." But I said that I didn't want to go. "It's not time for me to follow you!" But he grabbed my arms and tried to take me. I struggled with him and he tried to grab me. I was sitting in front of the rice barn, but he dragged me away. But I continued to struggle. As he dragged me by the front of the house [directly opposite the rice barn], I wrapped my legs around a stone and held on. Then I was able to pull my arms away and I ran! After that, my father left and I didn't see him again.

He tells the story as if he was living through it again, his voice quivering with fear and his gestures used to suggest and mime the unfolding action. At the end of the story, it was important for him I understand that though the dream, in his interpretation, foretold his death, he was able to change its prophecy by sacrificing a pig to his father's spirit, thus satiating his father's hunger for food and human companionship and returning him to his rightful home in the afterworld.

What was going on here? Nene'na Limbong remembered the dream as vividly as he did, in part, because at the time he recounted this dream, dream experiences in Toraja and the spirits that sometimes appeared in them were thought to be "real." He did not, then, recount an imaginary experience, from his point of view, but an actual one in which he very nearly lost his life. As he narrated the dream, he was absorbed by it, almost as if he was beginning to re-experience his father's attack, not simply recount it. What was previously a part of his latent memory and imagination was being re-experienced as something very present and outside of his self-conscious control. From the quotation above, we can see his "utterance meaning ... evolving over interactional time as an interpretive process" (Ochs 2012: 154). As Ochs notes, "ordinary co-narration ... can wander all over the temporal map and transport interlocutors into zones of the moral imaginary that are unexpected and at times startling" (2012a: 155). Although our conversation began with my asking about past dream experiences, it ended with Nene'na Limbong experiencing and expressing fear and anxiety in the here and now. What was promoting this temporal wandering, or "transference" or "linkage," in Loewald's terms, between implicit and explicit memory, between the self as narrator of past experience and the experiencing self (cf. Groark 2008, 2009, 2010)?

Certainly my pointed question has a part in it. It provides a strong prompt to memories and a framework for organizing them in a culturally recognizable way. But of course Nene'na Limbong was familiar with dreams and how the Toraja conceptualized and experienced them long before I came on the scene. He would have been aware at the time of dreaming that though it was common for Toraja to dream of their parents or ancestral figures, not all people had such dreams. And further, that many of those who did dream of ancestral figures, only rarely dreamed of parents or nene' actually attacking them. He would have been aware that such a dream did not happen by accident, that it must have a meaning, perhaps an ominous one, and that it would behoove him to discover what that meaning was. Which is why he did in fact seek out the counsel of a person experienced in dream interpretation who could help him see that his father's spirit needed to be placated, having been angered by the failure of Nene'na Limbong, and perhaps other members of the family, to feed and acknowledge him properly.

As Wellenkamp and I (1994, 1996) learned, this pattern of waiting for an ill omen to occur before an offering was actually made to an ancestral figure was not uncommon in Toraja in the 1980s. While in theory, many people would say or imply that offerings to the ancestors should be made on a regular and voluntary basis—most easily and readily in the context of community feasts –in practice, many people simply could not afford to make such regular offerings. They instead waited for some actual sign that a specific ancestor was in need or had been offended before making a concrete offering. Nene'na Limbong never specified to me what he thought he or his family had or had not done that had offended his father's spirit so intensely, but given that he was not a poor man by village standards, he may have worried that any stinginess on his or his family's part would have been particularly offensive to his father. Or, if stinginess was not involved, then he likely worried that any other offense committed, whatever it might have been, was particularly egregious. Nene'na Limbong's worry or concern about the intensity of his dead father's anger would only have been amplified by the fact his father had himself been a high-status person in life whose spirit would have expected the kind of deference and respect worthy of an elevated social position.

From the point of view of cultural phenomenology, we can see that Nene'na Limbong's experience, memory, and narration of the dream is inconceivable without this cultural orientation and structuring. Indeed, one of the reasons he remembers the dream at all (or any of his other dreams for that matter) is for the simple reason that the Toraja considered them to be meaningful, possibly prophetic, and so worthy of attention. This orientation very likely increased the emotional, imaginal, and memory-making impact of the dream as dreamt (cf. Kracke 1979, 1981, 1987; Laughlin 2011; Lohmann 2003, 2010; Mageo 2003), but it certainly increased the likelihood that it would be remembered post dreaming experience and carried into the future. It also helps to explain why Nene'na Limbong as the narrator of the dream begins to experience the dream as if it were happening again because in the Toraja phenomenology of dreams, the past *is* the present in the sense that the father's spirit has not gone anywhere. It is just as "alive" and present and capable of taking offense and attacking Nene'na Limbong at the dream's telling as it was when the dream was first experienced. The narrating of the dream triggers Nene'na Limbong's latent awareness of the continuing presence of his father's spirit, which in turn infuses his "memory" of the dream with immediacy and emotional force. In Loewald's terminology, aspects of explicit self and memory become experientially linked with more implicit, less conscious aspects; an ancestor becomes partially ghostly once again. So while the cultural and phenomenological field shapes a certain type of dream experience for Nene'na Limbong, the emotionally charged memory of that experience then orients him to the social and cultural surround in a particular way, making him more sensitive to some stimuli and engagements than others (see also Hollan 2012a), such as my pointed questions about his prior dream experiences.

But there are aspects to this dream, its narration, and its reexperience that remain obscure unless we know more about the particularities of Nene'na Limbong's previous life experiences and the psychodynamics they engender. For example, as I mentioned above, though many people dreamed of their deceased parents and relatives during my fieldwork, Nene'na Limbong was the only one I knew of who had dreamed of being physically attacked by a nene'. More typically, ancestral spirits expressed their displeasure in dreams by stealing or destroying dreamers' valued possessions (or their symbolic representations) or by causing their domestic animals or crops to become sick or die. Such dreams did not fool anyone: people knew what they "really" meant and that their portents were ominous. But the indirect expression of displeasure and hostility was more in keeping with the prevailing cultural ethos, which emphasized emotional control and discretion (Hollan 1992). So the direct attack on Nene'na Limbong stands out in a dramatic way. The father's spirit is not just angry, he is angry enough to kill Nene'na Limbong, by dragging him away to the afterworld. What accounts for such open expression of hostility?

Nene'na Limbong was cautious in discussing his father with me. When I asked during the interviews what his childhood and upbringing had been like, he reported that his father had hit him occasionally, but he wanted me to understand that the blows were not meant to hurt or injure him, but only to discipline him. At other times, though, he described his father as a "skilled" or "professional" angry person and mentioned that his mother would plead with his father not to get so upset and angry with people. He also wanted me to know how he differed from his father: while he, Nene'na Limbong, might talk harshly or angrily to people, the way his father used to do, it was only for rhetorical or strategic purposes. In his heart, he still felt love or compassion for people, implying that his father's anger was more "real" and hurtful than his own.

While Nene'na Limbong's father might indeed have been a touchy, angry person, some of the imperviousness that Nene'na Limbong imputed to him might also have been linked to his father's relatively high social status. Especially at the time Nene'na Limbong was growing up, Toraja attempted to maintain a distinction among high-status persons, referred to as *to makaka*, common people, and lower-status, dependent people. Nene'na Limbong's father was a to makaka who owned several rice fields. Such high status and relative wealth would have "entitled" him to an authoritative attitude toward many people and would have made any impatience, demandingness, or harshness on his part difficult to challenge or even to acknowledge. By the 1980s, however, high-status privilege and impunity had eroded, in part because commoners and low-status people could by then earn money in the cash economy and themselves gain considerable status and prestige by slaughtering animals at community feasts. Nene'na Limbong's comments about the difference between his own "strategic" anger and his father's more "real" anger indirectly reference, I believe, this shift in social and political attitudes. What had once been the unquestioned rights, privileges, and attitudes of higher-status persons had become actively contested and challenged.

Nene'na Limbong mentions that his mother would attempt to protect him and others from his father's anger. There is a possibility that this protectiveness was itself something that might have angered or incited his father at times. In the dream, Nene'na Limbong is sitting in front of the rice barn before being dragged past his house, which he clings to desperately to escape his father's grasp. At this time in Toraja, both rice barns and houses were explicitly associated with women and women's work. Indeed, in certain traditional rituals, houses became the symbolic equivalent of women: they were ascribed wombs and pregnancy. Both literally and metaphorically the dream depicts a father attempting to forcibly separate a son from a domestic scene associated with women and femininity.

The dream seems to be capturing, then, the high level of acrimony that actually existed among Nene'na Limbong, his father, and other members of the family and community, perhaps exacerbated, as I have noted, by Nene'na Limbong's father's sense of entitlement as a high-status person. From a psychodynamic perspective, the strong fear that Nene'na Limbong displays in both the dream and its retelling might also be motivated by a fear of retaliation for his own anger and hostility towards his authoritative father. But whether the hostility depicted is an accurate expression of a father's ill temper and harshness towards his son, a son's indirect expression of ill temper towards his impervious father, or more probably a combination of both (cf. Hollan 2003a), its intensity and open expression are distinctive. This is important to underscore because it indicates how the particularities of people's life experiences can affect the way they engage and embody the cultural beliefs, practices, and semantic networks that mutually constitute their phenomenal worlds (Hollan 2012a). While it is true, as suggested above, that we cannot begin to understand this dream and my encounter with Nene'na Limbong without knowledge of the social, cultural, and political scapes in which it is embedded, it is equally true that their form and content could never have been predicted from that knowledge alone. Nene'na Limbong is *living* his culture in a way that is particular to the circumstances of its learning and ongoing articulation and expression. As Ochs has noted,

> ...there is a way of *living* experience that comes close to Husserl's (1991) and Gadamer's (1986) idea of experience and the life world as a process. In this perspective, semiotic enactments are temporally unfolding experiences, whose configuration at any moment is influenced by the voices, bodies, and dispositions of others present and non-present and a calculation of the situation at hand.
>
> (2012: 153; emphasis in original)

It matters, therefore, that Nene'na Limbong became exposed to ideas and experiences about deceased relatives appearing in dreams at a time when he and his own father were at odds with one another because it leads him to emotionally engage with those ideas, collapse them into himself and selfscape, in a way that is different from the way others might. This pointed, emotionally charged learning also leads him to emotionally associate, both consciously and unconsciously, a set of thoughts and images about ancestral figures that years later make his own dream image and its narration so unique, characterized by its open expression of hostility and fear.

We see, then, the circular, mutually constituting, autopoetic nature of the phenomenal field here: the preexisting cultural scapes of symbols, ideas, objects, and people shape Nene'na Limbong's sense of self and imagination in certain ways. But it is his active imagination and emotional experiencing that animates that cultural world, links and embodies its various parts in unique ways, and then represents them to the phenomenal fields of others.

But there is another ghost lurking here, namely, the transference between Nene'na Limbong and myself in a more conventional sense. As I mentioned previously, many of the dreams Nene'na Limbong recounted to me were about serious social, political, or physical threats to himself. I have no doubt these were dreams he had actually experienced, but why do these dreams come to mind in this moment and not others? Although I was much younger than Nene'na Limbong at the time of our conversations, and though I always felt fairly sheepish around him, knowing how dependent I was on him to willingly participate in interviews with me, I think I also posed a certain type of threat to him.

Nene'na Limbong was a man who had spent much of his adult life trying to retain and defend the relative wealth and high status he had inherited from his parents, and he had experienced numerous blows and setbacks in this regard. For example, as a young man, prior to War War II and the Indonesian revolution, he and many other higher-status people had allied themselves with the Dutch colonial government. Nene'na Limbong was designated a "head of village" during this time, and in return for his service, he was granted several special privileges, including a certain amount of free labor from the lower status and dependent men in his area. With the arrival of the Japanese during World War II, all this began to change, however. Tainted by his relationship with the Dutch, he was relieved of his official position and privileges, and from that point on, through the revolutionary period and the eventual establishment of the Indonesian national state, never again was given a government position. Concurrently with all of this, he was seeing his social and political position eroded even further by the spread of education in Toraja. The gradual establishment of schools throughout Toraja, especially after World War II, enabled many lower-status people to educate themselves and earn money in the cash economy throughout Sulawesi and Indonesia. As I mentioned above, this cash income was then often used to gain local status and prestige back in Toraja through the conspicuous slaughter of buffalo at community feasts. By actively participating in this system of competitive slaughtering, lower-status people had come to rival, and sometimes even exceed, the status and prestige of the traditional elites. As a result of such changes in the social and political landscape, Nene'na Limbong had become quite sensitive to social slights or threats of almost any kind, fearing that his social and political position could be eroded even further.

My presence and my work in the community, I now believe, played into some those sensitivities and scapes of memory and emotion. Just by virtue of my foreignness, my own relative wealth by Toraja standards, and my residence in the village, I think I became Nene'na Limbong's unwitting rival for people's attention and deference. And my persistent, even if very respectful, requests for interviews could easily have been perceived, I now understand, as an inappropriate assertion of power and status over him—perhaps in the same way he saw the social climbing of lower-status people as an inappropriate assertion of power. There is a resonance here between the dream themes he recounts and the challenges my presence poses to him. Although I do not literally attack him the way his hungry, possessive father does in the dream, I am hungry and possessive in my own way, and I need reminding that he is a man of renown who has withstood many social and political challenges in his life, even from those as powerful as his deceased father. For a while, then, my pointed questions lead to a reorganization of the phenomenal field between Nene'na Limbong and myself such that his awareness of me is allowed to mingle with his experienced past. In turn, his experienced past comes to animate the interview situation, his enactment of social and cultural forms, and my understanding of Toraja culture and life. A particular kind of selfscape emerges at the interface of social contingency and embodied emotion and memory.

My current understanding of how my residence in Nene'na Limbong's village might have affected him developed only after my active interviews with him had ended. As Nene'na Limbong and I sat on the reed mat covering the floor of our small, two-room, split-bamboo house and I asked him about his dreams that day, I was most consciously aware of being grateful that he had come for the interview on the day and time we had agreed to[9] and that he seemed to be in a fairly good mood and engaging with me in a serious way. As he began to recount his dreams to me, I remember noticing that many of the dreams seemed to do with surviving serious challenges to himself, but my thoughts about this were certainly not as clear and well formed in that moment as they later came to be (see Hollan 2003a). When he told the dream about his father attacking him in the excited and agitated way he did, I remember feeling excited and agitated as well, though mostly from a sense of confusion about what was happening in that moment and from the surprise of seeing this usually self-possessed, stoic elder slide into a state of fear—not because I was experiencing the recall of the dream in exactly the same way Nene'na Limbong was.

I underscore this point because although Nene'na Limbong and I were engaging in an event in which we were both perturbing and affecting each other's emotions and implicit memories in the ways I have been discussing, we yet were experiencing and understanding this encounter in distinct ways. So although this moment was grounded in basic intersubjective processes of mutual orientation and attunement, it eventually led to a state of what I would refer to as "cosubjectivity." That is, our contingent copresence was stimulating certain implicit memories and emotions in each of us, but only some of these were readily apparent to each of us in that moment. We were bumping up against each other's emerging selfscapes, and each other's conscious and unconscious willingness to reveal or explore these with one another. This cosubjectivity, growing out of the "fog" of our intersubjective engagement, led not only to our growing awareness of how we were affecting and understanding one another, but also very significantly, to our growing awareness of the differences between the two of us and to the gaps in our understanding of one another.

Conclusion

Hallowell was right to emphasize the importance of culture is shaping self-awareness and experience. It matters that in a place like Toraja in the 1980s, dream experiences were valued and could be used to assume and to prove the existence of spirits and their influence on human lives. Were this not the case, Nene'na Limbong would not have dreamed about his father in the particular idiom and emotional tone in which he did, nor would he have come to articulate and experience the emotional residues of his challenging experiences in the way he did. But I think Hallowell was also right to suggest that a psychodynamic perspective could complement the cultural one. Psychodynamic theories keep us focused on how the conscious parts of ourselves are related to the less than conscious parts and how this relationship is affected by our interactions with other people. I highlight Loewald's contributions here because of his phenomenological approach to the self-other relationship, emphasizing that articulations of self and other are dynamic temporal organizations of an integrated perceptual and phenomenal field, and his contention that conscious and unconscious parts of mind and memory mutually influence and inform one another throughout life.

Metaphorically speaking, we all have "ghosts"—less conscious, less organized parts of our minds and memories—that are stirred by our interactions with other people and objects. The particularities of our culturally, socially, and politically influenced encounters with others help determine which ghosts haunt us, which are stirred in our encounters with others, and which cultural forms are used to manifest and articulate them. As Loewald suggests, without such cultural articulation and shaping, our latent minds and memories remain just that, latent and disconnected from our conscious lives, sometimes in a haunting way.[10]

But equally important is the way in which the stirrings of latent mind and memory lead us to embody, enact, animate, and ultimately transform social and cultural processes and other people in the ways we do. Social interactions of any kind, including the one that unfolded between Nene'na Limbong and myself, remain open, emergent, and never completely predictable, in part, because each of the participants brings their ghosts into them, which may be roused and brought to life by "the blood of recognition" in new interactions. This is why I have argued previously (Hollan 2000, 2012a) that the enactment of cultural forms is always a "subjectification" in Obeyesekere's use of that term (1981, 1990); that is, a refashioning of received forms through the cauldron of individual fantasy and imagination, because no enactment can escape the imprint of a person's highly particularized embodiment, memory, and imagination. Although ancestral spirits were a very common element of the Toraja behavioral environment at the time I worked with Nene'an Limbong, his experience of and interaction with them were in some ways quite specific to himself, dependent on his own unique history of embodied memory and emotion. This means that I as the anthropologist learned a particular version of the Toraja story about ancestral spirits from him, not the only or definitive story. Nene'na Limbong brought Toraja ideas about ancestral spirits "alive" in a way that was particular to his time, place, and embodied experience. The corpus of Toraja ideas and practices surrounding ancestral spirits has, in a very real sense, never been the same since then.

Here and elsewhere (Hollan 2003, 2004, 2005a, 2008, 2009), I have used the concept of "selfscapes" to help focus and articulate complementary insights from phenomenology and psychoanalysis about self processes. The notion of a selfscape is meant to suggest that human self-awareness is always contingent on a variety of "scapes" that a person simultaneously traverses and engages continuously throughout the course of a day and night. Appadurai (1996) and others have discussed some of the social and cultural scapes that people traverse and encounter in the contemporary, globalized world[11] and that may become integrated into their lifeworlds and identities. Byron Good (2012b) and colleagues (Biehl et al. 2007; DelVecchio Good et al. 2008) have added an explicitly political and power-related dimension to how these local and global scapes of knowledge, technology, ideologies, and institutions affect subjectivity and lived experience. But the concept of selfscapes ties these varieties and complexities of the social world to an equally complex and dynamic terrain of embodied memory and emotion. The social and cultural scapes that people traverse are never lived and experienced in exactly the same way by two individuals—no matter how similar their overt behavior might be—because they bring to the engagement, and simultaneously traverse, different embodied histories of memory and emotion. Nene'na Limbong's dream reports were different from those of the other Toraja I knew and interviewed because his embodied memories and emotions were different as well.

This observation should complicate considerably our notions and theories of social and ethical action,[12] since it means that we must consider how embodied memory and emotion lead actors to become engaged with the social environment not uniformly, but in particular ways. Actors act in environments not just of competing norms, values, desires, and institutions, but ones in which the people around them have been affected by, and affect, these various elements in different ways. It matters *who* one's coactors are, at the level of embodied emotion and memory, not just what statuses, roles, or norms they happen to be representing or enacting in the moment. This adds a level of complexity to action that a concept such as "habitus" misses almost entirely, implying as it does a uniformity of motivation, attitude, and proclivity that is presumed but never demonstrated. It is these often unaccounted for differences in embodied memory and emotion that helps explain why actors everywhere are not infrequently surprised or mystified by the actions and reactions of those around them, even in situations where behavior is ostensibly highly scripted or constrained, and why, as I mentioned above, action is often more emergent and unpredictable than many prevailing social theories would suggest. This perspective resonates with Ochs's observation that

> informal situations are at once regulated and emergent on-line, as it were. Even seemingly mindless conversation routines have unexpected turns and as such are "interactional achievements" ... And in informal conversation, topics [may] wander recklessly far from expectations, conflicts and misunderstandings erupt, and emotions turn hot or cold in a flash.
>
> (2012: 155)

I have suggested here one of the reasons why such unexpected turns and emotional volatility in social interaction occur: because even in the most mundane of conversations, people's "ghosts" can be roused and brought to new life by the blood of recognition in the words or manners of those with whom they interact.

Finally, at a moment in the social sciences when the *inter*subjective aspects of human behavior are so carefully noted and theorized (e.g., Duranti 2010; Jackson 1998; Toren 2000, 2009), the "self-" part of the selfscape concept is a reminder that though our consciousness and self-awareness is very much dependent on, and shaped by, our transactions with other people and the world, all humans develop and maintain, most of the time, even if only contingently, significant distinctions between them*selves* and the world around them. These range from the most passive and unconscious biological ones, such as immune response and somatic markers (Damasio 1994, 1999, 2010) of various kinds, to the most active and self-conscious ones, such as ethical decision making. This self-fashioning is surely an autopoietic one that very much depends, as I have noted several times before, on continuous transactions with the world, but which nevertheless produces and regulates its own unique typology and organization of embodied memory and emotion (Thompson 2007).

What is important to note about this is that intersubjective processes lead to autopoietic *self* formations, including existential and subjective states of apartness, separateness, alienation, and aloneness, as well as those of sharing, communion, and empathy. At some level, no matter how perturbed or influenced by others, we are all stuck with ourselves. Given this wedding of intersubjective influence and embodied emotion and memory unique to the individual, the extent to which two people actually share a state of mind or experience, no matter how intersubjectively influenced, must always remain an empirical question. Indeed, probably much more common than is generally thought, the copresence of people leads not to high degrees of intersubjective sharing per se, but to rather to moments of what I have referred to as *co*subjectivity. By cosubjectivity, I mean moments when the copresence of people stimulate, in a contingent way, a flow of memories and emotions in those copresent, but when many of these subjective stirrings remain largely invisible or hidden from one coparticipant to another. This kind of experience resembles in some ways what psychoanalysts refer to as transference and countertransference reactions, though transference and countertransference are usually thought to be almost entirely unconscious, whereas moments of cosubjectivity as I define them may include thoughts, feelings, and memories that may be fully conscious, but left unspoken and unexpressed. Such moments are important because they can have profound implications for future actions and for all the participants involved.

Most obviously, when people have strong, or even subtle, emotional reactions that we are unaware of, more times than not we end up being puzzled by their behavior, if not upset and distressed by it—as I was initially puzzled by Nene'na Limbong's display of fear and anxiety when recalling the dream of his deceased father. And of course we are all often puzzling, if not upsetting and distressing, those around us with our own unacknowledged emotional reactions. Despite our openness to others at the most basic levels of subjectivity, these moments of cosubjectivity, illustrating the ever-present contingent boundaries between ourselves and others, can be, when left unexplored and unquestioned, a major source of miscommunication and misunderstanding among people, not only in the present moment but also as they feed forward into future interactions. They suggest the limits of empathy or the barriers that empathy must transcend, even in the midst of intersubjectivity.[13] The concept of selfscapes helps us capture such complexities by drawing our attention simultaneously to the social and embodied scapes and clines from which autopoietic processes emerge.

Acknowledgments

I thank again all the Toraja people who over the years have shared their thoughts and concerns with me. I am also grateful to my three reviewers for their very helpful and constructive comments.

Notes

1   The idea that humans are born with innate capacities to orient to the people and objects about them is now widespread among ethologists, evolutionary psychologists, developmental psychologists, and neurobiologists.
2   Freud discusses the distinctions between primary and secondary process thinking throughout *The Interpretation of Dreams*, but especially in a section near the end of the book entitled, "The Primary and Secondary Processes—Repression" (1965: 635–650).
3   For an excellent introduction to object-relations theories and how they differ from "classical" psychoanalytic perspectives, see Greenberg and Mitchell (1983).
4   The psychoanalyst, Steven Mitchell (2000); the sociologist, Nancy Chodorow (1999); and the social philosopher, Jonathan Lear (2003), among others, have all drawn inspiration from this article.
5   Ewing (1990) also attempts to capture the complexity of self-processes. She notes especially the way people maintain an illusion of self-coherence and wholeness

despite rapid shifts in self-representation from context to context by utilizing certain kinds of rhetorical and defensive strategies. I admire this model, and it has influenced my thinking for over 20 years. In contrast to Ewing, though, my notion of a selfscape draws upon the work of the neuroscientist, Antonio Damasio, to suggest that certain aspects of self-processes are deeply rooted in the brain's mapping of the body as it moves through space, and that some aspects of this mapping process and its internal organization may operate fairly independently of how the self is represented to others. My emphasis on the overall dynamic nature of "self-systems" per se is also heavily influenced by Gregory Bateson's notion (1972) of an "ecology of mind" and by the concept of autopoiesis, or developmental self-fashioning, especially as developed by people like Evan Thompson (2007).

6 For more on how states of sleeping and dreaming are related to waking life and vice versa, see Hollan (2013).

7 Nene'na Limbong was a peasant farmer, like all the other people Wellenkamp and I worked with, and in his dress and daily life, he was indistinguishable from any other villager. He was "wealthy" only in the sense that he and his family owned enough of their own rice fields that they could afford to eat rice throughout the year, rather than be forced to supplement their diet with less desirable foods such as sweet potatoes and cassava, which is what most other people in the village had to do.

8 For more information about how "person-centered" interviews are conducted and their significance for the development of anthropological theory and ethnography, see Levy and Hollan (2015) and Hollan (2005b).

9 Nene'na Limbong often did not show up for the interview appointments we had scheduled or canceled them at the last minute. When he did show up as arranged, I was always very happy and relieved. Only after the interview process was completed did I come to appreciate that his unpredictability might have been an indirect way of communicating to me that I needed to know and remember my proper place: he was the high-status elder deserving of respect and deference, and I was the foreign guest *owing* respect and deference. He would cooperate with me, but in his own good time.

10 For other perspectives on how people come to be "haunted" by the past, whether through direct personal experience or in a less direct, more social and political ways, see Gordan (1997), Derrida (1994), Royle (2003), and Good (2012b).

11 Specifically, Appadurai (1996) examines "ethnoscapes," "mediascapes," "technoscapes," "financescapes," and "ideoscapes."

12 Anthropologists have recently reinvigorated the study of morality and ethics, especially from the point of view of how values and conventions actually become embodied and enacted, both consciously and unconsciously, in the everyday flow of life. See, for example, Robbins (2004), Zigon (2008), Lambek (2010), Fassin (2012), and Mattingly (2012).

13 For more on the anthropological study of empathy, see Throop and Hollan (2008), Hollan and Throop (2011), Hollan (2012b), and Hollan (2014).

References

Appadurai, A. 1996. *Modernity at Large: Cultural Dimensions of Globalization*. Minneapolis: University of Minnesota Press.

Bateson, G. 1972. *Steps to An Ecology of Mind: Collected Essays in Anthropology, Psychiatry, Evolution, and Epistemology*. Chicago: University of Chicago Press.

Biehl, J., B. Good, and A. Kleinman, eds., 2007. *Subjectivity: Ethnographic Investigations*. Berkeley: University of California Press.

Chodorow, N.J. 1999. *The Power of Feelings*. New Haven, CT: Yale University Press.

Csordas, T.J. 1994. *The Sacred Self: A Cultural Phenomenology of Charismatic Healing*. Berkeley: University of California Press.

Csordas, T.J. 2012. Psychoanalysis and Phenomenology. *Ethos* 40(1):54–74.

Damasio, A.R. 1994. *Descartes' Error: Emotion, Reason, and the Human Brain*. New York: Avon Books.

Damasio, A.R. 1999. *The Feeling of What Happens: Body and Emotion in the Making of Consciousness*. New York: Harcourt Brace.

Damasio, A.R. 2010. *Self Comes to Mind: Constructing the Conscious Brain*. New York: Pantheon Books.

DelVecchio Good, M-J., S.T. Hyde, S. Pinto, and B.J. Good, eds., 2008. *Postcolonial Disorders*. Berkeley: University of California Press.

Derrida, J. 1994. *Specters of Marx: The State of the Debt, the Work of Mourning, and the New International*. New York: Routledge.

Desjarlais, R.R. 1992. *Body and Emotion: The Aesthetics of Illness and Healing in the Nepal Himalayas*. Philadelphia: University of Pennsylvania Press.

Devereux, G. 1967. *From Anxiety to Method in the Behavioral Sciences*. The Hague, Netherlands: Mouton & Co.

Duranti, A. 2010. Husserl, Intersubjectivity, and Anthropology. *Anthropological Theory* 10(12):16–35.

Ewing, K.P. 1990. The Illusion of Wholeness: Culture, Self, and the Experience of Inconsistency. *Ethos* 18(3):251–278.

Fassin, D., ed., 2012. *A Companion to Moral Anthropology*. Malden, MA: Wiley-Blackwell.

Freud, S. 1961. *Civilization and Its Discontents*. New York: W.W. Norton and Company.

Freud, S. 1965. *The Interpretation of Dreams*. New York: Avon Books.

Gadamer, H-G. 1986 Truth and Method. J. Weinsheimer and D.G. Marshall, trans. New York: Continuum.

Good, B. 1994. *Medicine, Rationality, and Experience*. Cambridge: Cambridge University Press.

Good, B. 2012a. Phenomenology, Psychoanalysis, and Subjectivity in Java. *Ethos* 40(1):24–36.

Good, B. 2012b. Theorizing the "Subject" of Medical and Psychiatric Anthropology. *Journal of the Royal Anthropological Institute* 18(3):515–535.

Gordan, A.F. 1997. *Ghostly Matters: Haunting and the Sociological Imagination*. Minneapolis: University of Minnesota Press.

Greenberg, J.R., and S.A. Mitchell. 1983. *Object Relations in Psychoanalytic Theory*. Cambridge, MA: Harvard University Press.

Groark, K.P. 2008. Social Opacity and the Dynamics of Empathic In-Sight Among the Tzotzil Maya of Chiapas, Mexico. *Ethos* 36(4):427–448.

Groark, K.P. 2009. Discourses of the Soul: The Negotiation of Personal Agency in Tzotzil Maya Dream Narrative. *American Ethnologist* 36(4):705–721.

Groark, K.P. 2010 Willful Souls: Dreaming and the Dialectics of Self-Experience Among the Highland Maya of Chiapas, Mexico. In *Toward an Anthropology of the Will*, edited by K.M. Murphy and C.J. Throop, pp. 101–122. Palo Alto, CA: Stanford University Press.

Hallowell, A.I. 1955 The Self and Its Behavioral Environment. In *Culture and Experience*, pp. 75–110. Philadelphia: University of Pennsylvania Press.

Hollan, D. 1992. Emotion Work and the Value of Emotional Equanimity Among the Toraja. *Ethnology* 31:45–56.

Hollan, D. 1996 Cultural and Experiential Aspects of Spirit Beliefs Among the Toraja. In *Spirits in Culture, History, and Mind*, edited by J.M. Mageo and A. Howard, pp. 213–235. New York: Routledge.

Hollan, D. 2000. Constructivist Models of Mind, Contemporary Psychoanalysis, and the Development of Culture Theory. *American Anthropologist* 102:538–550.

Hollan, D. 2003a. The Cultural and Intersubjective Context of Dream Remembrance and Reporting: Dreams, Aging, and the Anthropological Encounter in Toraja, Indonesia. In *Dream Travelers: Sleep Experiences and Culture in the Western Pacific*, edited by R.I. Lohmann, pp. 169–187. New York: Palgrave.

Hollan, D. 2003b. Selfscape Dreams. In *Dreaming and the Self: New Perspectives on Subjectivity, Identity, and Emotion*, edited by J.M. Mageo, pp. 61–74. Albany: State University of New York Press.

Hollan, D. 2004. The Anthropology of Dreaming: Selfscape Dreams. *Dreaming* 14(2):170–182.

Hollan, D. 2005a. Dreaming in a Global World. In *A Companion to Psychological Anthropology*, edited by C. Casey and R.B. Edgerton, pp. 90–102. Malden, MA: Blackwell.

Hollan, D. 2005b. Setting a New Standard: The Person-Centered Interviewing and Observation of Robert I. Levy. *Ethos* 33:459–466.

Hollan, D. 2008. Selfscapes of Well-Being in a Rural Indonesian Village. In *Pursuits of Happiness: Well-Being in Anthropological Perspective*, edited by G. Mathews and C. Izquierdo, pp. 221–227. New York: Berghahn.

Hollan, D. 2009. The Influence of Culture on the Experience and Interpretation of Disturbing Dreams. *Culture, Medicine, and Psychiatry* 33(2):313–322.

Hollan, D. 2012a. On the Varieties and Particularities of Cultural Experience. *Ethos* 40(1):37–53.

Hollan, D. 2012b. Emerging Issues in the Cross-Cultural Study of Empathy. *Emotion Review* 4(1):70–78.

Hollan, D. 2013. Sleeping, Dreaming, and Health in Rural Indonesia and the Urban U.S.: A Cultural and Experiential Approach. *Social Science and Medicine* 79:23–30.

Hollan, D. 2014. Empathy and Morality in Ethnographic Perspective. In *Empathy and Morality*, edited by H. Maibom, pp. 230–250. Oxford, UK: Oxford University Press.

Hollan, D.W., and C.J. Throop, eds., 2011. *The Anthropology of Empathy: Experiencing the Lives of Others in Pacific Societies*. New York: Berghahn Books.

Hollan, D.W., and J.C. Wellenkamp. 1994. *Contentment and Suffering: Culture and Experience in Toraja*. New York: Columbia University Press.

Hollan, D.W., and J.C. Wellenkamp. 1996. *Thread of Life: Toraja Reflections on the Life Cycle*. Honolulu: University of Hawaii Press.

Husserl, E. 1991. *On the Phenomenology of the Consciousness of Internal Time (1893–1917)*. J. B. Brough, trans. Dordrecht, Netherlands: Kluwer.

Jackson, M.D., ed., 1996. *Things as They Are: New Directions in Phenomenological Anthropology*. Bloomington: Indiana University Press.

Jackson, M.D. 1998. *Minima Ethnographica: Intersubjectivity and the Anthropological Project*. Chicago: University of Chicago Press.

Jackson, M.D. 2012. Commentary: The Complementarity of Intrapsychic and Intersubjective Dimensions of Social Reality. *Ethos* 40(1):113–118.

Kracke, W.H. 1979. Dreaming in Kagwahiv: Dream Beliefs and Their Intrapsychic Uses in an Amazonian Indian Culture. *Psychoanalytic Study of Society* 8:119–172.

Kracke, W.H. 1981. Kagwahiv Mourning: Dreams of a Bereaved Father. *Ethos* 9:258–275.

Kracke, W.H. 1987. Myths in Dreams, Thought in Images: Some Amazonian Contributions to the Psychoanalytic Theory of the Primary Process. In *Dreaming: Anthropological and Psychological Interpretations*, edited by B. Tedlock, pp. 31–54. New York: Cambridge University Press.

Lambek, M, ed., 2010. *Ordinary Ethics: Anthropology, Language, Ethics*. New York: Fordham University Press.

Laughlin, C.D. 2011. *Communing With the Gods: Consciousness, Culture, and the Dreaming Brain*. Brisbane, Australia: Daily Grail Publishing.

Lear, J. 2003. *Therapeutic Action: An Earnest Plea for Irony*. New York: Other Press.

Levy, R.I., and D.W. Hollan. 2015. Person-Centered Interviewing and Observation in Anthropology. In *Handbook of Methods in Cultural Anthropology*, 2nd edition, edited by H. Russell Barnard and C.C. Gravlee, pp. 313–342. Lanham, MD: Rowman and Littlefield.

Loewald, H.W. 2000. *The Essential Loewald: Collected Papers and Monographs*. Hagerstown, MD: University Publishing Group.

Lohmann, R.I., ed., 2003. *Dream Travelers: Sleep Experiences and Culture in the Western Pacific*. New York: Palgrave.

Lohmann, R.I., ed., 2010. How Evaluating Dreams Makes History: Asabano Examples. *History and Anthropology* 21(3):227–249.

Mageo, J.M., ed., 2003. *Dreaming and the Self: New Perspectives on Subjectivity, Identity, and Emotion*. Albany: State University of New York Press.

Mattingly, C. 2012. Two Virtue Ethics and the Anthropology of Morality. *Anthropological Theory* 12(2):161–184.

Mitchell, S.A. 2000. *Relationality: From Attachment to Intersubjectivity*. Hillsdale, NY: Analytic Press.

Obeyesekere, G. 1981. *Medusa's Hair: An Essay on Personal Symbols and Religious Experience*. Chicago: University of Chicago Press.

Obeyesekere, G. 1990. *The Work of Culture*. Chicago: University of Chicago Press.

Ochs, E. 2012. Experiencing Language. *Anthropological Theory* 12(2):142–160.

Robbins, J. 2004. *Christianity and Moral Torment in a Papua New Guinea Society*. Berkeley: University of California Press.

Royle, N. 2003. *The Uncanny*. Manchester, UK: Manchester University Press.

Thompson, E. 2007. *Mind in Life: Biology, Phenomenology, and the Sciences of Mind*. Cambridge, MA: Harvard University Press.

Throop, C.J. 2003. On Crafting a Cultural Mind: A Comparative Assessment of Some Recent Theories of "Internalization" in Psychological Anthropology. *Transcultural Psychiatry* 40:109–139.

Throop, C.J. 2010. *Suffering and Sentiment: Exploring the Vicissitudes of Experience and Pain in Yap*. Berkeley: University of California Press.

Throop, C.J. 2012. On Inaccessibility and Vulnerability: Some Horizons of Compatibility between Phenomenology and Psychoanalysis. *Ethos* 40(1):75–96.

Throop, C.J., and D.W. Hollan, eds., 2008. Whatever Happened to Empathy? Special Issue. *Ethos* 36(4):385–489.

Toren, C. 2000. Mind and Inter-Subjectivity: An Anthropological Perspective. *Journal of Intelligent Systems* 10(1):1–25.

Toren, C. 2009. Intersubjectivity as Epistemology. *Social Analysis* 53(2):130–146.

Willen, S.S., and D. Seeman. 2012. Introduction: Experience and Inquietude. *Ethos* 40(1):1–23.

Winnicott, D.W. 1996. *Playing and Reality*. New York: Routledge Press.

Zigon, J. 2008. *Morality: An Anthropological Perspective*. London: Berg.

9 Relational, but Also Singular

On the Varieties and Particularities of Selfscapes

Let me begin by posing a bit of a thought experiment: Do you know whether I dreamed last night, and if I did, how that dream might be affecting my sense of self as I begin to write this chapter? If you are neurobiologically inclined, you are probably guessing that I must have dreamed something last night, since that is what most mammals do when they sleep, even if I might not remember today what I was dreaming last night. If you are more culturally inclined, you might be tempted to guess that whatever I might have been dreaming last night, it was likely greatly influenced by my social and cultural world, both in terms of who and what I was dreaming about, as well as the likelihood that I would consciously remember what I was dreaming or not. You might surmise that most people tend to dream, either literally or symbolically, about the most "important" people in their lives, as socially and culturally determined, and about the scenarios, or imagined scenarios, in which they could be entangled with those people, including the many potential conflicts and contradictions that could arise within them (Mageo and Sheriff 2021). You might also guess that I would be more likely to remember and pay attention to my dreams, affecting my sense of self in a more conscious and significant way, if my social world took dreams seriously and offered me ways of interpreting them (Kracke 1979, 1981), including whether some of them might be considered prophetic of my future life and well-being.

So far, so good. But at this point, let us complicate things a bit further. Suppose I confirm for you that I dreamed of my deceased father last night, someone who had and has great significance in my life. When he was alive, my father and I had a complicated, and at times, troubled relationship. I not only admired him greatly but was also wary of him. He was an unbending man who could hold very critical, harsh views of anyone, including me, who disagreed with him about what he considered to be significant matters. Although I wear the watch he took off his wrist and gave to me just before he died, and although I think about him in some way almost every day, I rarely remember a dream about him, so that when I do remember such a dream, the dream always catches my attention and I wonder, why this dream now?

It is at this point that the social and cultural analysis of my dream begins to reach its limits. Even if you knew exactly what I dreamed about my father

DOI: 10.4324/9781003529118-11

last night, and even if you had guessed or investigated my social background and thought you knew something, or even a great deal, about father–son relationships in people from my background, you would not know how I *experience* my father and the dreams I have of him and how they affect my sense of myself. If you knew I had four siblings (one deceased), you might think that they could give you some insight into the kind of relationship I had with my father, since we all lived together in the same house with him for many years, my two brothers and I sharing one small bedroom, but you would be getting some version of how *they* experienced me and my father, not *my* experience of *my* father. As the middle child of five children and as the middle son of three sons, both of whom had even more troubled relationships with my father than I did, I had my own particular experiences of and with my father that were quite singular and distinct from any of my other siblings, even within this small monocultural, monolingual nuclear family. Although we all shared a common biological progenitor, from an experiential point of view, my siblings' father was not *my* father. *My* father is mine alone and you can get a glimpse of him and his impact on me only if I am moved to share or say something about him, as I have done above.

The point of this brief exercise is to suggest that while my consciousness of myself is entangled with the material, social, and cultural world from the moment of its inception, once in existence, I have been involved in a process of autopoiesis in which my selective memories of, actions in, and emotional associations and reactions to the world, some of which are completely unconscious, have been developing and maintaining a boundary or separation among *myself*, *my* experiences, and *my* consciousness and everything else in my world that does not have the imprint of my consciousness. This boundary is surely a selectively porous, permeable, dynamic, and evolving one, as is true of all autopoietic processes (Thompson 2007), in which the "moulding [sic]" of the boundary by past experience (James 2021: 100) comes to influence what is allowed or likely to be experienced in the future.[1] But it is a boundary nonetheless, and one that separates *my* thoughts, *my* experiences, and *my* awareness of *myself* from yours and from all other forms of consciousness in the world. This is the point that William James underscores in Chapter 9 of *The Principles of Psychology*, in which he notes the "absolute insulation" (James 2021: 97) of one person's thoughts and consciousness from those of any other person or consciousness—unless of course they are disclosed to others either explicitly or implicitly. Each mind,

> keeps its own thoughts to itself. There is no giving or bartering between them. No thought even comes into direct *sight* of a thought in another personal consciousness than its own. Absolute insulation, irreducible pluralism, is the law. It seems as if the elementary psychic fact were not *thought* or *this thought* or *that thought*, but *my thought*, every thought being owned. Neither contemporaneity, nor proximity in space, nor similarity of quality and content are able to fuse thoughts together which

are sundered by this barrier of belonging to different personal minds. The breaches between such thoughts are the most absolute breaches in nature.

(James 2021, 97, emphasis in original)

James notes that *our* thoughts and memories have a "warmth," "intimacy," and "immediacy" to them that dearly distinguish them from anyone else's thoughts and memories (James 2021: 102). We may have knowledge or conceptions of other people's thoughts, memories, and feelings, but we do not have *felt* ownership of them, as we do our own.

Consciousness of ourselves, then, while always entangled with the world it both reflects and co-creates, is also quite singular and "insulated," to use James's language. It is this insularity, with the imaginative capacities it both affords and amplifies, that helps explain how and why people are affected differently by, and so react differently to, similar circumstances. The slippage between received circumstances and the personal experience *of* such circumstances also accounts for much of the pluralism of the world, according to James, and for the inevitable transformation of social, cultural, and institutional forms as they are interpreted, enacted, and lived anew by different individuals (Hollan 2012; Obeyesekere 1981, 1990). None of us come at the world and experience it as blank slates. No one simply internalizes and then reproduces the world they find around them (Strauss and Quinn 1996). We are historical creatures and our histories matter in how we come to experience and interpret the circumstances around us.

I underscore James's views on the insular aspects of self-consciousness, as a few others have recently[2] (Chodorow 2020; Kirschner 2019, 2020; Strawson 2017), to counterbalance the contemporary move toward a strong relational perspective on self-experience, one in which almost any notion of a private, singular, or insulated self is thought to be illusory or an artifact of Western "individualism."[3] As I have suggested elsewhere (Hollan 2012; Hollan 2022), it is clear from James's overall work that he is not naively romanticizing the concept, philosophy, or psychology of "the individual," nor is he claiming that experience is sealed within an isolated mind. Rather, he is merely drawing attention to the existential fact that things happen to one person that do not happen to another and that this difference in happenings continues to leave its mark on the way people experience and interpret the world. As James remarks,

No two of us have identical difficulties, nor should we be expected to work out identical solutions. Each, from his [sic] own angle of observation, takes in a certain sphere of fact and trouble, which each must deal with in a unique manner ... Each attitude being a syllable in human nature's message, it takes the whole of us to spell the meaning out completely.

(1982[1902]: 487)

Even with this singularity of "attitude," however, no human conscious-ness exists apart from the material, social, and cultural worlds from which it emerges and with which it is always entangled. The recursive processes involved in autopoiesis result in selves that have their own, unique internal topography and functional boundaries, but they would not have emerged without those material and social worlds and they die when no longer im-mersed within them. The semipermeable boundaries of selves mean that they are *both* relationally constituted and maintained *and* unique and singular at the same time. Both things are true of all selves all the time, though, at any given moment, selves are more or less reacting to the world or more or less acting in and on the world.

Varieties and Particularities of Selfscapes

Consciousness of self emerges and maintains itself in the material, symbolic, and imaginative space between body and world, I use the concept of "selfs-capes" to gesture toward this space (Hollan 2008, 2014). Drawing on Dama-sio's extensive work on embodied mind and emotion (1994, 1999, 2010), a selfscape is the emerging self-system's implicit moment by moment mapping of its own representations of its own past embodied experiences onto the space and time of the contemporary socially, culturally, and politically consti-tuted world. The "-scape" part of the term refers to both the intraself topogra-phy and other-than-self terrains that the self-system *simultaneously* navigates, maps, and represents during the course of a day and night—the mapping continues at night, especially in the form of dreams (Hollan 2003, 2005, 2017), as the example of my own dream above is meant to suggest—and from which a contingent and dynamic sense of self emerges moment by moment. The mapping is not only a complex and dynamic one in which contemporary experience of the world and received circumstances may reshape a person's topography of memory and emotional proclivities, but also one in which the reverse may occur. A person's experientially acquired ways of perceiving and interpreting may impose themselves on the world, transforming and reshap-ing that world, and becoming a significant part of the social ecology that others must contend with.

The notion of selfscapes, then, is a bridging concept meant to capture the integrity of self systems, not only their singularity of "attitude" and relative insularity, from a Jamesian point of view, but also their contingency and looping dynamism in relation to their entanglements with the world. While such a concept allows us to consider the porosity of selves (Throop 2017), and the many ways they are shaped and influenced by their entanglements with the world, it is also meant to underscore the slippage between received circumstances and the personal experience *of* those circumstances that I emphasized above. It is this slippage, related to the fact that the prior expe-riences of uniquely situated persons always affect their current and future experience, that makes any notion of "conventional" behavior so suspect, since overt behavior that appears conventional and common from the third-person point of view may yet be experienced and thought and imagined about quite differently by the people who are enacting those behaviors. There is a perceptual, imaginative, and symbolic gratuitousness to human experience (Rapport 2008) that far exceeds the limited forms of overt behavior we actually observe and which greatly expands upon and refashions the always limited and finite material and symbolic resources from which it emerges. In the remainder of the chapter, I use ethnographic and clinical examples from Indonesia and the United States to illustrate both the relational and singular aspects of selfscapes, but I emphasize how even those embedded within the same local world may yet experience and react to that world in unique ways.

An Earnest Man in Toraja

When I got to know Nene'na Tandi in the 1980s and 1990s, he was an older man in his 60s, living in a remote mountaintop village in rural Toraja on the island of Sulawesi in eastern Indonesia. Like most other villagers living in this area, he was a wet rice farmer living just above the subsistence level, worried about whether he would harvest enough rice to last through the year. And like many other people there, he was attempting to find a middle ground between the demands and expectations of traditional Toraja culture, including the competitive slaughtering of pigs and buffalo at elaborate funeral ceremonies, and the more "modern" teachings and lifestyle of Christianity as passed down by Dutch missionaries in the 1920s and 1930s, including the increasing value placed on education, whether actually affordable for most people or not. Like most other Toraja as well, he was concerned by the increasing outmigration of young people to other parts of Indonesia for work and education, and by his minority, and sometimes stigmatized, status as a member of a traditional and Christianizing group of people in a province and nation that was dominated by Muslim groups and institutions.

In all of these ways, Nene'na Tandi was a fairly typical Toraja elder in the village where I lived and worked, entangled with and enacting the social, cultural, and political world he had been born into at a particular moment in Indonesian history, And yet he was also identified by himself, by his fellow Toraja, and by me as being someone who was exceptional in many ways. For one, he was a gifted orator and communicator, not only someone who was capable of making even the most grim of people laugh, but also someone who was well known for offering "sweet" words of comfort and support to those going through hard times, even to people who might not have deserved such empathy from a conventional Toraja point of view. Such rhetorical skills made him a much more influential person than his commoner background and lack of education would otherwise have warranted, and because of this, he had become a person to be reckoned with on almost any issue of consequence in the village.

But his reputation as a clever, entertaining, outspoken person was balanced by an earnestness he had about the importance of valuing and respecting what the ancestors and God considered to be proper and moral ways of living. He would often say that the advice of the ancestors and wise elders was like "gold," its value unrivaled by anything else in a person's life, and he often gave his own advice to people freely, whether they had asked for it or not. Given Nene'na Tandi's outgoing and rambunctious nature, I was initially puzzled by this earnestness, which I eventually came to understand better only after a long series of open-ended interviews with him about his past and current life experience.[4]

In his own telling, Nene'na Tandi had been a very wild youth, strong-willed, and defiant. He knew in theory, and from his elders' teachings and admonitions, that God and the ancestors were watching over him and would reward him for proper behavior and punish him for improper, but in William James's terms (2013: 21), he had not yet experienced the "truth" of those beliefs, they made no "practical difference" for him, Rather, because he was enjoying his misbehavior and had not yet suffered any negative consequences for it, he was becoming more and more transgressive, up until the point his family finally ran out of patience with him and exiled him to a distant village. A true act of desperation on his family's part, given how much Toraja love and value children and consider them to be essential social and economic assets.

Yet even after being sent away, Nene'na Tandi said he remained defiant. As soon as he found an opportunity, and against his parents' wishes, he left his first wife and joined a group of young men heading to New Guinea to find employment. Once there, however, he quickly discovered that New Guinea would not be the haven he had hoped for. Almost immediately upon disembarking, he fell seriously ill with malaria, and then struggled to find work. He remembered being hungry for days on end, and fearing that he might actually starve. It was during this troubling, despairing time that he began to comprehend and accept what his elders had always told him: that God and the ancestors were keeping score and would eventually punish those who defied their ways, especially those like himself who consciously and knowingly defied their ways. He feared that these spiritual forces would allow him to die far away from home and family, and he was enormously relieved when a ship's captain took pity on him and offered him free passage back to Sulawesi. When he returned to Toraja, he said he was a changed man. He moved back to his home village, he married a woman his parents approved of, he began to work the family's rice fields and gardens, and he eventually became the respected elder that I knew and interviewed. This return to the fold did not solve all Nene'na Tandi's problems, however. Over the years, Nene'na Tandi discovered that he was unable to have his own biological children, which was very distressing for him, given the importance of having children I mentioned above. To the end of his life, he worried that his difficulty having children was a spiritual or ancestral retribution for all the trouble and harm he had caused people as a youth.

One can see here how Nene'na Tandi was taking in his own "sphere of fact and trouble" from the world around him and developing a certain "attitude" toward it. Though many of these elements of fact and trouble were common to many Toraja people at that time—for example, how to balance obligations to self, family, and community, when and how seriously to take the possibility of spiritual or ancestral retribution—Nene'na Tandi was responding to these conundrums from his own "angle of observation," which was uniquely troubling to him. Unlike many of his fellow villagers, Nene'na Tandi worried that he was especially worthy of retribution and punishment for his misbehavior as a youth because he had knowingly, willfully, and self-consciously acted in a way that had distressed and hurt others. Although he still took great pride in his assertiveness and boldness even as an older man, he realized that it was these same qualities that, as a youth, had led him to act so badly. While others might have conveniently "forgotten" about their own past intentions and willfulness, or found convenient ways of mitigating them, Nene'na Tandi could not allow himself such excuses. He knew that he had acted badly, and he knew that he was continuing to pay the price for that misbehavior, no matter how good his life had become in other respects.

It was Nene'na Tandi's deep sense of regret about his own misbehavior and the childlessness that had resulted from it that contributed not only to the strong sense of empathy he had for others, but also to the unusually earnest approach he took to encouraging respect for God and the ancestors. As someone whose "conversion" to actual belief in spiritual forces came relatively late in life, only after he had allowed himself to suffer the consequences of his previous disregard of those forces, he wanted to help others avoid a similar fate. He became an astute observer of the signs and indexes of spiritual displeasure directed at himself or others. His self-consciousness about these issues led him to inhabit and enact Toraja conceptions of ancestral figures, justice, and morality in a way that went far beyond that of most of his fellow villagers. He thereby helped create a particular kind of world for himself and his fellows, one that was, in some respects, unlike any other Toraja world either before or since. The attitudes and beliefs that Nene'na Tandi had developed through his own problematic encounters with the world had come to affect the lives of others in a unique, unmistakable way, illustrating an important aspect of the looping dynamics of person and context (Hollan 2014); in this case, how an interior scape of emotion and memory can lead a person to construct a particular kind of lifeworld for himself and his consociates.

Nene'na Tandi inhabited his world in other ways that were unique as well. Although he had been unable to have children in his waking life, he was more successful in his dream life. When I once asked him about his dreams, knowing that many Toraja people at that time believed that people's spirits could wander away from their bodies during dreams at night and comingle with other such wandering spirits, he surprised me by asking me in return if I had ever noticed how much one of the children in his village looked like him. He then told me that his spirit and that of the boy's mother often had sex in his dreams, and so he thought of himself as the boy's spiritual father, which explained the similarity in appearance, regardless of who the actual biological father was. While such dream experiences, and the thoughts that flowed from them, drew from widely shared beliefs about dreams, it is the creative way in which Nene'na Tandi used those common elements to express and experience something important about his own particular desires and "sphere of fact and trouble" that made his emerging selfscape singular as well as relationally entangled.

Experiencing Shame in a U.S. Workplace

I came to know George, a white, middle-class man, in my research psychoanalytic practice in southern California. George was troubled by a very unhappy childhood and family situation. He had grown up as the single child of parents who themselves had severe problems, according to George. His mother was often depressed, to the point of being hospitalized at times, and his father drank and gambled heavily and had a terrible temper. Both parents were also quite emotionally dependent on George, and throughout the time I knew him, he felt a grave responsibility to look after and care for his parents, even when this compromised his own chances at friendship and intimacy. George was certain that it was this unhappy upbringing and his ongoing entanglements with his parents that contributed to his own sense of depression and social awkwardness, as if there was a sheet of glass that kept him separated from other people.

Despite these troubles, though, George had been able to become educated in a highly technical field that had enabled him to find employment in a large corporation. He had been working at this corporation for many years when I got to know him, and it was his hope that he could continue to work there until he retired, since the position suited him so well: it was a job that rewarded him for, and made him feel proud of, the unusual kind of cognitive and intellectual skills he possessed; it allowed him a very flexible work schedule, so that he could sleep late in the morning and work until late at night, which was his preference, and also allowed him to care for his parents; it allowed him to work in solitude for long periods of time, which enabled him to avoid the anxiety and awkwardness he experienced around most people; and it had the kind of benefits—good pay, health insurance, retirement pension—that were becoming more and more rare in U.S. corporate life. It was only with the safety, security, and benefits of this job that George had finally decided to try psychotherapy as a way of improving his personal and family life.

So while George was very unhappy and depressed in his private life, he felt fortunate to have the job he did and he took great pride in his work life and accomplishments. All this began to change around 2007, though, with the coming of a severe economic recession in the United States and around the world. George's corporation had begun downsizing before the recession of 2007–2008 emerged, but with its arrival, the offloading of expensive jobs to lower-paid and compensated foreign workers began in earnest. For months, George watched as many of his colleagues were being laid off, many of them being asked to spend their last weeks of employment training the very people who had become their replacements. When George himself got laid off, it came as no great surprise to him, because he had seen the writing on the wall weeks in advance of his actual firing. In his case, however, the shame and humiliation of being fired was intensified by the fact that he was almost immediately asked to come back to his old job as a short-term contract worker, minus many of the benefits he had previously received, which was like rubbing salt into an open wound for him. Feeling angered and humiliated, his first thought was to reject the job offer immediately, but he hesitated, knowing how much he needed the job for both financial and personal reasons.

During this week or so of hesitation, as George discussed with me all these mixed feelings and motivations, he recounted a disturbing dream he had had in which a gang of men had been pulling him into the darkness to attack him. This then led to a number of recollections of himself being bullied as a child, and how ashamed he had been that he had never been able to stand up for himself, either then or now. In his current situation, he worried about what others would think of him if he returned to work. Would they think he had no shame, or that he could generate no better prospects for himself? Eventually, George decided he could not afford *not* to return to work, no matter how humiliating. But in order to do this, he would have to swallow his pride yet again and submit himself to a standard background and financial check, as if his long employment history at this corporation had never occurred. It was in this context of freshly stirred anger and humiliation that he reported another dream: "I am in a classroom of some kind, towards the back, feeling distant from the teacher and other students up front." As he is recounting the dream, he says it reminds him of the second-grade teacher he has told me about before, the one who once pulled him out of class to tell him how disappointed she was with him. "You are smart enough to be at the front of the class with the other good students, if you would just put your mind to it," she told him.

Much of George's story will sound familiar to anyone caught up in the structural entanglements of the neoliberal corporate world, especially anyone who was entangled in that world and structure during the 2007–2008 global recession. And yet George is not just any disgruntled employee. He is disgruntled and humiliated in his own particular way. The humiliation that the corporate world inflicts on him does not come in an experiential vacuum. Rather, it resonates deeply with and is amplified by some of his earlier life experiences: his embarrassment about returning to work as a contract worker precipitates dreams about being assaulted and about sitting in the back of a classroom, feeling alienated and ashamed. These, in turn, stir up memories of never being able to defend or stand up for himself and of being reprimanded by a teacher for his lack of attention and ambition. George's manager, his colleagues, and others in the corporation might have anticipated that George would be embarrassed by his return to work as a mere short-term contract worker, but of course they could not have known from his overt behavior alone that he actually dreamed about and experienced this return as a violent assault on himself. George was "taking in" and being affected by a set of circumstances that were common to many people at that time, but he was doing so from his own "angle of observation," which was unique to him and his experience of the world and his past. His emerging selfscape was entangled in the world, but the tangles were getting knotted in nonlinear, looping ways around an association of thoughts, memories, and images that were unique to George.

Concluding Thoughts: Toward an Ecology of Selfscapes

I have used the concept of selfscapes to highlight aspects of self-experience that are sometimes considered contradictory. One is that self-experience is always deeply entangled in and informed by the social worlds from which it emerges and continues to maintain itself. My siblings and I all shared many experiences of growing up with our father. We share or shared many of the same memories of him, and we share or shared a collective identity based on those common experiences and memories. We are all relationally and mutually constituted in that way. Many of Nene'na Tandi's most compelling concerns in life were also those of his fellow villagers. He and they were all concerned with how to become "modern" Indonesians while also preserving their customs and identities as Toraja and as Christians. He and many of his fellow villagers were preoccupied with what role powerful spiritual forces, either ancestral or Christian, might play in their lives, and how those forces could be influenced to help and support rather than harm or punish. George's concerns about his disposability as a worker, and the precarity that created for him, were shared by many others who were employed in the neoliberal corporate cultures of the late 20th and early 21st centuries.

Yet I have also noted that selfscapes are singular as well as being socially and relationally constituted. The singularity arises because no one's "angle of observation" on the world, no matter how small or local that world might be, is identical with anyone else's, and these differences in positionality and perspective lead to different memory- and emotion-scapes, which then feed into and affect future engagements with and experiences of the world. This is the slippage that occurs between received circumstances and any individual's experience *of* those circumstances. The concept of selfscapes gestures toward these spiraling, recursive, autopoietic processes in which all people are engaged until the moment of their deaths. While people can and do attempt to consciously manage not only their entanglements with the world but also their emotional reactions to and memories of those entanglements, autopoietic processes often flow unconsciously, in unintended directions, as dreams so clearly demonstrate. It is an individual's unique organization of and response to their received circumstances that make all selfscapes both relational and singular, and which distorts their analysis, comprehension, or appreciation if taken from one of these perspectives alone.

My experiences with and dreams and memories of *my* father, however serendipitous and unintended, are mine alone, and they are "insulated" from those of my siblings unless or until I disclose them in some way, just as *their* particular dreams and memories of *their* father are insulated from me. Nene'na Tandi's particular experience of spiritual retribution was also his alone, and it led him to be much more concerned about the propriety of his own behavior and that of others than most of his fellow villagers. His desire to help others avoid his own fate led him not only to be more empathic than most other people, but also to be more vigilant about seeking out the signs and indexes of improper behavior, thereby contributing to a social climate that would have been very different without him. George appeared overtly to comply passively with the demands and interests of his corporation, as did many of his colleagues, no doubt, but as we have seen, his sense of shame at the loss of his job was actually dreamed about as a violent mugging, resonating with earlier experiences of being bullied and reprimanded that were unique to him. He was not just any disgruntled employee, but a very particular kind.

At the level of analysis of selfscapes, the social types of received circumstances—whether of race, class, gender, ethnicity, or any other—begin to dissolve into intersectionalities of all these types, as a specific person begins to experience and live them. Of course, in any particular historical moment, one or another of these social types may play an oversized role in how a person experiences the world, but at the level of selfscapes, we will always find those who defy the social expectations and conventions of the period and whose autopoietic processes forefront some less historically prevalent "attitude." When this happens, we find that people may impose them*selves* on other people and the world, as well as being imposed on, as Obeyesekere (1981, 1990) has observed, and with consequences that reverberate endlessly.

The concept of selfscapes suggests the limits of thinking of or with social types or categories alone, including relationality, because it ties the varieties and complexities of social worlds to an equally complex and dynamic terrain of embodied emotion and memory. People do not react to received circumstances; they do not become engaged in social worlds, uniformly, but in particular ways. As a result, they act in environments not just of competing values, norms, classes, institutions, and ways of conceptualizing and labeling things like gender and race, but environments in which the people around them have animated these various elements in different ways and with varying levels of conviction and emotional intensity. In one's proximate social environment, it matters very much *who* one's co-actors and interlocutors are and how they *inhabit* the world, at the level of "insulated" emotion and memory, not just what rules, norms, or statuses they may be enacting overtly in the current moment. There is a complexity, dynamism, and unexpectedness to social and ethical action and reaction at this level of analysis that is reminiscent of the interactions and reactions within complex ecological systems of any kind (Bateson 1972), in which even small changes in one part of the ecology, small changes in a person's selfscape, for example, may have very surprising and unintended consequences, as they feed forward and feedback into other parts of the social ecology. Nene'na Tandi, George, and I were all deeply and uniquely affected by the social ecologies in which we were entangled, but our very presence altered those ecologies and the people around us in turn, in ways we both knew or know about and will never know. It is this variety and particularity of social action and reaction that James is underscoring when he writes that it takes "the whole of us," each with our own unique "attitude" toward the world and our own "sphere of fact and trouble," to spell out the meaning of the human condition. And that meaning changes, no matter how insignificantly, with each change in a selfscape, and with each birth and death.

Notes

1 Devereux (1967, 321–324) makes a similar point when he emphasizes that the boundaries of the self are not just highly dynamic and "mobile," but they are *"actually* created in each instant" (324; emphasis in original).
2 I am particularly grateful to Suzanne Kirshner for reminding me of James's passage in *The Principles of Psychology* on the insularity of thought.
3 Views of the extent to which any notion of a private, singular, or insulated self is thought to be a historically and culturally bound Western concept have tended to oscillate over time; see, for example, Geertz (1984), Shweder and Bourne (1984), Howard (1985), Hollan (1992), Spiro (1993), Zahavi (2022). But we are in a moment when many scholars, in a variety of disciplines, are emphasizing the relationality of self-experience, rather than its uniqueness.
4 I refer to this type of interview as a "person-centered" interview. For a discussion of the value and utility of person-centered interviews, see Hollan (2005). For a discussion of how to conduct person-centered interviews, see Levy and Hollan (2015).

References

Bateson, G. 1972. *Steps to an Ecology of Mind*. Chicago, IL: University of Chicago Press.
Chodorow, N. J. 2020. *The Psychoanalytic Ear and the Sociological Eye: Toward an American Independent Tradition*. New York: Routledge.
Damasio, A. R. 1994. *Descartes' Error: Emotion, Reason, and the Human Brain*. New York: Avon.
Damasio, A. R. 1999. *The Feeling of What Happens: Body and Emotion in the Making of Consciousness*. New York: Harcourt Brace.
Damasio, A. R. 2010. *Self Comes to Mind: Constructing the Conscious Brain*. New York: Pantheon.
Devereux, G. 1967. *From Anxiety to Method in the Social Sciences*. The Hague: Mouton.
Geertz, C. 1984. From the native's Point of View: On the Nature of Anthropological understanding, In *Culture Theory*, edited by R. Shweder and R. A. LeVine, pp. 23–136. Cambridge: Cambridge University Press.

Hollan, D. 1992. Cross-Cultural Differences in the *Self. Journal of Anthropological Research* 48:365–379.

Hollan, D. 2003. Selfscape dreams. In *Dreaming and the Self: New Perspectives on Subjectivity, Identity, and Emotion*, edited by J. M. Mageo, pp. 61–74. Albany, NY: State University of New York Press.

Hollan, D. 2005. Dreaming in a Global world. In *A Companion to Psychological Anthropology*, edited by C. Casey and R. B. Edgerton, pp. 90–102. Malden, MA: Blackwell.

Hollan, D. 2008. Selfscapes of Well-Being in a Rural Indonesian village. In *Pursuits of Happiness: Well-Being in Anthropological Perspective*, edited by G. Mathews and C. Izquierdo, pp. 211–227. New York: Berghahn.

Hollan, D. 2012. 'On the Varieties and Particularities of Cultural experience. *Ethos* 40(1):37–53.

Hollan, D. 2014. From Ghosts to Ancestors (and Back Again): On the Cultural and Psychodynamic Mediation of selfscapes. *Ethos* 42(2):175–197.

Hollan, D. 2017. Dreamscapes of Intimacy and Isolation: Shadows of Contagion and immunity. *Ethos* 45(2):216–231.

Hollan, D. 2022. James and Radical Empiricism in Rural Indonesia, In *Philosophy on Fieldwork: Case Studies in Anthropological Analysis*, edited by N. Bubandt and T. S. Wentzer, pp. 337–352. London: Routledge.

Howard, A. 1985. Ethnopsychology and the Prospects for a Cultural psychology, In *Person, Self, and Experience: Exploring Pacific Ethnopsychologies*, edited by G. M. White and J. Kirkpatrick, pp. 401–420. Berkeley, CA: University of California Press.

James, W. 1982 [1902]. *The Varieties of Religious Experience*. New York: Penguin.

James, W. 2013. *Pragmatism and the Meaning of Truth*. Scotts Valley, CA: CreateSpace Independent Publishing Platform.

James, W. 2021 [1890]. *The Principles of Psychology*. New York: Henry Holt.

Kirschner, S. R. 2019. The Indispensable Subject of Psychology: Theory, Subjectivity, and the Specter of Inner Life. In *Re-Envisioning Theoretical Psychology*, edited by T. Teo, pp. 131–159. New York: Palgrave.

Kirschner, S. R. 2020. Beyond the Oversocialized Conception of the Subject in Psychology: Desire, Conflict, and the Problem of Social order. *Theory and Psychology* 30(6):768–785.

Kracke, W. H. 1979. Dreaming in Kagwahiv: Dream Beliefs and Their Intrapsychic Uses in an Amazonian Indian culture. *Psychoanalytic Study of Society* 8:119–172.

Kracke, W. H. 1981. Mourning: Dreams of a Bereaved father. *Ethos* 9:258–275.

Levy, R. L., and D. W. Hollan 2015. Person-Centered Interviewing and observation. In *Handbook of Methods in Cultural Anthropology*, 2nd Edition, edited by R, Bernard and C.C. Gravlee, pp. 313–342. Lanham, MD: Rowman & Littlefield.

Mageo, J., and R. E. Sheriff, eds., 2021. *New Directions in the Anthropology of Dreaming*. New York: Routledge.

Obeyesekere, G. 1981. *Medusa's Hair: An Essay on Personal Symbols and Religious Experience*. Chicago, IL: University of Chicago Press.

Obeyesekere, G. 1990. *The Work of Culture: Symbolic Transformation in Psychoanalysis and Anthropology*. Chicago, IL: University of Chicago Press.

Rapport, N. 2008. Gratuitousness: Notes Towards an Anthropology of interiority. *The Australian Journal of Anthropology* 19(3):330–348.

Shweder, R. A., and E. J. Bourne. 1984. Does the Concept of the Person Vary Cross-Culturally?. In *Culture Theory*, edited by R. A. Shweder and R. A. LeVine, pp. 58–199. Cambridge: Cambridge University Press.

Spiro, M. R. 1993. Is the Western Conception of the Self "Peculiar" Within the Context of the World Cultures?. *Ethos* 21(2):107–153.

Strauss, C., and N. Quinn. 1996. *A Cognitive Theory of Cultural Meaning*. Cambridge: Cambridge University Press.

Strawson, G. 2017. *The Subject of Experience*. New York: Oxford University Press.

Thompson, E. 2007. *Mind in Life: Biology, Phenomenology, and the Sciences of Mind*. Cambridge: Cambridge University Press.

Throop, C. J. 2017. Despairing Moods: Worldly Attunements and Permeable Personhood in Yap. *Ethos* 45(2):199–215.

Zahavi, D. 2022. Individuality and Community: The Limits of Social Constructivism. *Ethos* 50(4):392–409.

Index

stress 111, 119, 128; *see also* anxiety; depression; trauma
subjective well-being 107–108
subjectivity 1–14; consciousness and 3, 10, 61; and experiential potentials of groups 9–10; human 3, 10–11, 61; *see also* cosubjectivity; intersubjectivity
Sullivan, H. S. 40, 44, 68

teknonymy 27
theory: anthropology 143n8; of culture 45–50; entrainment 78; of interaction rituals 78–80; psychoanalytic 60; of psychocultural process 46
Thompson, E. 66, 142–143n5
Throop, Jason 61
Tolpin, Paul 96
To Minaa 54n17
tongkonan 112
Toraja 89n1; ancestors in 131; cultivation of rice in 111; culture 3, 28, 138, 151; data 24, 31n7; dream 122; feast 84, 87; ghosts and ancestors in 131; gradients of well-being in 111–114; households 112; market and administrative towns in 105n6; Nene'na Tandi in 151–154; self 26–30; selfscape 114–118; social terrain in 113; village 111–114

transference 80, 81, 122, 126, 128, 129, 137
trauma 7, 11, 36, 40, 52, 93, 96; *see also* anxiety; depression; stress

U.S. Workplace 154–156

varieties and particularities 147–158; Earnest Man 151–154; overview 147–150; U.S. Workplace 154–156
Vietnam War 51
Violence: A Micro-sociological Theory (Collins) 78

Wallace, A. F. C. 50, 71, 73n1
War War II 137
Weiss, J. 44
well-being 107–120; current states of 118; domestic 115; happiness and 110; implications for study of 108–110; overview 107; selfscapes of 107–120; sense of 111, 117, 118; social and cultural gradients of 110–111; socialscape of 114; states of 118–119; subjective 107–108; in Toraja 111–118
Wellenkamp, J. C. 23, 25, 31n3, 31n9, 97, 112, 131–133, 143n7
"Western" self 30
White, G. M. 19
Winnicott, D. W. 43, 126

For Product Safety Concerns and Information please contact our EU
representative GPSR@taylorandfrancis.com
Taylor & Francis Verlag GmbH, Kaufingerstraße 24, 80331 München, Germany

www.ingramcontent.com/pod-product-compliance
Lightning Source LLC
Chambersburg PA
CBHW070342270326
41926CB00017B/3948